Y0-DOK-960

"The value of a single child surpasses that of a galaxy of stars!"

Saint Augustine

"Today as never before, we are recognizing the urgent need in America for a revival of Character Education. Unless the youth of our nation embraces the values of excellence, integrity and courage, perseverance, and an authentic commitment to the welfare of others, America cannot long stand the test of time. *Living the Lessons*, by far the best book I've yet read on proven strategies for developing a values-based curriculum, is a vital resource for all who desire to create a classroom of the heart as well as the mind."

Guy Doud ~ National Teacher of the Year

"When parents and teachers feel at a loss to connect in life-giving ways with today's youth, read this book! Veteran teacher Olivia LaField uses stories and practical illustrations to document how unconditional love is the secret to building the whole person. This book will bring tears to your eyes while giving us all hope for the future of education."

Robert C. Andringa ~ Ph.D, President Emeritus Council of Christian Colleges and Universities

"The lessons described in this endearing book are not just for teachers. They're for everyone. And they don't seem like 'lessons.' They seem like blessings. I don't see how can anyone read this charming book without wiping tears of joy and gratitude. If you really want the world to be a better place, or you really want to be a better person, then take time to read these pages and let Olivia LaField become your friend."

Sarah Sumner ~ Ph.D. Dean, A.W. Tozer Theological Seminary

"A must read for novice and veteran teachers. Olivia's inspiring stories, examples and lessons provide models to develop students' academics. She demonstrates a powerful and heartfelt solution to reach every child, inspiring them to commit to honesty, respect, responsibility, and perseverance."

Glee Brooks ~ Ed.D. Dean of Education, Simpson University

"*Living the Lessons* is a store of treasures for every parent, relative, mentor, and teacher. Dig in and discover how you can shape a future with hope for the children in your life. The proven tools and true stories of transformation will help you unlock the God-given potential of the children in your sphere of influence."

Robert Lincoln Hancock ~ Founder of Endpoverty.org and Providence International

"Using practical examples and applications for families, schools, and communities, *Living the Lessons* provides a pathway to restore a future with hope."

Dick Dickerson ~ City of Redding Mayor, 2007

"Olivia LaField was called to teach. The students who cross her threshold each school year learn firsthand what it means to reside within a caring community, where each one is loved and valued. Most of my university colleagues and teacher credential students do not believe my description of her classroom until they experience it for themselves."

Tom Forbes, Ed.D. ~ Adjunct Professor of Education, Simpson University

"This book was written for those with a passion to teach, shape, and love children. That is the cry of the heart of Living the Lessons. It will inspire you, but more than anything, it will show you selfless love, and love changes everything. This book will help you learn to love children in a way that changes them forever."

Nathan Edwardson ~ Lead Pastor of the Stirring, CA

"This life-transforming book should be read and implemented by every classroom educator! In it, Olivia paints a vivid picture of how to do the seemingly impossible: create a classroom that feels like home."

Charlene Maeder ~ K-12 teacher

"Community makes our classroom feel like home. It's like family. It's…happiness. It gave me a chance for a happy life. I think community in our class is like the Civil Rights Movement with Ms. LaField as our Martin Luther King. Imagine the world caring about each other! One big community! It would be wonderful. It would be safe. I have seen the power of community. You can too."

Student

LIVING THE LESSONS:
BUILDING CHARACTER AND BOOSTING TEST SCORES
Copyright © 2012 by Olivia LaField

RedArrow Media, LLC
Reding, California

All rights reserved.
No part of this manuscript may be used or reproduced in any matter whatsoever without written permission from the publisher, except in the case of brief quotations embodied in critical articles and reviews. For more information please contact customercare@redarrowmedia.com.
FIRST EDITION

Author Photograph © Serge Podtetenieff
Cover design by Samuel Nudds
Layout design by Renee Evans

ISBN: 9780983814023
Library of Congress Control Number: 2012930727
Printed in the United States

To the children,
for whom I am learning to live the lessons.

To Thomas Forbes,
my mentor and true friend, who shows me by example how to live the lessons with honor and integrity.

To the Truth,
without which it is impossible to live the lessons.

CONTENTS

Author's Note

The books we love best are the ones that draw us into their drama by artfully bringing the characters to life. They make us laugh and cry as we feel the ecstasy of their victories and the agony of their defeats. We become better people for having read them. I hope that *Living the Lessons* will be such a book for you and for all dedicated educators zealous to examine their lives and embrace change.

In one sense, *Living the Lessons* is an autobiography about how I got "from there to here" over the last thirty-six years of my life. Throughout the pages, I share much of my past in order to draw comparisons, illustrate points, and convey important lessons. My past has been my greatest teacher and, though a hard taskmaster, it has become my dear friend. Inextricably interwoven into my story is the foundational premise: *"The value of a single child surpasses that of a galaxy of stars!"* Each and every day my students' hearts and minds are transformed by the power of this theme.

Living the Lessons does not merely assert that you must learn to love children and then leave you wondering how; it shows you specifically what it looks like.

Much of the practical application component of the book is dedicated to the fine art of classroom management. As we all know, when our students are not listening, they are not learning. To help you capture and keep your students' attention, I have gone to great lengths to equip you with detailed blueprints and guidelines. As you learn to increasingly care for your students, you will naturally learn to manage your students better. Ultimately, you will create a classroom where your students learn to manage themselves and where they listen and learn because they *want* to, not because they *have* to.

You will create a classroom where your students learn to manage themselves.

Along with equipping your students to be self-directed, this book also shows you how to introduce your students to the attributes of a high moral character (Character Education) and thus receive a trained heart as well as a trained mind.

Theodore Roosevelt once wisely advised, "To educate a man in mind and not in morals is to educate a menace to society."

I believe history will one day confirm that somewhere in the last few decades the majority of us in education lost sight of "the heart of the matter." We wandered away from a values-based Character Education and arrived at the current "numbers" focus: largely annual API (Academic Performance Index) scores. *Living the Lessons* is not a critique of this focus; it is a solutions-based look into the classroom of one teacher, who believes that the answers to the "numbers dilemma" lie at the heart of the matter: values. Values like integrity, courage, perseverance, humility, selfless service, a commitment to excellence, and a strong work ethic eradicate the pressure for high API scores.

If it is your heart's desire to transform the lives of your students and to make the world a better place for them, *Living the Lessons* is my gift to you. We are each allotted a finite measure of time during which to touch and transform the lives of the children given to our keeping. May our students say of us when we are gone that we wasted not a moment, nor an opportunity to liberally bless them. May they say that, by our worthy example, we humbly imparted the gift of a strong, moral character, that we taught them to love the truth, and that we zealously strove to live the lessons with integrity. May we so transform our piece of the garden, our corner of the universe, that our students cherish the memory of their time with us and remember us in the light of the wisdom of Henry Wadsworth Longfellow: *"Lives of great men all remind us we can live our lives sublime and departing leave behind us footprints in the sands of time…"*

Gladly your servant and friend,

★ INTRODUCTION ★

CHAPTER 1

Like Chocolates

*T*he office assistant, who has only been working at the middle school for two weeks, gushes admiration for Olivia LaField as she escorts me across the campus. We enter a two-story building on the far side of the school and climb stairs to the second floor. When we reach what Ms. LaField refers to as the "Commons"—an open area in between all the classrooms—the assistant pushes a large, sliding glass door open and ushers me into what Olivia's seventh grade students refer to as "home."

Olivia's reputation is practically legendary. I've heard she carries a "presence" with students. Many are so greatly impacted by their time with her that they return to visit in droves…even twenty years later. As a fellow educator with a decade of local and international experience, I am not sure what to expect. With a tinge of envy, I wonder if her classroom could be *that* different from my own. Yet, I've heard that she possesses a key. It is a key that not only produces students who are masters of knowledge but also of thought. More significantly, as I am increasingly coming to understand, it is a key that helps them become successful at *life*.

What I notice first as I step inside "home" is how focused Ms. LaField and her students are. My entrance distracts no one. The room is surprisingly quiet, and all eyes are zoomed in on the overhead, which Ms. LaField is addressing genuinely. As I sit down at a student desk, I glance around the room. Surely there must be at least *one* student she will have to "Shush" to keep quiet! I am wrong. It's as if the students know that what she's discussing is vitally consequential for their life. They are fully, irrevocably engaged.

Olivia has copied a student's journal entry onto a transparency and is reading from the overhead.

"Wow!" she exclaims sincerely. "This person almost got angry but took the time to stop, think and act in the way she thought best. Instead of talking back to her mother, she remained respectful. She is working toward her goal very well!"

She glances toward the owner of the journal entry, Natalya, whose face beams with acknowledgement. As Olivia continues to read the entry, she takes time to laugh when Natalya mentions her pattern of being "distracted by boys" in the past, but how she is working on being "less distracted." At this point, Natalya's face turns red, but that does not last long. Soon, Olivia and the students are chanting in unison to her, "Keep it up, Natalya! We are proud of you!"

Words of affirmation. Belief. Sincerity. No one, not even the boys, are snickering or laughing at her vulnerability. And Natalya is radiating with a warm smile. I think to myself, *These students know what it feels like to be "safe." There is no "failure" in a safe classroom. They can just be… and find the courage to push past their limitations because Ms. LaField, no—everyone, students included—believes in them.*

In a conversation with Natalya later on, she is quick to tell me,

> Ms. LaField actually cares, and the biggest thing about her is forgiveness. Other teachers don't give us the chance to be trusted, but she believes we can be trusted. And if we mess up, we have another chance. I wish every teacher could be like her…

As I continue to watch Ms. LaField read several other journal entries, the students' eyes are still riveted on the overhead. Obviously she has asked them to reference how well they were living out their goals, which seemed to revolve around becoming a Person of Character. Rather than highlighting grammatical mistakes or incorrect word usage, Olivia focuses on each student's achievement. It starts to make sense. Earlier I noticed a sign that read, "You are entering a positive zone." What I was witnessing was the epitome of the power of positive reinforcement.

Minutes pass, and I begin to feel like I am in a recovery group, where the "group" has gone through intense emotional healing, due to their commitment to emotional intelligence. The thoughts and emotions streaming from the students' written reflections seem far beyond their age-level. I have to remind myself that they are only in the seventh grade.

After Olivia gives multiple kudos for students' journal entries on "successfully meeting their goals," she moves on to explain the rubric she used to grade their work. Then she emphasizes how she spent seven hours doing so. I can tell by the continued quiet profundity from the students that they are proud of Ms. LaField for what she has done for them. She calls each person's name and gracefully hands him or her a piece of paper. Each graded rubric gives specific observations and encouragement, and is colorfully decorated with stickers.

In a conversation with a student later on that day, he divulges to me,

> *Ms. LaField cares a lot! I mean, she spent seven hours grading our journals. Who does that? Most teachers have a big, huge bubble around them and they don't tell you the truth.*

And care she does—not just about their academic achievement, but their journey to becoming better individuals. I gaze around the classroom and notice a bulletin board that reads, "Martin Luther King Jr.'s 'Big' Words: *love, unity, peace,* and *freedom.*" One of his quotes is also emphasized: "Everyone can be great!" The Skills of Independence, which are the "skills" necessary to be a self-motivated student, are listed on another wall, as are the traits for a student to become a Person of Character. On yet another succession of bulletin boards are the steps to becoming a "Valued Employee," meaning the student is a hard worker and has advanced in his or her level of achievement just like he or she would in the real world:

1. You're Hired!
2. First Promotion
3. Second Promotion
4. Valued Employee

It is obvious by Olivia's interactions with her students and by the décor in her classroom that when students fail, she and the other students are there to pick them up and encourage them onward.

Another student says, "Ms. LaField teaches us to 'speak up!' And she's committed to what you have to say."

I think to myself, *Committed to what they have to say? How do they even understand that concept?* I quickly have the answer: Olivia's students have learned several significant lessons that promote them toward success:

* That she cares.
* That they can be emotionally intelligent.

- ★ That their emotional intelligence will lead to greater happiness in their personal lives, which will in turn lead to greater achievement academically.
- ★ That their emotional intelligence will guide them to become People of Character that bring positive change to the world.
- ★ That by bringing positive change to the world, they will find fulfillment.

This last lesson is embodied by one of Ms. LaField's favorite Confucius quotes, "The only way for a person to live a truly joyous life is to have a strong interest in the welfare of others." Could it be that Ms. LaField has found a way to avert potentially wayward character and indolence? I am determined to hear what the students have to say about her method of teaching. Have they internalized her concepts to the point of being able to verbalize them? Perhaps even to someone who has recently become an eager student—me? Children can't help but be honest. I sit in a circle of students working diligently, and independently, on the Elements of Literature, and ask one simple question: "Tell me about your experience in Ms. LaField's Core (English and History) class…"

I am quickly quieted by the spontaneous thoughts flooding from their stream of consciousness. They are eager to share about Ms. LaField and their Core class.

A smaller girl, with dirty blonde hair and green eyes, says as perfectly as an educated adult, "I think to myself every day, *Core is finally here!* And I lose the 'happy vibe' when I leave Ms. LaField's class."

The boy in the midst of the group says thoughtfully, "If every teacher were like Ms. LaField, school would be easier and we would succeed more in life." Olivia's success lies in her originality, and her perpetual empowerment and engagement of students. Her students' test scores attest to the fact that they are leaving her classroom having received emotional and familial healing, *and* a superior education. Before visiting her classroom, I did not understand how she attained this.

After several surprising and fulfilling hours in Ms. LaField's classroom, I exit into the Commons and smile to myself. My favorite student quote of the day depicts the wonderment of a child: "Ms. LaField is like a box of chocolates!" My mind is bombarded by ideas of how to implement many of her strategic lessons…and I wonder if my students will ever refer to me in the same way they have her. Am I actively *living the lessons* I so passionately teach to my students? I suppose it really doesn't matter if they remember my classroom, or me, as long as they leave academically stimulated beyond their years. And as long as they believe in themselves, their value and purpose, and most importantly, that they have attained the necessary tools to be successful at *life*.

Vanessa J. Chandler is an English and history teacher at a California Distinguished School ranked in the top 200 schools nation-wide.

CHAPTER 2
The Whole Child

*O*nce upon a time thirty-six years ago I proudly signed my first teaching contract and dove head first—and blindly I might add—into the relatively calm waters of public education. Things were pretty simple back then. I was handed the keys to my classroom, a set of books from which to teach and a yearly salary of $6,900. I survived those first two years for one overriding reason: *calm waters.*

The kids—generally speaking—smiled often, politely raised their hands, obediently observed my rules, completed their homework on time, and seldom complained. Most came from stable, supportive homes, where they received not only the love and nurturing of two committed parents but also the benefit of a strong moral, and often a strong spiritual foundation. Calm waters in those days meant less responsibility for my students' personal well-being, fewer demands by parents or administration, and infinitely less stress.

In those days there were no students on Ritalin, no Columbines, no violent video games and no free condoms. There was no need for a Just Say No Club, no pop-up porn on the Internet, little or no gang warfare, no AIDS epidemic (in the U.S.), and no national health crisis. Our students didn't live in motels, their parents weren't incarcerated, very few were raised in foster homes or by their grandparents, and Child Protective Services was an unknown entity. But that was way back before the waters got all stirred up by the erosion of the moral fiber of our nation—before the breakdown of the family unit, and before Christmas vacation became winter break.

So what's the forecast looking like? What's on the horizon for the public education system? Is it all just a guessing game or can we accurately predict foreseeable changes? Personally speaking, despite my positively optimistic, upbeat "fair-weather" propensities, I believe a titanic tsunami is headed our way.

Certainly many would disagree—understandably so. I am one teacher out of many thousands and can speak only from my own experience, but one year at a time I have watched the tide rise and the waters grow more turbulent. Never before, in my opinion, have our public schools faced such formidable challenges.

One daunting challenge facing the public schools is the principle upon which our country's entire economic system is based: good old-fashioned capitalistic *competition*. Charter schools and alternative education facilities are sprouting up all over the country. Parents now have choices as never before and are enthusiastically utilizing their options. Whereas in calmer water they could do little more to resolve a conflict than request a different teacher for their child—which they were usually denied—now they can simply transfer their child to another school! Indeed, in today's turbulent water, parents wield so much power that they can, and do, "threaten" to remove their child from the school if he/she is not placed with a particular teacher.

Administrators now take parent ultimatums extremely seriously for one obvious reason: *declining enrollment*. Trite but true, as the enrollment goes, so goes the school. Today, even the students understand the concept and are using it to their advantage. Competition is always good for the consumer (in this case the parent) and bad for the substandard business (in this case the school) that loses customers to the "better deal." In keeping with the principle of supply and demand, profits go to the business with the highest quality product at the lowest price.

An equally disturbing challenge, one inextricably linked to declining enrollment, is the ever-increasing numbers of students with *more*. A teacher need not have taught for more than a few years to recognize the growing numbers of at-risk students in our classrooms. Student apathy grows *more* widespread every year. An inordinate number of our students are instant gratifiers—addicted to their televisions, cell phones, computers, and video games. Whereas previous generations embraced a strong work ethic and the value of perseverance, this generation grows less industrious and more indolent. Whereas previous generations taught their children to be responsible, law-abiding citizens of high moral character, this generation has largely adopted the "If it feels good, do it" mentality.

One disheartened teacher told me that only about 10% of his students complete their homework and turn it in on time. Another highly devoted teacher I know offers study halls five days a week and often works on weekends. He faces the challenge of preparing his students for the state tests, which determine how well they have mastered the subject matter he has been diligently working to teach them. Understandably, he is more than a little concerned about the results of those tests.

I don't mean to imply that our classrooms are devoid of hard working, dedicated, responsible students with high goals and dreams of a bright future. What I am asserting is that the numbers are declining. Across America we have fewer students who aspire to reaching their full potential, fewer personally responsible for their choices, fewer self-disciplined, and fewer who are task and goal-oriented. On the other hand, every year there are *more* ... more emotionally troubled, more easily distracted, more likely to give up, and more likely to drop out. Every year in the classrooms across America, our at-risk population grows in number and severity.

I believe it is reasonable to predict that as the schools continue to focus primarily on the standards and fail to meet the needs of the growing numbers of at-risk, disconnected students, API scores in many schools will, at some point in the future, begin to fall rather than continue to rise. This drop in scores will, I believe, be exacerbated by the increasing numbers of concerned parents who, for whatever reason, transfer their children to schools that more successfully meet their high expectations. It's simply a matter of competition: The best schools will win!

It's simply a matter of competition: The best schools will win!

REMARKABLE RESULTS

Without equivocation, I will tell you that I have a heart for at-risk children, a heart that sees their pain and wants to help, wants to rekindle the light in their souls that, for many, was long ago extinguished.

As a result of my devotion to these children, for several years I chose to teach at-risk students in summer school. In my class were students who, for one reason or another, failed the seventh grade. The last year I taught summer school, my roll sheet came to a grand total of thirty-eight at-risk teenagers—all in the same room!

If only I could take you back in time to spend a day with those precious young people. Every day was a procession of breakthroughs. That last summer I asked several parents to comment briefly on their child's summer school experience. As you read the following reflections, keep in mind that summer school meets for a brief six weeks:

"The experience Jody had in summer school was wonderful. She is happier than she has ever been in school. I can't believe the change I have seen in Jody. She actually wants to go to school now. She has a wall full of awards that she shows to everyone. I have noticed that she cares more about everything in life now. She wants to help people around her and always do her best. She even uses her manners at home now!"

"First off, Nick never complained about going to summer school. Boy, was that easy! Nick made a connection with his teacher. He did not feel left out or behind other students. He feels smarter. He now stops talking when I ask him to. He's more positive and feels like he finally fits in with his teachers. God sent Ms. LaField down to earth especially for Nick!"

"Kelsey was only in summer school for a total of four weeks but felt it changed her life in some ways. When Kelsey spoke about the class it sounded as though it was life affirming and confidence building for her. Few teachers go out of their way to make the child feel special and important."

"Since Casey started summer school I am seeing signs of my 'old Casey' who once more loves school, friends and his teacher."

This was not "fun and games" summer school. My former "failures" were expected to stay focused and on task for six hours a day—and they did. While others in nearby rooms were playing and having fun, my students were poring over math packets, writing an expository essay on their goals for graduating from eighth grade, and working diligently on improving their reading comprehension skills. By the end of each day, they had amazed themselves with their own diligence and self-discipline.

It is true that I had developed a strong curriculum and enjoyed the ardent support and expertise of both a devoted aide and an extraordinary student teacher. It is also true that over the years I have developed an extensive repertoire of finely tuned classroom management skills—not to mention a file cabinet overflowing with creative awards and inspirational ideas for motivating my students. Add to that thirty years of experience, and you have the basic ingredients of a solid remediation program, one with a strong probability of meeting the academic needs of many at-risk children. But I was committed to achieving much more than meeting my students' academic needs. As the parent comments reflect, their appreciation extended far beyond the curricular focus of their child's summer school experience. The comments included the following elements about each student:

* is happier
* feels smarter
* cares more
* more positive
* more confident
* feels good about himself/herself
* motivated through self-esteem
* loves school, friends, and teacher

Pretend that all those comments were written about one student. Now, make a critical connection: What do those changes represent for the *academic* focus of summer school? Is a happy child more willing to listen and obey the teacher? Is a happy child more apt to stay on task? Does a happy child produce not only more work but higher quality work? What about the satisfaction of the parents? And because we all are vested: Is the teacher of that happy child a more gratified teacher?

THE WHOLE CHILD PHILOSOPHY

Woven throughout *Living the Lessons* are many references to what I fondly call the Whole Child philosophy. To fully understand this paradigm for education, which governs my approach to teaching, you must first understand the Whole Child concept.

The Whole Child philosophy is based on the fact that human beings are multi-faceted. It seeks to determine:

1) a child's essential facets and

2) how educators ought to address these facets in the classroom.

On the first point, proponents of the Whole Child approach to education disagree. One group separates the child into four parts, the other group includes a fifth. The first group argues that the classroom ought to address a child intellectually, socially, emotionally, and physically. The second group, to which I subscribe, incorporates a fifth category: the moral component of the child. Just as the Constitution supports, strengthens, and unites our nation, avid proponents of this second group contend that the moral piece supports, strengthens, and unites the Whole Child.

A majority of educators do not support the Whole Child approach to education. Not because they don't believe children have multi-faceted needs, but because they don't see how they could "fit everything in." Meeting the intellectual needs of their students, they contend, is their sole responsibility; the social, emotional, moral, and physical needs of the child should be addressed in the home. Teachers have their hands full enough with academic standards and numbers.

A child with unmet social, emotional and physical needs will not reach optimal effectiveness intellectually or academically.

The problem with this attitude is that it goes too far in compartmentalizing the facets of a child, ignoring how each facet is deeply connected to and influences the others. A child with unmet social, moral, emotional and physical needs will not reach optimal effectiveness intellectually or academically. I am fully convinced that reaching our potential as human beings increases in exact proportion to the adequate provision for the needs of each part. The more fully our needs are met, the more fully we actualize mentally, emotionally, spiritually, and physically as well-balanced, healthy individuals.

The real question is this: Who should meet children's needs and where should they be met? In a perfect world, all children would enjoy the love, support, and stability of a strong family. Within the confines of the home, a loving father and mother would abundantly provide for the social, emotional, intellectual, moral, and physical needs of their children. When the children in a perfect world turn five, they would be, in the truest sense of the word, ready for school and ready to learn.

In the perfect world, the school would act as an extension and support of the home. It would establish and maintain a safe and caring environment that effectively stimulates the growth of all children on all levels, especially the intellectual level. For thirteen years, the school would faithfully fulfill its role as an extension and support of the family, which would continue to reciprocate by supporting the school. As the children grow, the home would depend more and more upon the school to provide for the intellectual development of the children.

In the perfect world, because the home and the school have corporately fulfilled their roles, children would be fully prepared for whatever lies ahead by the time they don their graduation caps.

Obviously, we do not live in a perfect world. My point in the illustration is to highlight just how *far away* from the perfect world we have wandered. Further away today than yesterday. Further away yesterday than last year. Further away last year than when I was a child—and did not have even a single friend whose parents were divorced! With the passing of each year, homes in America are less equipped to provide for the needs of their children. The family structure in America is growing more fractured, more dysfunctional, more *im*perfect.

What are those of us in education to do about the students in our classrooms who fail to come to school prepared, eager and ready to learn because their needs were not met at home? For that matter, what are we to do with those in our classes who do not want to come to school at all? What are we to do with the stark reality that we had more at-risk students last year than the year before and that we will predictably have more next year?

OUR OPTIONS

We have several options. We can close our eyes and pretend it will go away. We can talk about it *ad nauseam* and then walk away frustrated with another fruitless, circular discussion. We can grow more and more disenchanted with each passing year, less and less willing to "deal with it." We can do our best to hang in there one day at a time. The problem with all these options is that *nothing will change.*

The option I am offering, which will bring change, is the Whole Child approach to education. I believe in it because it works, and I can prove that it works. My students prove that we can, indeed, "fit it all in," and that when we meet the social, emotional, and moral needs of the children in our classrooms, they are more prepared to have their intellectual needs met.

The Whole Child approach to education is designed to nourish the intellectual, social, emotional, moral, and physical needs of all students, not only our most needy. Even those students from "model" homes who come to us well prepared need robust development in order to maximize their potential. Our duty as educators is to do our utmost to empower every one of our students. As their teachers, we have an opportunity to equip our students with the skills and knowledge that will lead them to success and personal fulfillment.

Please remember that the foundational ideas and methods for implementing the Whole Child approach in *Living the Lessons* were designed with my seventh and eighth graders in mind. Nevertheless, most of them can be easily adapted for kindergarteners through seniors. The basic principles can also be customized for teaching math, science or other subjects. As you read along, it is of supreme importance that you continually ask yourself, "How can I apply this to my students?" Be creative. Take what I have to share and build on it. I am confident that there is something in this book for every teacher on the planet.

On community...

Community is like a rainbow of people, beautiful on their own but even more extravagent as one. ~Roxy

★ EMOTIONAL ★

CHAPTER 3
Emotional Intelligence

*T*hey were typical four-year-olds. In many ways they were different on the outside—racially, culturally, and economically—yet much alike on the inside. Not one of them had a clue that they had been chosen to take part in an experiment. The purpose of the experiment? To test their emotional intelligence.

The test was simple. One at a time, each child was led by a friendly man into a pleasant room. After inviting the child to sit at a small table, the man sat down across from the child and pointed to a marshmallow in a bowl on the table. He explained that in a moment he was going to leave the room, at which time the child could eat the marshmallow if he or she wanted. But, the man explained, if the child waited to eat the marshmallow until his return, then he would reward the child with another marshmallow.

When the man was sure the child understood, he left the room. A hidden camera zoomed in to capture the child's dilemma as a television audience of millions held their breath. Would the child delay gratification and be rewarded with the double portion, or would the child opt for instant gratification and receive no more upon the man's return?

A couple of the kids devoured the marshmallow without a moment's hesitation. For others the decision was total agony. They wanted so much to wait, but they just could not seem to stop themselves from indulging their appetites. These children were the instant gratifiers. They wanted their marshmallow now!

Most fascinating to me, however, were those children who prevailed and waited for the man's return. Some actually covered their eyes with their hands to keep from looking at the marshmallow. Some locked their little hands behind their backs to keep from giving in to the temptation.

The people who were watching must have been enthusiastically applauding those brave little champions who, armed with a degree of self-control that leaves many adults in the dust, fought the good fight and won the battle of the marshmallows. The children who delayed gratification received the double portion.

Years later, when I first read Daniel Goleman's #1 bestseller, *Emotional Intelligence*, I learned that the experiment had been devised by Walter Miscel, a psychologist who, in the 1960s, experimented with the four-year-old children of the faculty members of Stanford University. His intent was to determine whether the ability to delay gratification at an early age could be used as an accurate predictor of future success. Goleman quotes Miscel:

> *At age four, how children do on this test of delayed gratification is twice as powerful a predictor of what their SAT scores will be as is IQ at age four.* [1]

And also describes,

> *Those who subscribe to a narrow view of intelligence, arguing that I.Q. is a genetic given that cannot be changed by life experience, and that our destiny in life is largely fixed by these aptitudes, ignore the more challenging question: What can we change that will help our children fare better in life? What factors are at play, for example, when people of high I.Q. flounder while those of modest I.Q. do surprisingly well? I would argue that the difference quite often lies in the abilities called emotional intelligence, which include among others: self-control, zeal, and persistence, and the ability to motivate oneself. And these skills can be taught to children, giving them a better chance to use whatever intellectual potential the genetic lottery may have given them.* [2]

WHAT IS EMOTIONAL INTELLIGENCE?

According to the first model proposed by Salovey and Mayer (1990) and supported by Goleman (1995), we can divide it into five distinct domains:

★ **Knowing one's emotions:** self-awareness, recognizing a feeling as it happens.

★ **Managing one's emotions:** handling feelings appropriately.

- ★ **Motivating oneself:** marshaling emotions in the service of a goal, emotional self-control (impulse control), delaying gratification.
- ★ **Recognizing emotions in others:** empathy.
- ★ **Handling relationships:** managing emotions in others. [3]

As you read this chapter, I encourage you to return often to this model and thoroughly familiarize yourself with these domains. Without a clear grasp of their dynamics, you cannot create a curriculum that fosters emotional intelligence in your students. Even more importantly, begin to *We can't effectively impose lessons on our students that we ourselves fail to live with integrity.* scrupulously observe and evaluate your own level of emotional intelligence. We can't effectively impose lessons on our students that we ourselves fail to live with integrity.

My purpose in this chapter is certainly not to recreate my own version of Goleman's exhaustive study. As far as I am concerned, his book stands alone as recommended reading on the topic. My purpose is to inspire you to seriously consider the possibility of infusing emotional intelligence into your curriculum in order to meet the emotional needs of the Whole Child. To this end, I will share with you both my own methods of introducing the concept of emotional intelligence, as well as an extremely practical, yet highly effective tool I devised. Basing the tool on Goleman's premises, I use it as an instrument for helping my students increase their levels of emotional intelligence.

MAY I HAVE YOUR ATTENTION, PLEASE?

My first step in teaching the concept of emotional intelligence to my students is simply to introduce the concept and then explain it. That probably sounds like a pretty boring approach, one that might just put kids to sleep—and rightly so. If you are seriously determined to teach your students a particular concept, then you had better be creative in your approach and delivery.

You first have to ask yourself, "How can I get their attention?" Remember, all your students sitting quietly at their desks eagerly looking at you does not necessarily mean you have their attention, although it surely does help. Just because kids look like they are listening does not mean that they are. Getting their attention means getting their minds engaged and capturing their interest. That is more than half of the battle—the rest of the battle is keeping their interest.

To capture my students' attention, I often use visual aids. In the case of my introductory emotional intelligence lesson, I use two pictures: Mother Teresa and Albert Einstein. At some point in the first week of school, I draw my students' attention to the whiteboard, where the pictures are prominently displayed together. I ask, "Who are they?"

Rather than answering the question then and there, I give my students each a copy of both pictures with the assignment to find out who they are. They are allowed to use any available source, including family members, etc. Then they are required to research a few facts about these two people and come back to class the next day prepared to share what they learned. This allows a greater number of students with a broader base of knowledge to be involved in the discussion.

The following day, the discussion begins in earnest. After everyone has a chance to share something they learned, I ask for the most outstanding fact about Einstein.

The majority of the class always responds, "He was really smart!"

Then I ask about Mother Teresa's most outstanding quality.

They say, "She was really kind," or "She helped a lot of people."

Next I ask: "Do you think Mother Teresa was smart too?" Here they are always a bit confused and wonder what I mean. This is the point at which I introduce the idea that people are smart in different ways. I do not complicate it with an explanation of the seven different intelligences. I use simple terms: Einstein was *head* smart, and Mother Teresa was *heart* smart.

"What might it mean to be *head* smart?" I ask. "What about *heart* smart?" As much as possible, I only ask questions. Once they get the general idea, I ask them to think about people they know who are (or were) head smart or heart smart. Examples help tremendously, and I always add a few of my own.

Next comes a crucial question: If they had to pick one or the other, which would they rather be—head smart or heart smart? Why? Posed with this thought-provoking question, they are challenged to "go deep" for an answer; consequently, the discussion comes to life. After everyone has a chance to share, it is my turn.

Do they want to know which one I would choose if I had to make the choice? Of course, they do! I begin by telling them that we ideally want to be both, but in general are a mixture of the two. But if I were forced to pick, I would choose to be heart smart. In simple terms, I explain the difference between thinking with our heads and thinking with our hearts. They are only seventh graders, and it is always best to keep it simple, especially at the beginning of the year. I do believe, however, that even children in the third or fourth grade could understand my explanation.

Using Einstein as an example, we talk about what an amazing math wizard he was and that math has little to do with the heart—with feelings. I make sure they understand that it is wonderful to be super smart like Einstein but that his head-smart intelligence was no guarantee that he was a happy, loving man. If I had to choose between one or the other, I would much rather struggle with math and the more difficult subjects like chemistry, and instead be a kind, loving person with lots of friends. In other words, I would choose the heart smart intelligence over the head smart.

WHY BE MORE HEART SMART?

In this initial discussion, I tell my students that I am happy if they make straight A's without opening a book, but that their grades do not impress me most. What does impress me? Students with heart—who treat others with kindness and respect. I tell my students that there are many incredibly head-smart people in the world who are failures in their personal lives. And then I share what for many of my students is the best news they have ever heard from a teacher: Even if they do their very best but still make average grades, they can still be successful in every area of their lives. They can, I assure them, be much more successful than many of their peers who are "so smart" and make such good grades. How? They can learn to be heart smart.

I explain that we can keep getting more heart smart every day of our lives. How? If we care. If we are willing to do the work. If we are committed and never quit. And the more heart smart we get, I tell them, the happier and more successful we are.

Never shall I forget the day we reached this point in the discussion and I noticed a cute little redhead named Katie quietly crying at her seat. When I tenderly asked her what was wrong, she answered—in front of the whole class— that they were happy tears because she realized for the first time that there was hope for her. She explained that no matter how hard she studied, she had never made grades high enough to please her parents.

Katie told us that she had always felt like a failure but that now she knew she could have a good life without perfect grades. Katie decided then and there that she was going to be heart smart in every way she could. Made to feel inadequate because of grades on a report card, she had equated her own self-worth with those low marks—even though she had done her best! But now she had hope.

On the subject of hope as it relates to emotional intelligence, Goleman notes:

Hope, modern researchers are finding, does more than offer a bit of solace amid affliction. People who are hopeful evidence less depression than others as they maneuver through life in pursuit of their goals, are less anxious in general, and have fewer emotional distresses. [4]

I was a "Katie." Compared to my siblings, who virtually made straight A's all the way through college and beyond, I was an average student who dreaded report card day—especially in high school. At thirteen I was diagnosed with epilepsy, and the seizure medications—which included an unspeakable variety of uppers and downers—made focusing difficult. Because of the epilepsy and the low grades, no one in my family ever believed I would do more than have babies or perhaps succeed as a secretary. Certainly, they never expected that I would actually go to college—much less graduate and become a teacher. You can be sure that I felt Katie's pain that day. And you can be sure I tell my students my story at some point in that first discussion because my journey to achieve my dream of becoming a teacher was, to a great degree, all about emotional intelligence.

To recapture and then sustain my students' interest, they have to know what's in it for them.

The follow-up discussion the next day always begins with a review. What do they remember? Who did what? The important questions to review are the ones that bring the topic back to how it relates to their own personal lives. To recapture and then sustain my students' interest, they have to know what's in it for them. With that in mind, it makes sense that my review is comprised of the singular question: "Who would like to be more heart smart?" Of course, everyone's hand goes up.

After the review, I introduce the more precise terminology. Perhaps, depending on the age of your students, you may decide to keep the terminology simple and refer only to the terms head smart and heart smart. I choose to teach my students the more sophisticated language. I.Q. (intelligence quotient) is about head smart. E.Q. (emotional quotient) is about heart smart. As middle schoolers, they are certainly old enough to understand the connection.

THE ASSESSMENT TOOL

Once they are comfortable with the new terminology, they are ready for "My Emotional I.Q." questionnaire, the tool to which I referred at the beginning of the chapter. After reading Goleman's book, I created an inventory that includes all the attributes of emotional intelligence found in his book, as well as a few of my own that I consider to be closely related. Although I occasionally revise the list to personalize it for specific students, it has successfully withstood the test of time. Please take a few minutes to thoughtfully study the inventory at the end of the chapter.

After the kids complete their inventories and choose their three personal goals, I store them away for safekeeping and bring them out once a quarter for the next three quarters. At these times my students review their numbers and analyze their progress. I never fail to precede those lessons with an intense anticipatory set regarding the seriousness of their reevaluations. Each time I exhort them to care about their lives. I talk passionately about reaching their full potential, about being the architects of their lives. I look deeply into their eyes as I talk heart-to-heart, and they cannot help but interpret my intensity as coming from a place of love. So when I release them back to their seats to complete their inventories, I hope it is with a strong sense that "This is really important, so I'm going to take it seriously."

After thoughtfully and truthfully analyzing their growth and recording their new numbers, my students are invited to share their progress, especially in their three areas of weakness. What wonderful tales they share! They are excited, proud, and best of all, happier. And they are increasingly convinced of the capacity of emotional intelligence to dramatically transform their lives for the better.

The quarterly Emotional I.Q. Inventory assessments are important because if we expect our students to remain committed to their pursuit of increased emotional intelligence, we must provide them with opportunities to examine, analyze, and most importantly, celebrate their progress. However, the overall success of the quarterly assessments would be impossible without the daily work conducted throughout each quarter.

EMOTIONAL IQ INVENTORY

1 = Never ★ 2 = Seldom ★ 3 = Sometimes
4 = Most of the time ★ 5 = All the time

	1	2	3	4
1. I like myself.				
2. I lose my temper.				
3. I am an instant gratifier.				
4. Becoming a better person is important to me.				
5. I judge people by their outward appearance.				
6. I treat everyone with the same kindness and respect.				
7. I work well with others.				
8. I set goals and reach them.				
9. I let the crowd influence me.				
10. I strive to do my best.				
11. I make wise choices.				
12. I am responsible with my chores at home.				
13. I give up easily.				
14. I think I am better than others.				
15. I think for myself.				
16. I care about the feelings of others.				
17. I have self-control.				
18. I worry about what others think of me.				
19. I think before I act.				
20. I get upset easily.				
21. I have a positive attitude.				
22. I let others control me.				
23. Others trust me.				
24. I get along well with my friends.				
25. I am happy.				
26. I enjoy school.				
27. I have a good relationship with the people in my family.				
28. I compare myself to others.				
29. I am grateful.				

	1	2	3	4
30. I think about myself first before considering the needs of others.				
31. I feel remorse when I hurt others.				
32. I learn from my mistakes.				
33. I accept the responsibility for my actions.				
34. I resolve my conflicts easily.				
35. I forgive others.				

Janice
AM CORE

My Emotional IQ

I am a person of character!

		1	2	3	4
1	I like myself.	4	4	5	5
2	I lose my temper. ★	2	3	2	1
3	I am an instant gratifier.	5	5	4	3
4	Becoming a better person is important to me. ★	3	4	5	5
5	I judge people by their outward appearance. ★	3	3	2	1
6	I treat everyone with the same kindness and respect. ★	3	4	4	5
7	I work well with others.	5	5	5	5
8	I set goals and reach them.	4	4	4	5
9	I let the crowd influence me.	2	2	1	1
10	I strive to do my best.	5	5	5	5
11	I make wise choices. ★	3	3	4	5
12	I am responsible with my chores at home. ★	3	3	4	5
13	I give up easily.	1	1	1	1
14	I think I'm better than others.	1	1	1	1
15	I think for myself.	5	5	5	5
16	I care about the feelings of others.	4	4	5	5
17	I have self-control.	4	5	5	5
18	I worry about what others think of me.	3	3	1	1
19	I think before I act.	4	4	4	5
20	I get upset easily.	3	2	2	2
21	I have a positive attitude.	4	4	5	5
22	I let others control me.	1	1	1	1
23	Others trust me.	4	4	4	5
24	I get along well with my friends.	4	5	5	5
25	I am happy.	4	4	4	5
26	I enjoy school.	4	4	5	5
27	I have a good relationship with the people in my family.	4	4	4	4
28	I compare myself to others. ★	3	3	2	1
29	I am grateful.	5	5	5	5
30	I think about myself first before considering the needs of others	1	1	1	1
31	I feel remorse when I hurt others.	5	5	5	5
32	I learn from my mistakes.	5	5	5	5
33	I accept responsibility for my actions.	5	5	5	5
34	I resolve my conflicts peacefully.	4	4	5	5

I ♥ life

I ♥ miss Lafield

5-All of the time	4-Most of the time	3-Sometimes	2-Seldom	1-Never

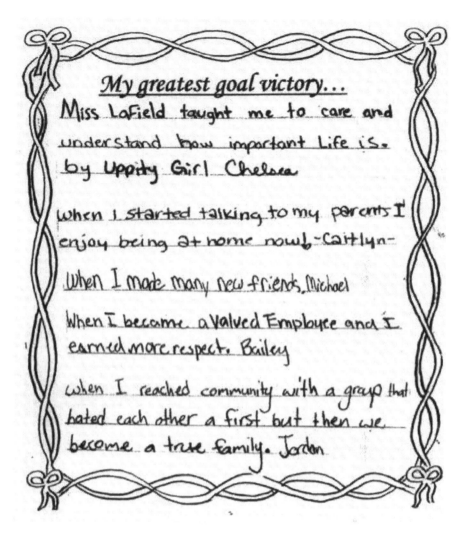

My greatest goal victory...

Miss LaField taught me to care and understand how important Life is.
by Uppity Girl Chelsea

When i started talking to my parents I enjoy being at home now! ~Caitlyn~

When I made many new friends. Michael

When I became a Valued Employee and I earned more respect. Bailey

when I reached community with a group that hated each other a first but then we become a true family. Jordan

CHAPTER 4
The Skills of Independence

I want all my students to experience the sense of personal empowerment that springs from a self-controlled, self-directed life. In short, I want my students to *manage themselves!* Self-management is the cornerstone of emotional intelligence.

I have avidly sought new ways of creating a self-directed classroom, where optimal learning thrives and students are motivated to manage themselves and achieve their best—despite impediments. Recently, I created a tool that is revolutionizing my classroom: *The Skills of Independence.* My inspiration sprang from an expression of unprecedented student maturity, which I shall never forget.

One afternoon my students left the classroom on their way to the library. Everyone went ahead of me except for a few students who detained me with a barrage of questions. By the time I left the room about five minutes later, I expected to find the awaiting students wandering aimlessly outside the door. To my utter amazement, however, they were all gathered around the tables diligently working. With no instruction whatsoever from me, they had chosen to manage themselves. They were twelve and thirteen-year-olds behaving like mature adults!

That evening I could think of little else. What new strategy could I possibly introduce to promote such self-disciplined behavior? Convinced that if my students had done it once they could do it again, I set to work at my computer and quickly generated the following list of the essential habits that characterize the self-directed student—habits that would perpetuate that afternoon's uncommon delight.

THE SKILLS OF INDEPENDENCE

Students who master the Skills of Independence:

- ★ Are self-starters, who don't wait for the teacher to tell them what to do.
- ★ Make wise use of their time.
- ★ Are not easily distracted by their peers.
- ★ Can be trusted to stay on task—even when no one is there to make sure.

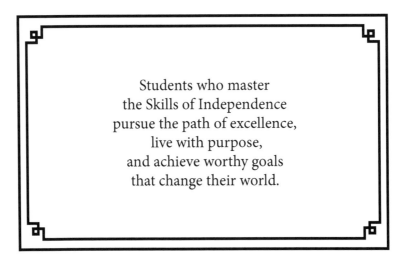

Students who master
the Skills of Independence
pursue the path of excellence,
live with purpose,
and achieve worthy goals
that change their world.

The following day, after applauding my students for their extraordinary behavior the day before, I displayed the newly conceived *Skills of Independence* on the overhead projector. With all eyes glued to the screen, I methodically explained each attribute and how they had demonstrated it. I began with their choice to get on task without direction from me and ended with their choice to stay on task without my intervention. They had perfectly illustrated the *Skills of Independence*.

Next, I asked for their comments and suggestions. We talked at length about their experiences in classrooms where the teacher could not leave the class unattended for even a moment, and about classrooms where teachers did little more than police student behavior. We talked about their responsibility in creating a climate where they had to be controlled by the teacher because they could not, or would not, control themselves.

Next, I directed the discussion toward the big picture: I asked them what happens in the real world when people don't learn to control themselves and must be controlled by societal constraints, and conversely, what happens to those who learn to control themselves long before they leave home and school. How would mastering the Skills benefit them as students? How would our class benefit as a whole? How would I benefit as their teacher?

Through this discussion my students understood that this was not a set of clever new rules to govern their behavior. They began to comprehend the far-reaching consequences that accompany mastering—or failing to master the *Skills of Independence.* And after grasping my reasons to adopt the *Skills of Independence* as our new standard, they agreed to adopt it as well.

One key factor for implementing this new standard was restructuring the students' entry into class. I set the standards even higher than my previously high expectations. After taking their seats, I wanted no more talking, no more questions, no more wasting a moment just "sitting there." I sat at my computer and observed them with occasional sidelong glances. For days, I firmly refused to answer any question that was not an emergency. Ninety-nine percent of their questions had to wait. They soon learned the difference between what I considered an emergency and what questions could wait. I was giving them time to practice their newfound empowerment, and I had to create an atmosphere conducive to success.

I was giving them time to practice their newfound empowerment, and I had to create an atmosphere conducive to success.

After ten minutes or so of independent, self-directed time on task, I greeted them in my usual enthusiastic manner, and we spent a few minutes evaluating their performance. Studying the Skills on the overhead, they compared their behavior. Some happily surprised themselves with leaps forward, while others progressed with baby steps, but every single one of them, without exception, was making progress. The change was unmistakable.

At the beginning of week three, I introduced a system of daily self-evaluation. Using the form at the end of the chapter, students measured their progress using the Skills on a daily basis and then averaged their marks on Friday, after which I recorded them on our computerized grading program. To date, I have only had to question two students on the veracity of their self-evaluation.

Recently, I required my students to write a paragraph summarizing their perception of the success of the *Skills of Independence* on a personal and a class level. With difficulty, I chose the following sample:

"The Skills of Independence have changed my life in three ways that stand out. To begin with, I am striving my best not to get distracted. In other periods people always distract me, but now I ask them nicely not to. In Ms. LaField's class we rarely get distracted anymore because as soon as we come in we go right to work. Furthermore, I don't wait for instructions from my teachers anymore; I go straight to work as soon as I come in. Our class, working hard on the Skills of Independence, now works before the bell even rings! Finally, when the teacher leaves the room, I am still on task. In the past most of us would notice and start to talk. But now we have the Skills of Independence, and it's going much better!"

Undoubtedly, incorporating the skills into our curriculum will result in higher state test scores. That makes my principal happy. I will continue to enjoy my students more and more as they acquire the emotional intelligence that allows me to facilitate with ease rather than control with difficulty. That makes me happy. But that's not why we teach students the *Skills of Independence*. It's about what makes my *students* happy, both now and for the rest of their lives. That's why I'm a teacher…I can still be touching my students' lives even after I'm gone. Teachers who give their students the tools to lead happy, successful, meaningful lives are never forgotten.

Teachers who give their students the tools to lead happy, successful, meaningful lives are never forgotten.

Skills of Independence Weekly Self-Evaluation

Name_____

	Mon	Tues	Wed	Thurs
1. I was a self-starter: I didn't wait for the teacher to tell me what to do.	___/	___/	___/	___
2. I made wise use of my time.	___/	___/	___/	___
3. I was not easily distracted by my peers.	___/	___/	___/	___
4. I stayed on task—even when the teacher wasn't watching.	___/	___/	___/	___

5>All the time 4>Most of the time 3>Sometimes 2>Seldom 1>Never

This week I improved on_____

Next week I need to _____

Teacher comments_____

"Self-discipline: the ability to make yourself do what you should do, when you should do it, whether you feel like it or not."
~Elbert Hubbard

CHAPTER 5

Blending E.Q. into the Curriculum

*T*he Emotional I.Q. Inventory would prove to be an effort in futility if I failed to create a curriculum that sustained its success. Over the years, as I have focused to greater degrees on the subject of emotional intelligence, I have also developed more creative approaches to its integration into standard academic curriculum.

Goleman states:

> *With the curriculum already besieged by a proliferation of new topics and agendas, some teachers who understandably feel overburdened resist taking extra time from the basics for yet another course. So an emerging strategy in emotional education is not to create a new class but to blend lessons on feelings and relationships with other topics already taught. Emotional lessons can merge naturally into reading and writing, health, science, social studies, and other standard courses as well.* [1]

I believe it is safe to assert here that, well beyond its intentional integration into the standard curriculum, my class is permeated with a distinctly recognizable aura of emotional intelligence.

From a visual standpoint, one need only to examine our walls, which are rife with inspirational quotes that foster emotional intelligence as well as attractive displays featuring the attributes of People of Character and Right Heart (two concepts to be discussed later). These images weave their way into my students' minds and hearts.

From a group dynamic standpoint, the primary focus on community in our classroom is fertile ground for planting viable seeds of emotional intelligence. As my students work together, they learn essential social skills without which they cannot possibly enjoy happy, healthy, mutually respectful relationships—skills such as empathy, regard for the feelings of others, and peaceful conflict resolution.

You may also see emotional intelligence in the fabric and foundation of our classroom from a **Character Education standpoint**. Goleman states, "There is an old-fashioned word for the body of skills that emotional intelligence represents: *character*." [2] I appreciate Mr. Goleman's tongue-in-cheek reference to character as an *old-fashioned* word. I hope you agree that it is incumbent upon us, the teachers of America, to bring the word back into fashion.

...it is important to understand that emotional intelligence and Character Education are inextricably interwoven.

Because I address the topic of Character Education in other chapters, I will not elaborate here; however, it is important to understand that emotional intelligence and Character Education are inextricably interwoven. When we are talking about one, we are, in some form or another talking about the other.

From a teacher/student relationship standpoint, my students' immersion into emotional intelligence begins the moment they walk into our classroom. I shake each one of my students' hands every day as they enter our room, and as we shake hands, the student and I recite the weekly *Live the Lesson* quote on the whiteboard. One week, for example, the quote was, "Decide what you want to be, pay the price, and be what you want to be," by John A. Widtsoe. My students were completing their list of family, school, and personal goals that week, so I picked a quote that supported the topic.

On the day I introduce a new quote, we spend a few minutes discussing its meaning and then a minute or so practicing it—with enthusiasm! Usually, if the quote is long enough, I divide it into three parts. I lead with the first part, my students say the second, and then we say the last part in unison. So at the door that week as I shook each student's hand, I said, "Decide what you want to be," they said, "pay the price," and together we said, "and be what you want to be." This daily ritual helps them to memorize and internalize the quote. As real-life opportunities to apply the quote's wisdom present themselves, it arises spontaneously to their awareness. At that point the quote is no longer mere words; it is revelation—they get it. Once that happens, they begin to live it.

The morning ritual's counterpart is the closing ritual. Each day as the kids are cleaning their workspace and preparing for the final bell, I look around and consciously try to recall something that happened during the course of the day that merits a quick accolade. One day it was for Kevin, a boy who from the first day of school had separated himself from all of his classmates and me. I had, in fact, suspended him for two days for treating his Task Manager disrespectfully in my absence the previous week. It was obvious to us all that at some point in his time away from us, Kevin had made a decision to "join" our class. He was altogether different—soft, happy, willing, focused, and smiling.

That afternoon, I announced sincerely and with deep appreciation, "I am proud of Kevin." I then went on to briefly explain why I was proud—after which the kids spontaneously chanted our "We are proud of you!" cheer. In all it must have taken no more than two minutes, but they were two minutes that Kevin will never forget. Kevin had made his debut into the world of emotional intelligence.

My students do not get an occasional shot in the arm of emotional intelligence; they are hooked up to an IV.

Our class is a successful marriage of the mind and the heart. My students do not get an occasional shot in the arm of emotional intelligence; they are hooked up to an IV.

INTEGRATING EMOTIONAL INTELLIGENCE INTO LANGUAGE ARTS

In the first five-paragraph expository essay my students write, the three main ideas must stem from the three areas of weakness they noted on their Emotional I.Q. Inventory. Their supporting details include such topics as: why that particular weakness is a problem, an anecdote to illustrate their point, their plan for personal growth, and how growth in emotional intelligence will enhance their lives.

Using the Emotional I.Q. Inventory as the focus of their first essay is effective simply because they spend a lot of time on that initial essay. The majority of my students will be required to revise their first essay three or four times before I accept it as their best effort, and with each revision their awareness of Emotional Intelligence deepens. The more immersed they are in writing and revising, the more conscious of their problems they become. Before we can ever hope to help our students change and grow emotionally, we have to first and foremost help them realize that they have areas where they can improve.

As a general suggestion I cannot over-emphasize the importance of thoughtfully choosing topics for your students' essays. Whenever possible, my students are asked to write about topics that require personal reflection and self-examination. Every one of my students could tell you by the third week of school what Plato had to say regarding thoughtful self-examination, because they have heard it repeated *ad nauseum*: "The unexamined life is not worth living." Never underestimate the power of a single quote to penetrate a child's mind and open wide the doors that lead to personal growth and transformation, doors that ultimately lead to higher emotional intelligence.

INTEGRATING EMOTIONAL INTELLIGENCE WITH GOAL SETTING

I also integrate emotional intelligence into the curriculum by incorporating it into our comprehensive focus on setting and reaching goals. Sometime during the first month of school, I require my students to carefully choose goals from each of the three main areas of their lives: personal, home, and school. Determining their school and family goals is fairly straightforward for my students, but generally speaking, they do not yet know what a personal goal is, much less how to choose one. That is where their Emotional I.Q. Inventory comes in. Upon close inspection, the inventory is a highly comprehensive assemblage of personal goals from which to choose.

Before we begin our search, I clarify the meaning of a personal goal so that my students clearly understand how it is different than a family or a school goal. With that accomplished, we are ready to proceed with #1 on the inventory: *I like myself.* As I explain it to my students, if you don't like yourself, you have a "major league" problem! Then we talk about it. Why do people dislike themselves? How do they feel when they don't like themselves? What do people do when they don't like themselves? We all agree that it is pretty depressing. But even worse is that the majority of my students can identify with those feelings and behaviors.

The more emotionally intelligent we become, the more we like ourselves.

Then I give them the good news: We can set a personal goal, and with commitment and perseverance, learn to like ourselves more and more. In fact, I assure them, the more emotionally intelligent we become, the more we like ourselves. And the more we like ourselves, the better life gets. Again, our explanations of emotional intelligence must be simple enough for young minds, but even more important, they must be compelling. They must move our students to action.

Every year I ask my students to put their heads down, close their eyes tightly, and raise their hands if they do not like themselves. I give them plenty of time to muster the courage and with stern semi-threats, I make absolutely certain that nobody is peeking. Every year more hands go up. Every year the wounded in my classroom multiply to the point that I honestly believe if things don't change, the seriously wounded will someday become the majority in our classrooms.

With heads back up, I announce the startling truth that many of their classmates also struggle with self-rejection issues. They realize, perhaps for the first time, that they are not alone. Once that revelation sinks in, I ask once again for all heads to go down and all eyes to be tightly closed. "Okay, kids," I say, "raise your hands if you really want to learn to like yourselves." Of course, every hand immediately goes up.

At that point I have buy-in. They all want to like themselves. It's not enough for us to just tell kids they should like themselves. That approach is about as effective as the well-intentioned but impotent "Just Say No" approach. We have to show them. I show my kids by appealing to their hearts. I empathize with them. I get them feeling. Only then are they moved to the action of setting a long-range personal goal to learn to like themselves—a very emotionally intelligent choice. By the time we are finished with the activity, they have hopefully chosen three appropriate personal goals that will, along with their family and school goals, dramatically increase their emotional intelligence.

THE NEXT ESSAY

Clearly, once our students have decided upon their goals, we cannot realistically expect them to be ever vigilant about moving toward them. Indeed, most adults fail dismally to consistently reach their goals. The reason is lack of emotional intelligence. The ability to persevere toward our goals when the going gets tough resides at the core of emotional intelligence. Equally important, reaching a difficult goal requires self-discipline, another hallmark of emotional intelligence. People who lack impulse control cannot hope to reach goals. They are the instant gratifiers who succumb to the temptation of that chocolate cake despite their goal to lose the weight they so despise!

Considering the odds against this generation of instant gratifiers, we must, if our students are to experience any degree of success, consistently provide them with ample opportunities to contemplate their goals. That is exactly what I do throughout the year, beginning with their second essay.

My students' second expository essay follows the same format as their first: Their family, school, and personal goals comprise the three main idea paragraphs in the body of the essay. In this essay they are asked once again to examine their behavior, reflect on possible changes, and, if need be, choose a new course of action.

Like the first essay, they write and rewrite, and through the writing process, they grow more conscious of their new goals. The more I require them to focus on their goals, the more likely they are to reach them. As a result, they grow more emotionally intelligent.

DAILY JOURNALS AND GOAL VICTORIES

Almost every day for the remainder of the year my students focus briefly on their goals with daily journals. Once everyone has thoughtfully determined their family, school, and personal goals, I pass out the journals.

My students are allowed to personalize their journal to their tastes. Many of the boys plaster their journal with pictures of their favorite athlete or team. The girls often include pictures of their friends or role models, but every student is encouraged to spend energy on creating a journal that reflects their unique personality. In other words, I teach them how to create a journal of which they are truly proud. From the beginning I emphasize that I will accept nothing less than their best.

Finally, in order to keep the momentum alive throughout the entire year, I use spare moments to invite my students to share their "goal victories" with the class. As one who cannot bear to waste precious time in class, sharing goal victories during "down times" is definitely a quality time-filler.

KEEPING THE TEACHER CONNECTED TO THE STUDENTS' GOALS

Over the years, I have found that these methods for keeping my students conscious of their personal goals are also powerful ways to connect deeply with them. By repeatedly reading their journals and learning of their progress during sharing time, I familiarize myself with their areas of focus.

The goals art project, which is displayed on one of our classroom's walls, is far more than a mere space-filler. This impressive display of my students' goals serves as a constant visual reminder to them and to me. For example, I can glance at the wall before I meet my kids at the door to shake their hands, and then inquire about their progress. I like to use the goals display to connect more with students who need a personal, caring touch. When our students realize that we truly care, they open the door to their hearts and let us in. Believe me, once that needy student knows that I actually remember his or her goals, I do not have to wait long for that personal relationship to blossom. We can begin to easily converse about matters that mean a great deal to them. I can help with advice. I can praise, encourage, and congratulate. I can literally act as a "goals advocate" for that child.

Kari was a quiet, reserved girl in one year's morning Core class. She never raised her hand, never talked when she was not supposed to, and never did anything but follow the rules and faithfully complete every assignment. She was, and probably always had been, that invisible child who is often tragically overlooked.

One of Kari's personal goals was to stop biting her fingernails. One morning as I shook her hand and welcomed her into class, I looked right into her eyes and, with a warm smile, asked how she was doing with the nail biting. If only you could

It takes so little of our time, effort, and energy to make so big a difference in the life of a precious child.

have seen her face. It was like I turned on the switch in a dark room and flooded it with light.

It takes so little of our time, effort, and energy to make so big a difference in the life of a precious child. Someday she will tell others that her seventh grade teacher was her favorite. Why? I valued her! Yes, I helped her with her goal to stop biting her nails, but what amazed her was that I actually took an interest in helping her. I gave her personal attention. We laughed together every day as I "inspected" her nails. It was a precious time for both of us and required so little effort on my part.

USING POETRY TO TEACH EMOTIONAL INTELLIGENCE

I also promote emotional intelligence with my choice of poetry. All of the poems that my students memorize somehow reflect a focus on one or more aspects of emotional intelligence. For example, on the last Friday of the third week of school, they recite their first poem, "Myself," which challenges them to examine their choices and realize that the choices we make every day create our tomorrows. They learn from the poem that loving and respecting ourselves depends on the choices we make.

A poem is an ideal tool for teaching the far-reaching effects of cheating, a topic which, if we are wise, we will address from a positive perspective. I use the poem "Myself" to teach my students that when we choose not to cheat, we are choosing to love ourselves. When I learn that one of my students is cheating, I remind them of the poem. I make sure that my students do not feel ashamed after we talk about their choice to cheat. I want them to feel inspired to change, and it has been my experience that students are less likely to cheat again if you don't condemn them.

Beginning as early as first grade, students can understand, memorize, and recite this powerful poem by Edgar Guest:

I have to live with myself, and so
I want to be fit for myself to know.
I want to be able as days go by
Always to look myself in the eye.

I don't want to stand with the setting sun
And hate myself for the things I've done.
I never can hide myself from me;
I see what others may never see.

I know what others may never know.
I never can fool myself, and so
Whatever happens I want to be
Self-respecting and conscience free!

EXAMPLES FROM HISTORY

History at every grade level provides unlimited opportunities for infusing emotional intelligence into the curriculum. I choose specific people—Confucius, for example—whose lives reflect the attributes of emotional intelligence. We also focus on particular historical events that conveyed either a lack of or an abundance of emotional intelligence.

Equally important, you will find that Character Education brings history to life for your students. My introduction to Character Education, in fact, came in the form of a brilliant lesson taught by my dear friends, Dr. Thomas Forbes and Dr. Al Rocca, who came from our local university to speak to my students about the perseverance of the soldiers at Valley Forge. As we help our students relate to people and events from a more "up close and personal" perspective, they become real people with the power to impact our students' lives.

THE POWER OF STORIES

Of all the mediums I have created over the years to infuse emotional intelligence into the curriculum, my students enjoy Storytime most. Stories capture children's hearts and change their lives without the intimidation of most of our curricular approaches.

The first and last story every year, "The Lesson," by Carol Lynn Pearson, focuses on the importance of taking personal responsibility for our actions, learning from our mistakes, and most importantly, accepting the fact that life is a series of problems, which we must solve for ourselves.

In "The Lesson," Robert, the main character, is introduced as a little boy first entering school. He enjoys the smell of new paper, recess, and most of all, the slippery slide and the teacher, who is used as a metaphor to represent life. One day the teacher gives him an arithmetic problem to solve, and beginning with that first simple problem, Robert's problems progressively grow both in number and intensity. Robert feels like he is being punished and becomes unhappy and resentful. But the teacher lovingly assures him, "Oh, Robert, I am not punishing you. It is just that you have problems, and you have to solve them!"

Eventually, Robert bravely faces every one of his problems, and as he solves each one, he feels very proud of himself and the teacher moves him up a grade. At the end of this marvelous story, Robert is an old man who, just before he dies, looks back on his life and smiles because by successfully solving his problems, he had lived a fruitful, well-spent life. For the remainder of the year, I revisit "The Lesson" whenever a student has a problem that somehow relates to a classroom issue.

For example, once my student Tanner lost his history worksheet and assumed I would simply give him another one. He assumed the teacher would solve his problem for him. I wait for these perfect moments. With the entire class quietly watching, I smiled at Tanner and told him gently but firmly, "Tanner, you have a problem."

I just wish you could have been there when, almost in unison, the whole class chanted, "and you have to solve it!" As you can imagine, we all had a great laugh, including Tanner, followed by a quick discussion about how Tanner could solve his problem. And, of course, because the whole class participated in the solution, the message was clear to everyone: When you lose a paper in Mrs. LaField's class, it is *your* problem.

I use "The Lesson" throughout the year to teach the imperative necessity of solving our own problems. Not only do my students grow more emotionally intelligent, but the problem of what to do when my students lose their papers is no longer an issue. Using the teacher's response from "The Lesson" completely alleviates negative reprimands, guilt trips, personal offense, and barriers that naturally result from confrontational teacher/student interactions…all from one story.

FINAL EVALUATIONS

At the end of the year, I always ask my students to examine their growth based on their Emotional I.Q Inventory and then write a short summary of their progress. As always, my students express it best:

(EMPATHY/SELF-AWARENESS)

"At the beginning of the year I never treated everyone with the same kindness and respect. If someone looked better or had more friends than me, I was mean to them. I didn't care about the feelings of others. I did not care if I had hurt someone mentally or physically. I figured that they could deal with it. Because of Ms. LaField I realized I was hurting everyone I knew, and that is when I realized I had to change. Ms. LaField taught us to say, 'I'm sorry. I was wrong. Will you forgive me?' That is who I am now."

(IMPULSE CONTROL/SELF-AWARENESS)

"My big problem at the beginning of the year was with my bad temper—because I had no patience. It has helped me keep myself under control, which really helps with my sister. It seems like everything Ms. LaField taught me this year ties into patience. For example, being patient when my friends are mad at me keeps me together. Being patient with my parents when they are mad at me keeps us from fighting every night."

(SELF-AWARENESS)

"At the beginning of the year I hated myself because I thought I was dumb. But then when I came to Mrs. LaField's class that all changed. She taught me that when I work hard I can make good grades like my friends. She helped me study for a really hard English test on sentence patterns and I made an A! That changed my whole life because it proved that I wasn't stupid after all. I just thought I was cuz I made all F's."

(SELF-AWARENESS/SELF-CONTROL)

"My biggest problem was with losing my temper. I'd get mad about small things like if I don't have ketchup for my garden burger. I have definitely improved since the beginning of the year because I have learned that the world doesn't revolve around me. Losing my temper was just a way to blow off steam, and I have discovered other ways such as exercising. Now my mother and I are getting along so much better!"

(EMPATHY)

"My first problem was not being a giver towards my mother. I used to never ask her how her day was or ask if she needed any help around the house. Now we give back and forth to each other. Also, I used to compare myself to others and think I was so much better than them. Now I don't even think twice about whether I have cuter clothes or prettier hair."

EMILY'S MIRACLE STORY

Emily is a remarkable young lady who, minute by minute over the course of her year with me, bravely battled every one of her dragons—and won. Our time together would make an Academy-Award-winning movie. Nothing less than a miracle story, it proved to me conclusively that love does, indeed, heal all wounds. Emily came to me bleeding profusely as a result of her emotional woundedness, and our class served as both an emergency room and an intensive care unit. Emily did not just get Band-aids—she got better. See why in her moving story:

"Mahatma Gandhi once said, 'Our greatness lies not so much in being able to change the world but in being able to change ourselves.' In other words, we can spend our entire life trying to make the world a better place, but if we don't change ourselves for the better, we will achieve nothing. I am so grateful to God and Ms. LaField for helping me change for the better. Change is one of the most important things I will ever learn.

This year in my core class many things helped me to change. One was the Emotional I.Q. Inventory assignment. This one assignment sparked many changes for me, but four really stand out from the others: being happy, having a positive attitude, caring about the feelings of others and the importance of becoming a better person.

61

At the beginning of the year I wasn't happy with anything, big or small. It seemed I was always upset with something. I was continually complaining about how my life wasn't worth living, yet I did nothing to try to make things better for myself. Then I walked into Ms. LaField's class.

I was not happy with that either. Right away I wanted to switch classes. She made me uncomfortable. She wanted so much more than just our attention and completed homework! So one day early in the year I decided I was finished with her class, and I told her I was getting out.

Ms. LaField took me into the Commons and we had a long conversation. Though I don't remember most of it, I do remember her telling me that I would make it through, that I could succeed in life, and that all I needed to do was believe. From then on, I began trying my hardest to be the person I was created to be.

Yes, there were setbacks and times I felt there was no hope, but with God guiding me and Ms. LaField encouraging me, I slowly began to emerge from my dark corner onto the path of enlightenment.

My friends used to enjoy teasing me about my wicked glare. My gaze was so furious and full of rage it would even scare the teachers. But since I have changed so dramatically, now I can't scare anyone! Before my transformation I did not have a positive attitude about anything, not even the good times. I consistently found something wrong with my life and having a negative attitude was sinking me deeper and deeper into depression. What was scariest about that was that I'm bipolar, and several of my close relatives who were bipolar committed suicide.

The Emotional "IQ" question, "Do you have a positive attitude?" really made me think. I decided that in order to do what Jesus would do, I needed to think like Jesus would have thought. So by listening to Ms. LaField and the Lord, I began to change my attitude.

I started with little things like cleaning my room without a fuss and doing my homework without arguing. Having a positive attitude became easier and easier. Now everyone notices how much I've changed. I won an award for having a positive attitude and my family now enjoys spending time with me.

Even as I write this, I am about to cry because I, Emily Ball, the girl who got kicked out of fifth grade for being unable to control her emotions, the girl people were afraid of and who did not like herself one bit now has a positive attitude and that is a miracle!

Before I got into Ms. LaField's class, caring about the feelings of others had never been a big priority on my list. I was incredibly selfish and did not care about anyone's feelings but my own. I went around spitting out harsh words on everyone, and that made me even more bitter. I was definitely a terrible Christian example.

I got called up to the office many times for violent acts, mostly kicking people. So not only did I not care about the feelings of others, I did not care about their physical well-being either. I didn't even care about my family.

I used to hit my older brothers all the time, and I wasn't just playing. Life was miserable for me because I was making it miserable for others. But Ms. LaField taught me about being unselfish. The heart on the Right Heart bulletin board that said 'unselfish' seemed to be staring at me day after day until I finally decided it was time to change.

I began with my brothers. I started trying really hard to get along with them and very quickly our relationships really improved! That was encouraging. Since I was having such great results with my brothers, I started trying to care about the feelings of everyone. People that were my enemies became my friends because I cared.

Now I am not lonely and miserable because I am following the Golden Rule. I am so happy because I make other people happy. Life is good! Ms. LaField continued helping me by teaching me to be a servant to others, so now I am not only caring for others but also serving them!

So many changes have filled my life. I wish I could share them all, but these four from the Emotional I.Q. Inventory sum up my big transformation. Some people tell me I'm lucky to have realized this so early in life, but is it luck that put me in Ms. LaField's class? Good fortune maybe? I believe it is a blessing from God. I believe he put me in Ms. LaField's class so I could help others like you! Yes, you, the person who is reading this right now!"

YOU CAN TOO

I would love to introduce you personally to my students and invite them to tell you, face to face, how they examined their lives, set goals, persevered, and became better people—People of Character. If you asked them how they did it, it is highly unlikely that they could explain the deliberate, sequential process that led to the changes, and at this point in their lives the actual process is inconsequential. But if you asked them to (describe the difference) in the quality of their lives, they would have no problem explaining it. I am confident that they would, by their authentic testimonies, convince you, and I would have succeeded in accomplishing my original intent: to make you a believer in teaching emotional intelligence as part of your curriculum.

CHAPTER 6
Discipline with Tough Love

*D*iscipline with tough love is another powerful avenue for teaching emotional intelligence, though sadly it is understood by few and employed by even fewer. Every time our students break a rule or somehow fail to meet our expectations, we have an opportunity. We can either chastise them, and in so doing create a resistant barrier, or help them create an awareness of their problem and their need to fix it. One approach builds walls; the other builds character.

Frankly, not all kids are lovable; in fact, some are downright disagreeable! In other terms, which don't sound quite so harsh, some kids are devoid of emotional intelligence. They are the ones who desperately need our attention and commitment, especially when they push us to our limit.

When we care for our difficult students unconditionally—despite themselves—we are teaching them emotional intelligence. Conversely, when we fail to care for our "unlovely" students, we are robbing them of the "education" of emotional intelligence that can only be taught through us personally displaying it in action.

JOSH

When he first came into my life, Josh, like so many of today's young people, was angry. Not just a little angry, mind you, but very angry. Angry kids are miserable kids. In extreme cases they are impulsive, short-tempered, mean-spirited, explosive, verbally abusive, defiant, and self-destructive. These wounded children, often grow up to be wounded adults capable of rampant destruction, both to themselves and others.

Josh definitely had good days, but on his bad days...well, let's just say he was the ultimate test of my limits. Josh had his first really bad day in early fall. I wasn't there to see it, but my poor substitute teacher certainly tangled with his "emotional intelligence issues." Without going into details, I heard the lurid story the moment the kids walked in the door the next day. All accounts coincided, and the verdict was unanimous: guilty without excuse. It was one of those moments when we feel like strangling the culprit on the spot, especially when the problem involves a substitute. It was one of those moments where we must take a few breaths and intentionally try not to inflict pain.

THE CARDINAL RULES OF TOUGH LOVE

Tough Love Cardinal Rule #1: Never humiliate a student by correcting him or her in front of his or her peers.

As I do with any confrontation, I politely invited Josh to join me in the Commons, where we could privately talk. Josh denied nothing. He "owned the truth," as we say in our class. I was encouraged, but not for long. Following his admission of guilt, Josh failed to display even a shred of remorse. In fact, he adamantly refused to admit that he was wrong. Though I said all the right words, and said them with compassion, patience, and respect, we reached a complete standstill. He refused to budge even a fraction of an inch.

What were my options? Give him detention? Call his mother? Send him to the office? Get mad and give him the emotionally unintelligent, "Okay, young man, you can just stay out here until you say you are sorry!" routine—equivalent in his mind to "Stay out here 'til you rot!"? Formerly, I would have opted for leaving him to rot. But what would it have taught him? Nothing except that I was like all the other teachers in his life who reacted to his anger with their own anger. This would certainly not help him to grow more emotionally intelligent; in fact, it would have undoubtedly set him back even farther.

Thankfully, I can say that I chose the path of love—tough love. But first I made sure Josh understood the basic core issue that he needed to face and overcome: his stubborn nature. Later, when our relationship was firmly established and he trusted me, we talked about the origin of his stubbornness, how much it hurt him, and ways to overcome it, etc. But for the moment, I left him in the Commons with a sincere promise to help him every step of the way should he decide to face his monster. I told him I would

I told him I would be waiting anxiously for him to come back in and join us—but only under my terms.

66

be waiting anxiously for him to come back in and join us—but only under my terms. He would have to admit that his disrespectful treatment of the substitute was out of line. In other words, Josh would have to admit he was wrong. I walked away leaving him to seethe and figure out what he was going to do.

The next morning I greeted him with a smile as if nothing had happened and asked once again with warmth if he would be joining us that day. Josh chose to remain outside the classroom, but I could feel his tough guy mask coming off and his heart softening.

Tough Love Cardinal Rule #2: We must never forget to separate the problem from the child.

Each step of the way, I focused exclusively on Josh's *problem*, not on Josh's *person*. Because Josh did not feel personally attacked, he did not feel that he was being punished unfairly. And because he did not feel resentful about his self-imposed predicament, rather than projecting his anger on me, he was able to turn inward.

You must believe that children like Josh can be reached! A cherished quote on our wall so aptly expresses this message: "People are not bad. They are wounded!"

WELCOME BACK, JOSH!

Later that morning I reaffirmed my hope for Josh's speedy return, but I did not try to convince or coerce him in any way. He had a big choice to make, and I wanted the victory to be entirely his when he ultimately made the right choice. I left him alone, convinced of two things: I meant to stand by my word, and I meant to care for him regardless of his choices. I would show him tough love.

 I left him alone, convinced of two things: I meant to stand by my word, and I meant to care for him regardless of his choices. I would show him tough love.

That afternoon Josh walked somewhat humbly into our classroom. We were all thrilled to see him and welcome him back into the fold. In the quiet pause followed our heartfelt welcome, with all eyes expectantly watching, Josh apologized sincerely and admitted to the entire class that he had been wrong to disrespect the substitute.

What followed was one of those magical moments that a teacher never forgets; certainly it was a moment Josh will never forget. Every child remained quietly seated around and upon the risers and watched intently as I arose from my beanbag and, without taking my eyes off Josh, stepped down and deliberately wove my way toward him through the mass of arms and legs scattered about on the floor. With every eye in the room fixed intently upon him, Josh stood alone, waiting and watching as I met him with open arms and personally welcomed him back. I stood next to him with my arm around his shoulder as I led the kids in the "We are proud of you!" chant and then proclaimed the event a true moment of transformation. With a million-dollar self-congratulatory smile at me and a triumphant glance at his supportive classmates, Josh nestled down comfortably on the floor next to a friend, and I returned to my beanbag to continue with our lesson as if the last few days had never happened.

It was a happy ending, but not *the* happy ending. Over the remainder of the year, Josh continued to "lash out"—though less and less often. Every single issue was anger-related and involved disrespect on some level. Each time, with the exception of the final incident, we had our same little talk that always ended with a reassuring pat on the back, a reconfirmation of my commitment and my parting words: "Stubborn people are lonely people."

COME BACK SOON, JOSH

I was simply finished—not with Josh, but with repeating myself.

In late April everything changed. I cannot say what was different that fateful day, when once again, I found myself out in the Commons with Josh. I do not recall the specifics of that final infraction. All I know is that our little talk took a whole new turn because I had come to the end of the line with Josh's outbursts. I was not tired or angry or otherwise disagreeable. I was simply *finished*—not with Josh, but with repeating myself. I hope that if you asked Josh what happened that day, he would tell you that I was not sick of him personally, but I was definitely sick of his behavior.

I shall never forget sitting down next to him, and with sad resignation, telling him that there was nothing left to say because I had already said it a hundred times. I don't think I even repeated the quote about stubborn people. Instead I left him with four words that succinctly expressed my enduring sentiments: "Come back soon, Josh." It was clear to him that I was finished with his angry reruns, but at the same time, he was also convinced in his heart that the door was still open.

All his life, Josh had fought for control. His whole life had been a struggle to get what he needed, to get what he should have gotten from his parents. As a result, Josh was "mad as hell" about the emotional deprivation he had suffered since birth. He did not know why he was so mad; he just knew life was not fair. What did he ever do to deserve such a raw deal? In his mind, all authority figures were out to make his life even more miserable.

Those of us who suffered through childhood emotional abuse unconsciously create coping mechanisms. However dysfunctional, they equip us for survival. Mine was denial. Nothing short of fantasy worked for me—that is, until I hit that wall at fifty and opted for reality therapy. Some hold it all in and then one day quietly implode, like fourteen-year-old Cliff Evans of "Cipher in the Snow," who, when he could bear the rejection no longer, politely stepped off the school bus, fell into the snow and died without a word to a soul that he was starving for love. [1]

Unlike Cliff, who never once opened his mouth to defend himself, Josh came out of his corner fighting mad! But that day when I left him in the Commons, he was not mad. I had stopped being the authority figure "out to get him" and had finally become his friend. That meant something to him. Something big. And he did not want to lose it.

LOVE MADE A WAY

Walking back into the classroom, I wondered how long he would sit alone in the Commons this time. But no sooner had I passed through the sliding glass door… when I turned around to see, virtually following in my footsteps, a young man whose transformed outer countenance poignantly expressed his triumphant victory over the monster within. Josh had just made what might have been the first truly wise decision of his life. Time stood still for a brief moment, but my tears would not. After all, I had already waited seven long months for that moment.

Love made a way for Josh that day. It made a way for him to take off his gloves and give up the fight—at least with me. What clicked for Josh was the realization that *I was on his side*. No longer the enemy, no longer someone to push him around, no longer someone who failed to love him despite his monster within, I had become his advocate and ally, and, as such, I became the catalyst that moved him to finally let down his guard. Someone really cared. Someone really wanted him to come back soon. That day Josh no longer wanted to be among the stubborn, lonely people.

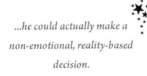

...he could actually make a non-emotional, reality-based decision.

For the sake of all the Joshes that you may someday have in your own classroom, please do not fail to grasp this transcendent truth: Because Josh trusted me enough to lower his angry, fear-based guard, he was empowered to immediately own the truth about why he was out in the Commons again. And then, wonder of wonders, he could actually make a non-emotional, reality-based decision. Because Josh could recognize my unswerving commitment to him. He could let go of his "stuff" and make an emotionally intelligent decision. And that is exactly what he did.

THE BEST OF THE STORY

Josh and I never shared another one of our little talks in the Commons, and, believe me, neither of us missed them. What we did share in the five weeks that remained is the rest of the story, the best of the story. It is the happy ending that will hopefully convince you of the awesome power of love to move mountains and master the monsters within. What Josh needed after that initial breakthrough was a challenge to further develop his emotional intelligence. I decided to offer him the big one in my class: to become a Valued Employee. (Valued Employee is the highest promotion one of my students can receive in my work incentive plan "You're Hired!" I will explain further in a coming chapter.)

Josh took the bait and went after this prize with all his heart. He chained that monster of his to a tight leash and tamed the rascal almost overnight. For the first time, Josh fully cooperated with his group and respected his Task Manager. He proved to be a team player, and his group reached community (explained in a later chapter). Instead of sitting as far away from me as I would allow, he voluntarily sat up front and, fully engaged, listened respectfully to my lessons. He raised his hand and participated. We soon learned how smart Josh was. For the first time, he started completing all of his assignments. He wrote a phenomenal essay, so outstanding that it earned the rare honor of a gold seal on the initial draft. It was, by the way, a persuasive essay. His objective? To convince his mother to stop smoking.

THE BIG TIME

In those last few weeks I was Josh's cheerleader. I believed in him, encouraged him, and praised him—and not just once in a while. He was going for the gold, and he needed a devoted fan who would go the distance with him, come rain or shine.

By late May, with only one week remaining in the school year, Josh hit the big time: Valued Employee. He was just in time to be honored at the Valued Employee's dessert banquet the next week. I went right home and made his medal. He wanted a black ribbon, but I would have made it solid gold if he had asked. Several kids gave up a few lines so he could be in the play we were performing, and he was set to go except for one problem—his parents were not coming.

Josh was okay with his mom not being there. She had a good excuse. But his dad, who lived across town, was another story altogether. His excuse was that he was too tired after work. Josh tried to convince me that he understood, but it was not hard to see that he wanted his dad there more than anything in the world. He wanted his dad to be proud of him.

The morning of the banquet I reached my absolute limit with his father's abject negligence, and I determined to intercede on Josh's behalf. I was not finished being his cheerleader, and by golly, I wanted his father to join me on the sidelines. Josh did not know his dad's phone number at work, so I called his mother to get it. She was reluctant, but I was not taking no for an answer and finally she relented.

My short conversation with his father could not exactly be described as a model parent/teacher phone call. I do not recommend informing a parent of what they will do or will not do, but that is exactly what I did that day. Emphatically, I instructed his father exactly where he was expected to be and exactly what time he was to be there. Furthermore, I refused to allow the conversation to end until I got what I wanted: a firm commitment that he would be there for his son.

It was a most glorious night for Josh, who received a special surprise honor with his dad in the audience. If only I could describe the look on Josh's face as he stepped confidently forward to receive the unrestrained approval from an audience of well over two hundred cheerleaders! The intensity of emotion he was obviously feeling at that moment emanated through now soft, sensitive eyes that saw the world from a radically new perspective: that of a friendly, accepting place, one that was finally in his corner. With one arm tight around his shoulders and the other gripping the microphone, I wept openly as I shared Josh's triumphant victory over the subversive contender in his own corner: *himself.*

In the midst of the thunderous applause for his son that followed, I remember catching his father's attention and giving him an enthusiastic thumbs up. Of course, I was really thinking, "It's just a darn good thing you made it, Buddy!"

OR THE LACK THEREOF?

Discipline with love—in Josh's case, tough love—was the key that opened the door to emotional intelligence for a boy who quite possibly may have harbored an arsenal of self-destructive anger the rest of his life. The frightful reality is that Josh might very well have left the confines of my classroom and grown up to become one of those "big monsters" that we read about, the ones who fill our prisons and leave behind a trail of tragedy.

Here is another sobering thought: Will you recognize your "Josh" when his monster rears its ugly head? Will you display emotional intelligence by controlling your impulses when he drives you to distraction? Or will you react impulsively out of your own lack of emotional intelligence?

Clearly, before we can hope to teach our students even an ounce of emotional intelligence, we must first have developed our own. And then we must model it for our students. We must *live the lessons.* It is not an option; it is absolutely, unequivocally mandatory. Legion are the teachers in the classrooms of America who have never considered, even for a moment, the wounds they inflict as a result of their own limited reserve of internal emotional resources. I should know. I was one of them for my first fifteen years in the classroom.

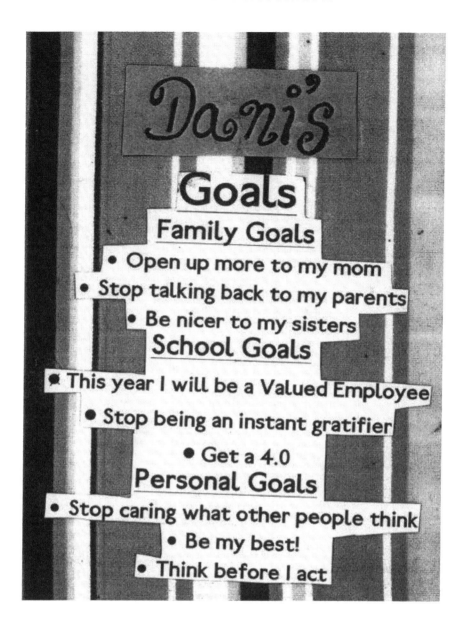

Name <u>Morgan</u>   Qtr. <u>2nd</u>

*Bravo! I can see that you
are very committed to
reaching your goals......☆☆☆
*You're examining your
life and changing......☆☆☆
*Feels honest......☆
*You obviously CARE!...☆☆☆☆☆
*Thank you for coming right
in and beginning to write......___
*I see improvement......___
*Punctuate carefully!!!......___
*Doesn't seem like you care...___
*Not enough written
reflection......___
*You need to get started
immediately!......___
*I'm doubtful that you are
working on your goals......___
*I know you can do better...___
*I can hardly read your
writing......___

Grade A+

Oh, sweetheart!!
I could just
cry I'm so
proud of you
You are growing
a big beautiful
Right
Heart
and I get
to watch
I love it

♡

SOCIAL

CHAPTER 7
Creating Home

*C*ommunity is more than a group of strangers who happen to live in the same vicinity; more than a group of citizens who gather together for the purpose of discussing mutual needs, interests, or problems; more than an occasional neighborly "get together" or a planned block party. It is, I fervently believe, the answer to many of the unresolved problems that confront and confound our world today. Community is the answer to the alienating conflicts that arise between and among neighbors, nations, friends, and families. Community is nothing less than the peaceful answer to "man's inhumanity to man." And community is the answer for that lost, lonely "invisible" child in my class, desperate for acceptance and a sense of significance.

As Marianne Williamson reminds us in *A Return to Love*, "We're all assigned a piece of the garden, a corner of the universe, that is ours to transform." [1] My piece of the garden is my classroom, which, transformed by the inclusive embrace of community, offers every one of my students a place in the sun to grow, thrive, and blossom.

Prior to my discovery of community, I had been searching for a different approach to education. Planted deeply within me was a profound knowing that my ways of controlling my classroom for the previous fifteen years were misguided. I had finally reached a point in my life where I was willing to own the truth about my control issues, and I saw that I needed a new "way of being" in the classroom. It was altogether unclear about what that new way of being would look like, hence, the search. By the time I was finished, very little remained worth salvaging except for the years of accumulated curriculum in my file cabinet.

EVERYTHING MUST CHANGE

The deep knowing came neither as a brilliant flash of lightning nor as an audible voice of authority from on high, but rather from a somewhat troubled spirit, a persistent thought that popped randomly into my conscious awareness: *Everything must change.* So, during that momentous summer when I heard the call for a new plan, I prepared for change—psychologically anyway. Patiently, I waited for direction regarding how to proceed with this nebulous new classroom idea, but when I had neither a hint nor even a vague notion by the last days of summer, I could do nothing but proceed as usual.

How vividly I recall my thoughts that first day of school. In the midst of roll call, as I hurriedly scanned the room seeking the unfamiliar face of the student whose name I had just called, the thought suddenly dawned on me that it was the first day of school and I was still waiting for "orders from headquarters." For a take-charge controller like me, that awareness definitely challenged my limits.

Having no recourse but to carry on with the old and wait patiently for the new, sure enough, the answer arrived within a very short time in the form of a book that was providentially placed in my hands: *The Different Drum*, by M. Scott Peck. [2] His book marked the end of my search and ultimately opened wide the door to community. With no foreknowledge of its content, I knew within minutes that I held in my hands the blueprint of my new classroom.

"I FELT LIKE I HAD COME HOME"

Until the age of fifteen, Peck attended Exeter Academy, a New England boarding school known at the time as the nation's leading training school for rugged individualism. He recalled, "As inmates will in a prison, the students had their own society, with norms that were often as vicious. The pressures for conformity were immense. At any given time at least half the student body occupied the status of outcasts." During his third year at Exeter, Peck recounts, "I dimly had the wisdom to know that I would soon suffocate in the air of that culture. It was not the thing to do at that time and place, but it was a matter of breathing for me: I dropped out." [3]

As it turned out, his adamant refusal to continue at Exeter proved to be not only his immediate saving grace but also the prelude to a pivotal turning point that would ultimately drive and direct the remainder of his entire life. Peck's parents discovered Friends Seminary, a little Quaker school in Greenwich

Village. There he flourished in the newly found solace of true acceptance and intimacy. Peck said, "I felt as if I had come home." [4]

I was to create a classroom that felt like home.

As I read those words, my heart, mind, soul, and spirit—everything in a human being capable of conscious awareness—resonated with the word *home*. With that single word, my search abruptly ended and the essence of the plan was unveiled: I was to create a classroom that felt like home.

I devoured the remainder of the book. It was like ripping open that Christmas present with the diamond of your dreams inside. Embedded within the pages of Peck's book lay blueprints for recreating that *home*, that sanctuary which constituted the heart and soul of Friends Seminary. From the first quick read, I began to understand what Peck referred to as a *true community*. I returned eagerly to the first page with the intent of meticulously dissecting the big picture into its separate and distinct parts.

I also learned that the general public's concept of community is a far cry from Peck's. Though it was definitely new territory, I quickly embraced the simple ABC's of a true community and in a matter of a few short hours assembled the pieces to fashion it. Without question, the design of my new classroom had been revealed. Just as Peck's search for acceptance ended with the discovery of community at Friends, my own search ended with the discovery of community via his astute account. I hope I can paint that same picture of a true community for you—though on a less complicated canvas.

A TRUE COMMUNITY DEFINED

At this point, a clear definition of a *true* community will be helpful. I believe we can say that a true community consists of a group of people who have learned to transcend individual barriers and value each other's differences, thereby creating a familial sense of unqualified acceptance and belonging. The community members feel safe to be themselves, to be vulnerable, and even to fail.

True community members commit themselves to the interests and needs of the group as a whole rather than to their own particular individual needs and interests. Deeply committed to maintaining the integrity and unity of their established fellowship, the members of a true community feel like a family; they feel at home with one another.

THE SACRED QUESTION

Perhaps you are now thinking, *Well, all that sounds pretty wonderful, but let's get real! How in the world can any teacher hope to replicate an unrealistic fantasy within the restrictive confines of the typical American classroom teeming with I-centered, self-absorbed takers?* That is a question of paramount importance. In response, I urge you to first contemplate a question of infinitely greater significance: *Would community be good for your students?* How quickly we neglect to consider first what is good for the kids. We must identify and embrace what is good before we ask "How?" And as I discovered, embracing the goodness of community opened the way to the process of finding how to build it in my classroom.

AN EVER-EVOLVING PROCESS

Creating community in my classroom has been an ongoing, evolving process. The initial question was how to break Peck's description of a true community into simple terms and create a format that the kids could understand and relate to. Essentially, my task was to design the ABC's of a *true* community. They had to be simple, clear and concise, short enough for my students to memorize and short enough for me to plaster on a bulletin board.

In twenty-four years I haven't altered a single word of those ABCs. The only changes have been jazzier, updated bulletin boards that proudly display the attributes of a true community. I'm sure you will recognize how easily they might be adapted to any age group or grade level:

The Seven Attributes of a True Community
- ★ We respect each other.
- ★ We help each other.
- ★ We work as a team.
- ★ We value each other's differences.
- ★ We solve conflicts peacefully.
- ★ We feel safe.
- ★ We feel like a family.

Simple yet sacred, these foundational components will, when consistently honored and obeyed, guide a group of people toward the creation of a family, a safe sanctuary and a home.

SHARING THE VISION

With the foundational attributes of a true community securely in place, the next challenge was how to begin the process of building that home. How would I create that place where, like the Friends of Peck's childhood, every child in my class is warmly welcomed and belongs?

The answer to that question is the story of the last twenty-four years. Just as life itself is a journey that we take one step at a time, so my journey of building that home began with a first step: sharing my vision with my students.

As I recall, it was the fall of 1988. We had begun the year with our desks in perfectly aligned rows. We were, by all standards, the traditional, teacher-directed carbon-copy of a thousand and one American classrooms. That was about to radically change.

Step One of the journey, sharing the vision, was an exciting day. My students quickly caught on to my unbridled enthusiasm about it and needed no convincing. They were immediately ready to begin what seemed to them like a great experiment.

We began by dividing the class into groups. I don't recall how the decisions were made regarding who would go into which group, but I do remember the excitement of moving the desks out of rows and into those first group configurations.

Once they settled into their groups, we were ready for Step Two — explaining the Seven Attributes of a True Community in detail. I had already created a wall display that helped to keep them focused visually on each attribute as we discussed it. They were happy to be in groups, and they had a sense of where they were going. That was the easy part.

Step Three was the hard part: How do we get to where we are going? Obviously, they needed guidance, but so did I! I envisioned a system of leadership in each group. I dubbed my student leaders Task Managers. Over the years, I expanded their roles with new and upgraded ideas. They have become an indispensable element of both the community aspect of our class and my classroom management strategies. Honestly, I cannot imagine life without them. Finding a Task Manager with a heart for a needy student is like finding the Hope diamond. Like Evan and Richard helped David, devoted Task Managers can literally help boost their peers from failing grades to honor roll status. Such is the case with Dani, who shares her feelings about helping Lai, a struggling boy in her group:

"There's a boy in my group named Lai. Because he gets in trouble and needs so much help, I've really been trying hard to help him get on a better path. I come every day to lunch study hall and help him with whatever he doesn't get—mostly math. So far he's been doing great, and he really has been choosing to care. Just yesterday he got a B-on his weekly math progress report! Ms. LaField and I were so proud of him! He was proud too, but he's pretty shy about it. His science grade is an A now, and he's working hard in all his classes. Someday I'm hoping to get him on the honor roll and maybe even a Valued Employee."

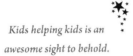

Kids helping kids is an awesome sight to behold.

My Task Managers call the kids in their group when they're absent, come to study hall to help them, and help them stay on task. To provide even more help for the kids in their group who have severe difficulty staying organized, I have a daily progress report that my Task Managers fill out for their "challenges," which includes all the homework and upcoming tests, etc. as well as a brief analysis of his or her on-task behavior that day. The student's responsibility is to show it to their parents each night and bring it back signed. Being a Task Manager is a giant commitment to be sure, and I try to remember to thank them every day. We must never underestimate our students' desire to reach out to their peers with support and encouragement. Kids helping kids is an awesome sight to behold.

THE BREAKTHROUGH MOMENT

As Task Managers learn to lead their groups using the Seven Attributes, they are building community while consciously working toward the ultimate goal of "reaching community." Because the entire concept of community, as well as the initial process of building community, is entirely alien to my first-quarter students, Task Managers must diligently lead their group for at least three weeks to a month before reaching community. Inevitably, some groups struggle until the "final hour."

What a happy day it is when the first group reaches community that first quarter. At one of our regular meetings, eventually one of the Task Managers will, with a mixture of uncertainty and excitement, tell me and the other Task Managers that they *think* their group has reached community. That is the breakthrough moment I have been eagerly anticipating.

The ensuing discussion revolves around the obvious question: "Why do you think you have reached community?" By this time, each of them knows the Seven Attributes of a True Community by heart, so I easily guide that first Task Manager through all seven, the last one being, "In a true community we feel like a family." This last attribute is the clincher. Up to that point, I have been assuring the Task Managers that when their group reaches community, they will know it by the safe, familial feeling that pervades their group. Everyone knows what a family feels like, or should feel like. If that Task Manager resolutely confirms that his or her group feels like a family, we have our first authentic community.

Every time a group reaches community, we celebrate! I excitedly gather all the kids around me on the rug. First comes the announcement—followed, of course, by enthusiastic applause. As we all know, enthusiasm is contagious, and

After all, a celebration without enthusiasm is no celebration at all.

I, the queen of enthusiasm, am lit up like a Christmas tree as we cheer for the Task Manager and kids in the new community. After all, a celebration without enthusiasm is no celebration at all.

Following the applause, I invite the group to discuss the same question with the class: How do they know they are a true community? I immerse the class in a quick review of the Seven Attributes, focusing on the seventh. Drawing from the experiences of the members of the new community, which now feels like a family, we continue our discussion until they all fully understand the dynamics of a true community.

I mentioned earlier that the groups change every quarter. Does every one of those groups reach community? No, each year we have several that cannot, despite monumental efforts by their Task Manager and myself. In those cases, I make certain that the Task Manager doesn't take the blame for the group's inability to reach community. The Task Manager must not feel like he or she failed.

Keep in mind that my training techniques are continually evolving and that my way is not necessarily the way that will work best for you. Also, keep in mind that my students are seventh graders. The younger the students, the less responsibly can your Task Managers "manage" a group of their peers.

After twenty-four years, my passion for teaching community has not waned even a little. Just think of it: a group of radically different students learn to help each other, respect each other, work as a team, and, as a result, feel like a family. Do you think the students in that community enjoy school more? Do you think they learn more because they are enjoying school? Do you think that by learning to "Do unto others" they are acquiring lifelong skills that will not only enhance, but possibly even salvage their personal relationships? I know I do because I have seen it for myself.

I WANT OUT OF THIS GROUP!

I shall never forget one particular group that simply could not work through their differences despite repeated attempts. They went beyond mere frustration; they were sick of each other! I vividly recall the day we met in the Commons for what seemed inevitably to be the final attempt at resolution. Everyone, including me, had just run out of words. When most of us reach that stalemate, that impasse where resolution is an effort in futility, we just shut down. That day we came to a moment where we all just sat there, mute and exhausted. In the midst of that lingering pause, Katie, who was obviously the most exasperated of us all, broke the silence with disgust: "I want out of this group!"

What followed Katie's outburst was nothing less than one of those rare, luminous moments when somebody says or does something that jolts us awake, leaving us injected with x-ray understanding. Some people call them "Aha!" moments; I prefer to believe they are perfectly timed flashes of light that illuminate our minds with divine clarity. Such were the flashes that lit up the movie screen of my mind with a disturbing image of Katie *twenty years down the road*. Deeply embittered and hardened by disappointments stemming from broken relationships, I saw her in my mind's eye once again repeating those same words—but this time to her husband: "I want out of this … *marriage!*"

The effect of this revelation was sudden and dramatic. I don't think I even took a breath before the words spilled out. Drawn to the urgent intensity in my voice, I quickly captured my students' attention. I didn't have to think about what to say. The perfect words just came, and with those words I was able to turn their hearts back to considering the *possibility* of reconciliation. In fact, by the time I was finished a short five minutes later, possibility had miraculously exploded into *probability*.

I helped them see that what they were experiencing was no different than what happens to the untold number of marriages that fall apart because people—for whatever

I was able to make it very real for them, especially because most of them were the innocent victims of two parents who didn't settle their differences.

reasons—don't work through their differences. I was able to make it very real for them, especially because most of them were the innocent victims of two parents who didn't settle their differences. I got them feeling, relating and empathizing, which helped them lower their defenses.

GREAT LOVE AND UNSWERVING COMMITMENT

If we can penetrate children's hearts, we can help them see and understand other viewpoints, thereby empowering them with the tools to live harmoniously and peacefully in an imperfect world—a world teeming with people who need understanding, compassion, empathy and forgiveness. This principle is nothing less than the essence of emotional intelligence.

How do we penetrate children's hearts? *With great love and unswerving commitment.* How did "love" penetrate the hearts of my students and prevail that day in the Commons? First, last and most important, I was patient. Up to the very second that I saw the "vision" of Katie and her husband, I maintained a positive attitude. If I had not, there would have been no vision. Impatience would have given up, right along with the kids. It would have voiced its frustration, effectively blocking a peaceful resolution and precipitating divorce.

That day in the Commons we all witnessed a miracle. Five despondent students, all hopelessly resigned to failure, unanimously agreed to try again. As you can imagine, I was overcome with emotion, and extremely proud of them. But I quickly warned them of their need for more than a simple agreement. They had reached consensus but not community. They needed a plan to follow faithfully when future storms inevitably hit. Honoring the plan, I advised them, would require that they hold each other strictly accountable.

Then, I made a wise decision—I left them on their own to devise a plan. To continue guiding them would have deprived them of the pride they would feel when they reached community. Devising their own plan would award them the credit for success. When we rescue our students by solving their problems for them, we rob them of their power and its rewards.

When we rescue our students by solving their problems for them, we rob them of their power and its rewards.

With a sense of humility and awe, I returned to class and left them with a prayer for continued guidance and a speedy resolution. When they called me excitedly back into the Commons, the group members were like overblown balloons nearly bursting to reveal their plan. One part of the plan was to alternate Task Managers every two days. A significant part of their problem was a bossy Task Manager who, despite the best of intentions, had alienated himself. Once everyone had performed for two days, they decided they would vote for the best candidate. Happily, their former Task Manager, who was reaping the benefit of a second chance, heartily agreed. In addition, they had determined who would hold whom accountable.

I was fast approaching the speechless zone that, for me, always precedes a veritable bucket of tears. I didn't know they had intentionally saved the best for last: They had unanimously agreed that no matter what obstacles they might face, they would remain committed to the goal of achieving community. They had agreed that divorce was not an option! Five twelve-year-olds esteemed the concept of community above their own personal needs, above their own personal interests, and therein lay the miracle.

Did they reach community? You bet they did. Was I proud? Aren't mothers always proud when their babies learn to walk? Was the celebration spectacular? Absolutely.

The entire process was ripe with life-changing lessons. Here are several:

- ★ They learned the critical importance of commitment to a cause higher than themselves.
- ★ They learned about consensus and about holding each other accountable.
- ★ They practiced setting goals and successfully reaching them.
- ★ They learned ways of solving their conflicts peacefully rather than divorcing themselves from the problem.
- ★ They practiced perseverance through a trial.
- ★ They practiced being People of Character.
- ★ They were personally empowered by the entire process. Its success gave them hope for meeting and solving future personal and relational problems.
- ★ They practiced tolerance, compassion, empathy, and group cooperation with right attitudes.
- ★ They practiced *humility* and *unselfishness* in the sense that they set aside their entrenched attitudes.
- ★ They learned that "The prize is worth the price!"

Theirs was an example of a real-life scenario reenacted in the homes of thousands of couples every day throughout the world—the "I quit, I found something better, and I want out" scenario. Its aftermath leaves shattered lives, broken dreams, and the innocent victims who fill more and more of the desks in our classrooms with each passing year. My hope for those five students is, that in the days and years to come they will not succumb to the scenario but will courageously *live the lessons* they learned that day in the Commons when they were only twelve years of age.

WELCOMING NEW ARRIVALS

One of the greatest advantages of Caring Communities is the "instant" home they provide for new students who inevitably join my class the middle of the year. In my former days, they would have best been described as impositions. Their arrival never came at a "good" time; in fact, it was sometimes downright inconvenient. Their anxious, lost, puppy-dog looks only meant one thing: more work.

Recently, Travis joined our class and found, in the space of single day, a home with us. That we unreservedly opened our hearts to welcome him was even more significant considering the conditions to which Travis went home every night: a rundown motel where his mother, brother, and he made the best of what little they had. They were homeless. When I talked to Travis' mother that first night on the phone, we shared a very important connection during which I learned she had had walking pneumonia for several months, her family had abandoned her, and her youngest son was chronically ill. We didn't even talk about the absent father. Without that phone call, I would never have known why Travis was often tired, why he often failed to complete assignments, and why he was easily distracted. As a result of one initial phone call, I understood the why's. I was better equipped to give Travis what he really needed: encouragement, empathy, support, and extra attention.

As I do each time a new student joins our class, I asked the Task Managers to decide which group would be most appropriate for Travis to join. I never tire of seeing them argue over who "gets to have" the new boy or girl who, minutes later, is introduced and shown the ropes. As much as possible on that first day, I depend upon my caring and compassionate students to reach out and help meet the social and emotional needs of the new student. Certainly, they want to feel welcomed by the teacher, but far more important is their need to feel accepted by their peers.

I also invited Travis to have lunch in our room, where a group of happy "regulars" eats every day. There, amidst laughter and lightheartedness, he could relax as the all-important birth of new friendships began.

SEVEN INSPIRED WORDS

I realize that those of you who decide to incorporate community in your classrooms will have many questions that I have not addressed here. But I assure you that just as I created the Task Manager system from the ground up, you too can create your own system. Any teacher committed to the core components of a true community, the Seven Attributes, can create a classroom that may look entirely different than my class but feel just as much like *home*.

As I close one of the most important chapters of *Living the Lessons*, I remind you of the compelling story of Scott Peck's fortuitous discovery of community at Friends Seminary and those seven words that unveiled the blueprints of my new classroom: "I felt like I had come home." What was it about those words? Why do they now still resonate with that voice that inwardly echoes home, home, home? They were the words that revealed my ultimate purpose for being a teacher. After fifteen years of getting most of it wrong, with Peck's seven words I realized what I was to do in the classroom for the rest of my career.

What does it feel like to come *home*? I contend that home is the place where we feel completely welcome and entirely safe. It is where we feel unconditionally accepted, included, and cherished. It is the place where we feel like we belong, where we feel like an integral member of a family that works together for a common cause, stands united against life's storms, learns together, laughs together, cries together, and loves together. And I contend that all of these things should be true of school.

Think about your students, especially those at risk, most of whom have no sense of home. Home is the one thing they need most in their lives!

Think about your students, especially those at risk, most of whom have no sense of *home*. Home is the one thing they need most in their lives! I was awakened that day to the needs of those "homeless" ones in my class. Some call it a magnificent obsession. I call it community. Peck called it home. It doesn't really matter what we call it—as long as it's good for the kids.

11/7/05   Monday

Dear Journal,

I got a D+ in Math last week on my progress report. Now that is dissappointing; however, I'm raising my grade and as of this moment it's an B. So my goall in getting good grades in math are extoardinarily easy. My personal + family goals are making me emotionally intellegent. They are making me emotionally intellegent because if I do them and acheive them then I get respect back in return. I also get less grounding. It makes me more respectfu My goal of being completely trustworthy has been acheived. I'm so excited. This worl will be a better place with the help of me

Yes!

      w/ ♥ Angela

      obedient

I'm very obedient which makes things easier in life.

CHAPTER 8
Forgiveness and Acceptance

*T*ormented. That's the word that comes to mind when I remember Tyler. Tormented externally by his peers and tormented internally as a result of their unabated, unabashed assaults on his personal dignity. If someone were to write a book called *The Anatomy of a Target,* Tyler would be the classic study case to include. He may as well have worn a sign around his neck: "I am a target. Go ahead and hurt me." Tyler came to me bleeding profusely from the accumulated gaping wounds of his childhood school days. Tyler was in pain, but his was a quiet, slow-boil pain. Tyler screamed quietly behind the pages of his latest fantasy escape book. Never once disrespectful, nor disobedient, nor disturbing, he was simply disconnected and wanted to stay that way... or so it seemed.

Before I changed my teaching style, Tyler could have hidden for nine months and then quietly slipped away; In those days I didn't shake a student's hand in the morning, look intently into his eyes, and recognize raging pain. In those days Tyler would have easily self-isolated because he would not have been required to sit in a group with his peers and build community. In those days I would have wondered why Tyler was so quiet, but I would never have ruminated over his pain.

As always, the real complaints began to surface around the first of October— after the kids have been in groups for a couple weeks. Tyler's Task Manager expressed frustration at his polite refusals to "put his book away and join the group." It was the first warning sign. I remember asking his Task Manager for patience with Tyler. He would obviously need time to learn to trust his new peer group, time to come out of hiding. You can't force a child out of hiding. You can't say, "Okay, Tyler, put your book away right now and talk to your peers." Well, you can, but it is a shortsighted victory.

Eventually, I talked to the entire group and helped them understand how best to care for Tyler. I helped them see that it was not about them, that Tyler had never received authentic understanding, acceptance and respect from his peers, that he did not trust their overtures. And why should he? I helped them feel his pain. It was about empathy—a practical application lesson in advanced emotional intelligence.

By the end of the quarter had Tyler visibly moved any closer to connecting with his peers? Not at all. During the second quarter I handpicked Tyler's new group. Everyone was fully aware of the first quarter struggle that had ended in disappointment, so it was only fair that willing volunteers surround him for the next attempt at winning his trust. But more than merely willing, they had to be fervently committed to the cause. They had to stick with Tyler despite his reclusive nature. They had to be prepared for non-aggressive refusals to participate. Which is exactly what they got. But despite Tyler's continued rebuffs, his second group never grumbled, lost patience or regretted their decision to join a group that might very likely fail to reach community, which—you guessed it—they did not.

When the time came for the third quarter Task Managers to pick groups, the overall feeling around the table was evident: Nobody wanted Tyler in their group. And why should they? Never once in all the years of picking groups have I even suggested that a Task Manager choose a certain student against his or her will. Certainly, I have offered suggestions, but my students know they are free to decide.

I have no clearly defined set of established rules for what to do in such cases. I can't say that I knew exactly what I was going to do when I stood up and told the kids I'd be back, but I went into the room, walked straight to Tyler's desk and asked him politely to follow me to the sliding glass door. Calmly, matter-of-factly, and non-judgmentally, I pointed to the Task Managers at the table in the Commons and told him point blank that they had reached a roadblock: He had not been picked for one of the groups.

Surprised? It does sound rather unfeeling and, in actuality, it was. But it was "the facts," and I knew Tyler could deal with facts. He was completely logical, rational, and well-acquainted with rejection. I began with questions. Had he ever been mistreated by his peers in his last two groups? *No.* Had they tried for months to include him? *Yes.* Had he ignored their persistent invitations? *Yes.* Had he kept two groups from reaching community. *Yes.* Did he care? Well, *he guessed so.* Did he understand why nobody wanted him in his or her group? *Yes.* Good.

We had all the cards out. No denials. He saw it as it was, as something new. He saw that he had the problem—not his peers.

The next question came without forethought: If one of the Task Managers would agree to giving him another chance, would he agree to be a team player? *Yes.* Naturally, I pressed the point. Did he mean it? *Yes.* Could we put it in writing? *Yes.* I was convinced. And then I asked him to look out the glass door and pick the one Task Manager in whose group he would most like to be. Chelsea. Having no idea what Chelsea would say, I prepared Tyler for disappointment and sent him back to his seat.

After relating the conversation to my Task Managers, I indifferently stated that he wanted to be in Chelsea's group. All eyes were on Chelsea. Not a moment passed before she flashed a brilliant smile of acceptance. We clapped. We cheered. I cried.

Tyler was true to his promise. Little by little he lowered his defenses. Sometimes he was downright disrespectful. He was taking some of his pain out on his peers. But mostly he was testing them, testing them to see if they were for real. But one day at a time, it got better. Tyler got better. And one day out in the Commons I caught them laughing together. Really laughing. I just stood there and watched from a distance. I watched, and, yes, I cried big tears for a little boy whose wounds were finally beginning to heal.

One happy day Chelsea's group reached community. As they stood together on the risers holding the "We Reached Community!" sign, I asked Tyler how it felt. The kids were all *It was, he told us, the first time in his life he had ever felt safe and accepted at school.* standing on the chairs as they always do for community celebrations—perfectly still. They could never have known the profound significance the moment held for Tyler's life, but they knew it was big. There was a long pause as he collected his thoughts. Tears welled up behind his glasses. He took a very deep breath. Time and the world stood still in Room 225. It was, he told us, the first time in his life he had ever felt safe and accepted at school. The first time. But not the last.

The rest of Tyler's story is the happy ending part. He decided to go to college and become a counselor so he could help kids like himself. He saw a purpose in his pain. He finally had hope.

Tyler wanted you to hear his story in his own words:

"School is a horrible place to be when you don't give in to the 'standards.' It starts in kindergarten—the first day of school, the first time away from family, and with complete strangers. No one knows how to act, so we learn from each other. It can start with just one kid who was raised wrong. Just one kid and it begins. That one kid has bad traits, and from there on, it becomes a disease. Every year it's spreading more and more. Every year more and more kids catch it.

It's like pneumonia: It gets worse until it's treated. This 'disease' is more than bullying. It's prejudice! It's greed! It's wrong! I have been picked on, pushed, punched, kicked, humiliated, disgraced, and spit on. It's like stabbing my soul with a knife. And it goes deep. It leaves a scar. If you could see my soul, it would look like it was hit by a train. The prejudice at school is much bigger than people realize. It is pain. It is sadness. It is worldwide. Ms. LaField is like my doctor. She is helping cure the disease with community. Community is like home. It's like family. It's... happiness. It gave me a chance for a happy life. I think community is like the Civil Rights Movement with Ms. LaField as our Martin Luther King. Imagine the world caring about each other! One big community! It would be wonderful. It would be safe. I have seen the power of community. You can, too."

FORGIVENESS

Forgiveness is the remedy for the inexorable certainty that as long as we live and breathe, we will hurt and be hurt.

Forgiveness is the remedy for the inexorable certainty that as long as we live and breathe, we will hurt and be hurt. Forgiveness is for the imperfect people living together in an imperfect world. We must scrutinize our relationships and expel every vestige of unforgiveness as we would an unwelcome intruder come to steal our most cherished treasures. And we must live the lesson with integrity before we ever endeavor to teach it to our students.

In ever-increasing numbers our students come to us with long histories of relational wounds and broken families. It is my contention that students cannot develop and maintain healthy social relationships if they harbor anger, bitterness, and resentment toward those who caused significant pain in their past. They must learn to forgive before they can move on to create better lives for themselves.

THE JOHN W. FORGIVENESS MOVEMENT

Every year I issue a forgiveness challenge to my student. One year this challenge spontaneously created a series of events we later dubbed the John W. Forgiveness Movement.

John, an eighth grader in another Core class, was possibly the most despised student on a school wide level that I had ever encountered. Hated by even the sweetest, most compassionate girls in our class, he was described by many as a monster. But unexpectedly John's breakthrough finally came. Melonie recalls,

> *"My forgiveness moment was when I forgave John W. He was mean to me since elementary school. I walked up to him in science and said, 'I forgive you, John.' After that everyone started to forgive him, and he began to be nice."*

I wish you could have been there when Melonie stood up and proudly announced to the class what she had done. Stunned with shocked disbelief, the entire class broke into a loud barrage of "Are you crazy?" Wisely capturing the emotion of the moment, I challenged the rest of them to follow Melonie's example. Though I did not know the boy, it was obvious from the way he bullied people all of his life that he was harboring some very deep emotional scars. Little by little I helped my students see his pain; little by little they learned to feel compassion for John W.

And then one day, John walked up to me in the Commons and introduced himself. After a warm smile, a firm handshake and a couple brief moments of "Oh, so you're the mean kid I've been hearing so much about," I asked him point blank if he enjoyed being so mean and so disliked. I wasn't implying judgment, or condemnation, and I wasn't trying to reprimand. I was only asking, "Why?"

It's amazing how much we can learn about people if we care enough to ask the right questions, and if we listen with an authentic intent to help.

It was as though he had been waiting all of his life for someone to finally ask. It's amazing how much we can learn about people if we care enough to ask the right questions, and if we listen with an authentic intent to help. Without hesitation, John admitted that he did not like the way he was, but he did not know how to change.

Isn't that exactly the way it is with so many of our students? They are our troublemakers, our unwelcome, obnoxious distractions, and because we are not yet far enough along on the journey, we fail to recognize their wounds. They are screaming for help in the most dramatic ways they know, and we miss it.

John's wounds began to heal, and the formerly infamous John W. gave up the ghost. The real John—buried deep under a pile of emotional garbage—rose to the surface for all to know and love.

The last week of school my students collected money to buy John a giant pizza so immense it had to be turned sideways to pass through the door. It was, as you can well imagine, quite a moment—John reclining casually on my beanbag, looking like royalty with all my students gathered around him like dogs begging for a morsel of his prize. As always, I cried. I cried for that wounded little boy, lost for so many years and finally found. Once again, miracles followed love in action.

On the last day of school our students meander around to different classrooms signing each other's yearbooks. When John wandered through my door, I immediately ushered him to a corner desk, handed him a pencil and paper, and asked him to write a brief account of the outpouring of love that had changed his life so radically.

I am so thankful I saved the note he scrawled that day, for he expressed his story far better in a few brief words than I could in an entire book:

> Ever since I was a little boy I have been picking on kids. Even though I knew it hirt peoples fellings I did it anyway. I did it for atintion. I never got it from my dad who diserted me when I was 2. Then when I was in 8th grade I meet this girle named melonie who told me shee forgave me for being so mean. Then other People sorted started forgiveing me. That really started changing my life. I started being nice to people and making friends. I finally stop picking on people because I got the atintion I needed.

THE DR. SEUSS APPROACH

One quote on our wall by Mother Teresa 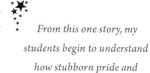 reminds my students that "to love, you must forgive." Another—my students' favorite— includes a picture from the Dr. Seuss book, *The Sneeches.*[1]   Using the overhead projector, I enlarged the picture of the northbound Zax and the southbound Zax, standing nose-

From this one story, my students begin to understand how stubborn pride and unforgiveness work together to destroy relationships.

to-nose, both refusing to step aside and allow the other to pass. It is a perfect representation of two angry people who "would rather be right than be happy." Above the picture I attached the words, "Stubborn people are lonely people," and below, "I'm sorry! I was wrong. Will you forgive me?" This is the story that I use to introduce the concept of humility. From this one story, my students begin to understand how stubborn pride and unforgiveness work together to destroy relationships.

I shall always remember the morning I was greeting my students at the door when one boy excitedly approached to announce that he and his best friend had been playing basketball and that, as usual, it had ended with an argument. But on this occasion, without even thinking, he had blurted out, "I'm sorry! I was wrong. Will you forgive me?" Not only had he amazed his friend, he had amazed himself. But most amazing to them both was they continued their game— something they had never done before! Think of the far-reaching ramifications of that one lesson.

AN IMPERFECT WORLD

Sometimes a situation requires more than the Dr. Seuss method. I model a step-by-step process for my students to follow when they hurt someone else. I will describe this process for you in detail as I myself would practice it.

Let's say, for example, that I am upset and impatiently accuse Rachelle of something before giving her a chance to share her truth. The entire class watches as Rachelle, who is completely innocent, retreats quietly to her desk. Class resumes, and I temporarily forget the problem. That night, as I examine myself with the intent of making sure I lived the lessons that day, I realized the consequences of my actions.

The next day I gather the kids around me and with a very serious countenance make sure everyone is aware that something extremely important is about to happen. I wait for complete quiet and with all eyes on me, I announce that yesterday I did something very hurtful to someone in the class. I ask if anyone knows what I am talking about. Everyone raises their hands. I am ready for step one.

I hold up the first of the five signs on my lap. It states, "We live in an imperfect world." I ask for clarification. A brief discussion follows which quickly leads to the point: We live in an imperfect world because people are imperfect. They make mistakes. We all make mistakes. Everyone agrees. But it's okay to make mistakes, I tell them, as long as we are willing to take personal responsibility for our mistakes. I am ready for step two.

I hold up the second sign, which asks, "What happened?" I clearly describe yesterday's incident with Rachelle. The focus in this step is to help my students realize that my responsibility is to own the truth about what I did to Rachelle, with no excuses. No matter how I felt or what Rachelle may have done, I was wrong. Nobody made me treat Rachelle disrespectfully.

Holding up the third sign, which asks, "What should I do about it?" I ask for their input. They know what I should do, but I continue to press the point: I should apologize. After all, I was wrong, and I care about Rachelle's feelings. I care about our relationship. My students, who by this time are virtually paralyzed with amazement, watch as I look intently into Rachelle's eyes and tell her with the utmost sincerity that I am so sorry for hurting her.

It is time for the fourth step—the step that heals: "Will you forgive me?" I hold up the sign, look once again at Rachelle, usually with tears, and humbly ask for her forgiveness, which she was long ago ready to bestow. I leave my place to hug her. All is now well between Rachelle and me.

It is time for the last step. I have owned the truth, sincerely apologized to Rachelle, and humbly asked her forgiveness, which she happily granted. We even hugged. What could be left? I hold up the last sign, which asks: "What can I learn?" I must examine the problem and seriously consider how to avoid repeating my mistake. A short discussion of possibilities ensues.

Unfortunately, far too many of us fail to complete that last critical step. We think we are finished all too soon and then wonder why we keep repeating the same mistakes. As I share in another chapter, our biggest and boldest sign in the room declares *We are here to learn.* We must teach our students to examine their behavior and learn from it. The ability to do so constitutes the very heart and soul of emotional intelligence.

This year's modeling process was different than all others, however, because the student's behavior that precipitated my inappropriate outburst was outrageously unacceptable. With great difficulty I finally convinced my students that no matter what the other person does, we have to own our part. They kept insisting that "she deserved it." Even my brightest, most aware students wanted to justify my behavior. A supreme example of a teachable moment, I milked it for all it was worth. It was a lesson that went deep and changed them. In the years to come, they will have many opportunities to live it.

A PUBLIC APOLOGY

Yet another way I teach forgiveness is with a colorful laminated sign that hangs on a nail in the far corner of our room. One side reads, "I'm sorry!" and the other, "Will you please forgive me?" Any time my students want to make a public apology, they merely get the sign, stand on the risers and wait for everyone's attention. Right there, in front of all their peers, they quickly model the five-step process. In this way I give them opportunities to practice the lessons. I even encourage them to make their own signs and use them at home. Simple yet powerful, it's a tool they can use all of their lives.

"ME FIRST AND THE GIMME GIMME'S"

Every year I ask all of those who need to forgive someone to raise their hands, and every year, almost without exception, every hand goes up. After a caution to avoid extremely sensitive personal issues, I invite my students to briefly share their stories. Always one of the first bonding times of the year, we open our hearts and learn to know each other on a deeper level. Then before the lesson is over, I earnestly challenge them to bravely forgive someone over the weekend and to be prepared the following week to share victorious "Forgiveness Moments" the last five minutes of each day of the next week. The following are a few of those victories:

> *"I forgave my dad for everything he has done to me and my mom and my brothers and sister. He ruined our entire lives when he left. I was one, and my mother had four little children to take care of all by herself."*

> *"I forgave myself. My little brother died in a car accident four years ago, and I have always held myself responsible for his death. I forgave myself and now I can finally be happy."*

"My mom and I got into a big fight, and she was making everything my fault when it was really hers. The next day I told her I forgave her, and she hugged me and said she needed that."

And finally, Kat, a precious child with a truly amazing heart, shares some very wise advice to us all:

"Let me tell you, Ms. LaField is big about forgiving and loving. I have changed a lot because she has introduced forgiving into my life. You have no idea how grateful I am that Ms. LaField has taken the time to teach all of her students—we are like her children—about choosing to care, forgiving, loving, humility, and so much more. She has all of these words up all over the walls reminding everybody to do their best each and every day of their lives. Just as Mother Teresa once wisely said, 'Loving must come as natural to us as living and breathing.' In other words, we must choose to love each other, and the more we do, the easier it is to do it.

To love, you must forgive. And to forgive you must pull out all of the arrows of hurt and pain that people have shot into your heart. Once at a Right Heart Club meeting, Ms. LaField started talking about loving and forgiving. She explained that when we were little kids, we didn't hold grudges, and it was easy for us to be happy. We didn't need people to tell us to be happy or teach us how. That was before we started getting insulted.

Ms. LaField put a picture of a little stick girl on the overhead who was happy. She had a perfect, happy heart at first, but then people starting hurting her, and little by little she had lots of arrows sticking in her heart. Ms. LaField began to erase the arrows one at a time, and she explained that each time the little girl forgave someone, another arrow came out and that by forgiving the people who hurt her, she got happier and happier like she was when she was little.

We must be like that little girl. We must forgive and forget. We can never love others or be happy with ourselves if we do not forgive. Please let this touch your heart and begin to take action. Pull out your arrows and forgive. Be a miracle and inspiration. Believe!"

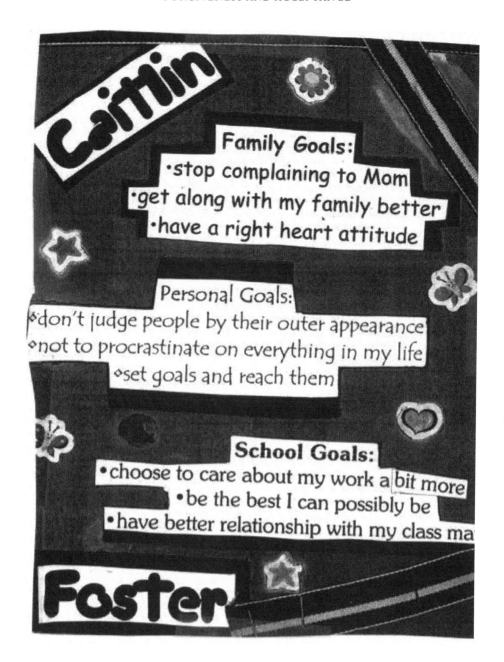

Caitlin

Family Goals:
• stop complaining to Mom
• get along with my family better
• have a right heart attitude

Personal Goals:
• don't judge people by their outer appearance
• not to procrastinate on everything in my life
• set goals and reach them

School Goals:
• choose to care about my work a bit more
• be the best I can possibly be
• have better relationship with my class ma

Foster

★ MORAL ★

CHAPTER 9

Character Education

I begin to address the *moral* needs of my student on the first day of school. I greet my class holding a rock in my hands and say, "Good morning, Class. I'm Ms. LaField, *and this is our Truth Rock.*" I explain that truth is the bedrock upon which character rests. Not a day goes by in our class without reference to the truth. If you were to ask my students what I love most, they would most likely first tell you that I love them, but they would also tell you that I love the truth.

As my students gaze around their new classroom on the first day, they are welcomed by a veritable plethora of words on the walls. I call them *"wall words."* One display consists of a colorful explosion of eight stars each boldly announcing: Courage, Truth, Perseverance, Integrity, Respect, Responsibility, Humility, and Kindness. In the midst of them all shines the biggest star emblazoned with the words, "People of Character."

I refer to these words often throughout the year. One day during Storytime I pointed up to the words and asked my students which word best represented the lesson in our story about the blind pole-vaulter.

"Perseverance!" exclaimed Kristen. After only a few weeks of school, most of them already knew the word and could easily recognize a real-life application.

"Yes," I told them, "People of Character are never quitters!" One inspirational story at a time, with the help of the indispensable wall words, I introduce my students to the attributes of true character and the tenets of morality.

About the wall words Jason says:

"Ms. LaField has a big star on her wall that says People of Character with lots of other words around it. Once those words got into me it was like my

soul was becoming cleaner. I took this knowledge to my family and friends and once again, they're amazed."

What are at first mere words on a wall gradually come to life for my students. Embracing them through repeated exposure, they are changed from within.

A STRONG FOCUS ON GOALS

Our goals focus is an indispensable venue for teaching my students high moral character. Challenged to examine their lives in the light of the truth, my students wisely decide on personal, family, and school goals that directly affect and enhance the development of their moral character. Choices to stop lying, disrespecting their parents, and acting irresponsibly dramatically transform their lives. Old habits soon give way to new ways of being so that, in a surprisingly short time, they begin to proudly share breakthroughs with their classmates.

My students' journals are the key to helping them maintain a sustained focus on their goals. One of their daily journal entry requirements is to "pick a wall word" and explain in one sentence how it applies to their life on that particular day. For example, at the bottom of the entry page, they might write "Courage" and then follow it with something like, "Today I had a lot of courage because I told Bobbie to stop picking on Donovan." Just one wall word a day, and in an amazingly short period of time, the words come alive.

A CHARACTER-BUILDING PROGRAM

A further means of teaching my students character-building traits is our You're Hired! program: a career-focused, incentive-based program created to teach my students a strong work ethic. You're Hired! is the most motivational tool I have encountered. I continue to be astounded by the success of the program to inspire my students to higher degrees of moral "maturity."

In order to receive the highest promotion in You're Hired!, Valued Employee, my students must prove to be courteous, respectful, responsible, hard working, and completely trustworthy. Furthermore, they must consistently display the qualities of a positive "team player" who obeys with a Right Heart. (Right Heart essentially means that their motivations are pure, but this will be explained in detail later on.) Once they fulfill all the qualifications in *my* class, they are dubbed Valued Employee "candidates" until all of their other teachers and their parents sign papers stating that they fulfill each and every requirement for them as well. Oh, the stories I could tell about those sweet, responsible Dr. Jekyll/Mr. Hyde students who charm their teachers in school, then tyrannize their parents at home! This program actually inspires students to respect their parents, some for the first time in their lives. A supreme example of real-life application, my "candidates" learn the meaning of integrity and go on to become Valued Employees by *living the lessons* everywhere they go.

INTEGRATION INTO THE ACADEMIC CURRICULUM

Another powerful approach to teaching my students to be people of high moral character is the planned integration of character themes throughout the academic curriculum. The poems they learn, the essays they write, the literature we read, and the history we study are carefully chosen for their character focus. If your commitment to creating character-based lessons is decisively strong, you are limited only by your imagination.

Let's say you are calling out the spelling words for this week's test. Naturally, you are going to use them within the context of a sentence, so why not dictate "character-based" sentences? How about doing the same in a punctuation lesson, or any English lesson for that matter? If you require your students to write sentences using their spelling words, why not assign a different character trait each week that they must integrate into their sentences? Then you can select their sentences to use as you call out the spelling words for the test on Friday. They'll love listening for their sentence.

Think of the holidays we celebrate like Martin Luther King Day and the Presidents' Days. What better time to highlight the attributes of People of Character? If you were to visit our class, you would see how I "showcase" Dr. King. As you walk through the sliding glass doors, your eyes would be drawn to a large, elaborately decorated bulletin board entitled "Martin's Big Words." Surrounding his portrait in the center are enlarged words like Love, Peace, Equality, surrounded by several of his famous quotes. Many times during the year I draw my students' attention to that bulletin board until, by the end of the year, he is more to them than a mere historical character; he is a true hero! No matter what time period we teach, we can always find clever ways to integrate outstanding examples from other time periods.

We also have a character-based quote of the week. One week the quote in our class was one of my favorites from St. Augustine: "Let us sing a new song—not with our lips, but with our lives!" As I have explained, we discuss the quote with an emphasis on one or more of the character traits embedded within. Augustine focuses on integrity, a sophisticated word for many students that becomes a part of their everyday vocabulary.

THE CONFUCIUS CHALLENGE

History overflows with examples of virtuous people throughout time, who often sacrificed their lives for their strong moral characters and lofty beliefs. Currently, I teach the history of the Middle Ages and never run out of examples of People of Character, like Joan of Arc, Martin Luther, and Confucius, who, as a result of their unfailing commitment to truth and justice, left their indelible mark on humanity.

One year we studied the Five Virtues of Confucius. I zeroed in on the fifth:

Children should honor their parents, and parents should treat their children well.

Right in the midst of the discussion a wonderful idea came to me: I challenged my students to honor their parents for one entire week as never before. Some did not even have the vaguest notion what honor meant, so we spent several minutes discussing possible approaches. Most took the challenge and every day thereafter I asked one or two to share a victory to keep the challenge fresh in their minds.

That Friday we had a Chinese festival in honor of Confucius. The kids each donated a couple dollars to help with expenses. I bought paper lanterns, chopsticks, fortune cookies, and about ten pounds of peppered chicken from a local Chinese restaurant. Our wonderful head cook provided buckets of steamed rice.

Some admitted to respecting their parents for the first time in their lives. We listened to Asian music as we played Chinese checkers and competed to see who could pick up the most beans with chopsticks. It was great fun, but the best part was the last half hour when we all gathered around the risers for the kids to share their challenge victories.

You had to be there to understand how deeply they were affected by the challenge. Some admitted to respecting their parents for the first time in their lives.

During that initial discussion of the challenge, I had introduced the concept of servanthood. Many talked of serving their parents as never before. They were proud of themselves because they saw how much it had meant to their parents. But most importantly, they saw that much of the negativity in their homes was their fault!

My students learned more of what it means to be a Person of Character with that singular idea. The next Monday I gave them time to write personal reflections about their challenge week. Kurestin wrote,

"My mom is usually mad and stressed because my brother, sister, and I fight like crazy, but last week I didn't fight with them at all. I really appreciate my mom being here, but I never show it. I am a snob towards her, but last week I did my absolute best to show her I appreciate her. My mom never says thank you for anything to me, but last week she realized it and said thank you for everything I did for her, and we actually got along. This challenge helped me realize that my actions make a big difference! I didn't do this for a week. I will continue for the rest of my life."

Tommy concludes…

"On a scale of one to ten I would say I achieved a twelve on treating my parents with respect during the week of the Confucius challenge. At first I was really worried because my mom and I were not in good shape at all; in fact, I had been silent to her for a few days. I was obedient when she asked me to do something, but I hated it! When Ms. LaField challenged us to honor and respect our parents for a week, I knew I had to take the challenge. It turned out to be possibly the best week of my life. I was respectful to my parents all week, and they respected me the same. I think they noticed because both of them were so happy! Thank you, Confucius, for inspiring me!"

STORYTIME LESSONS

Many years ago I began reading stories with powerful lessons to my students, and I soon discovered that they are perhaps our most effective tool for infusing character-building lessons into the curriculum. Reading a story at the close of the week eventually evolved into a cherished tradition fondly known as Storytime.

Without the vital heart connection, the lesson of the story cannot act as a change agent.

More than any other time of the week, I enforce the high standards of respect in our classroom, for unless my students are completely still and quiet, they will miss the impact of the story.

As a result of so much practice over the years, I have mastered the fine art of storytelling. We can never hope to sustain our students' attention for any length of time unless we are extraordinary oral readers, and if we fail to sustain their attention, we will fail to convey the lesson. It is, therefore, incumbent upon us to fine-tune our oral reading skills until our students hear our stories with their hearts as well as their ears. Without the vital heart connection, the lesson of the story cannot act as a change agent.

Captivating storytellers must first have a story worthy of telling. I am forever searching for new stories to add to my collection. Last year, for example, discovering "The Sneeches" by Dr. Seuss was like discovering buried treasure. The lesson of the story is of paramount importance for so many of our students. Entertaining and provocative, it compellingly conveys the message that "being stubborn is bad because it hurts us so much." The storyline doesn't simply declare, "Don't be stubborn!" It shows the listener why stubbornness is so harmful by illustrating its hapless consequences.

At the conclusion of a story like "The Sneeches," I challenge my students to raise their hands if they will admit to being stubborn. After the snickers subside, they scan the room, relieved to learn that they are not in the minority. At that point, we are ready for the most important part of Storytime: *the personal application discussion.*

First, I ask for volunteers to share their own experiences with stubbornness. As these volunteers reveal the truth about themselves, the other students consider the truth about themselves as well. This is the prerequisite to personal application. After a few students share quick stories about a time they were stubborn, I ask, "Why does being stubborn hurt us?" It is important to give the students adequate time to process. I encourage them to probe for the answer, and most often someone "nails" it. The crucial point is that they buy into the "why" and then apply it to their own lives

In addition to having a story worth telling, we must read with expression, and we must know the story well enough to look up from our reading often and make eye contact with our students. Most adults assume that seventh graders are too old or perhaps too "cool" to gather on the rug near their teacher. Admittedly, the students are a little wary the first couple of stories, but soon they anticipate

Storytime with great enthusiasm. Each time I joyfully shout, "It's Storytime!" cheers fill the room as they chase each other to the rug to secure their favorite spot.

STORIES OF CHARACTER

Over the years I have collected a substantial anthology of powerful stories that, year after year, capture my students' hearts and effectively teach them the critical importance of becoming people of high moral character. Invariably, every story spotlights one of the many character traits or themes that I emphasize in our class, and whenever possible I select stories that support the focus of that particular week.

For example, every year I stress the value of being a giver, so early in the year I read *The Giving Tree* by Shel Silverstein. Quite often the stories correlate with one of the themes in the core novel we are reading. When we read *The Outsiders*, we spend a considerable amount of time discussing the dangers of stereotyping others, so I always read "The Wemmicks," a powerful story by Max Lucado about judging others by their outward appearance. Some of the stories relate to history, especially when we study slavery and the Civil Rights movement, and I always look forward to Black History Month as a time to read stories that denounce racial discrimination. At Thanksgiving and Christmas the stories emphasize the virtue of gratitude and the joy of giving.

Valuable stories can also be drawn from our own personal life experiences. Most of the stories I share with my students convey a lesson learned from experiences I had as a teenager. They are captivated by these stories, which help them see me as a human being, not just their teacher.

Some of my precious students expressed the following thoughts and feelings about Storytime:

"Every story that was read at Storytime inspired me, especially the one about the blind kid who pole vaulted. Storytime has really helped me grow, just like the Emotional I.Q because it showed me what I need to work on and what kind of person I am."

"I will never forget when Ms. LaField read Me First and the Gimme Gimmes. That really changed my life forever. I used to be so self-centered and rude. I

always wanted things my way. The Gimme Gimmes really showed me what I was doing. It explained it better than anything I had ever seen or heard."

"I like Storytime because I can relax and relieve my week's stress."

"At the beginning of the year Ms. LaField said Storytime was sacred. I laughed thinking it was a joke. But then as the weeks went by I found that 'Storytime the big joke' was now something to look forward to. And then towards the last part of the year, I found that Storytime really was sacred."

THE HONOR SYSTEM

Still another means of meeting the moral needs of the Whole Child in our class is the Honor System, a time-*honored* method of offering students opportunities to develop trustworthiness. I establish a strong trust base with my students in the first week of school by introducing one of our most important themes: "The true test of who I am is what I do when nobody is watching." Each time I allow my students to grade their own tests, I reaffirm the importance of being a Person of Character who can be trusted.

My students are never left feeling condemned because Ms. LaField caught them cheating; on the contrary, they are inspired to "come up higher" the next time.

Do my students ever cheat as they grade their own tests? Of course they do. Many have been cheating for years and never thought anything of it. Over the course of the year, as they are exposed more and more to the attributes of People of Character, they learn that not only does cheating rob them of self-respect, but it makes it impossible to develop and maintain lasting, intimate relationships.

Invariably, when I "catch" a student cheating, I use it as an opportunity to teach the value of truth, trust, honor, and integrity. My students are never left feeling condemned because Ms. LaField caught them cheating; on the contrary, they are inspired to "come up higher" the next time. At some point in the year, virtually every one of my students finally understands why cheating really is "so bad." It's about authoritatively *telling* versus compassionately *showing*.

TEACHABLE MOMENTS

One of the most powerful methods for meeting the moral needs of the Whole Child is *teachable moments*. I cannot overemphasize the value of dropping everything to capture a moment ripe with the potential for transforming the hearts and minds of your students. We must create situations whereby our students experience a revelation of the character words, through which they firmly grasp the concept. Only then can they ever hope to apply it to their lives with any lasting success. Teachable moments are powerful for one primary reason: They encourage our students to feel, to be "in their hearts" as I call it. When they are feeling, they are most receptive to the lesson at hand.

Early on, my students learn to recognize a forthcoming teachable moment. The moment often begins when I stop the lesson, pause for a second to gain their attention, and then say, "Something wonderful just happened. Can anybody tell us what it was?" Often they recognize who did what; however, they usually don't understand the embedded lesson. Almost without exception, the focus of the message is one particular wall word, one important character attribute.

For example, one week six of my students failed to have their parents sign their reading logs, and I was, as my grandmother used to say, fit to be tied! Suddenly, the realization struck me: They could have easily forged their logs, but they did not! Without a moment's hesitation, I asked for my students' attention and praised the six for their honesty. As always I concluded with something like, "I'm proud of you. You become People of Character each time you choose to do the right thing." Surely, the next time those students are tempted to forge their logs, they will remember that teachable moment and choose to fail—*honestly.*

WE MUST LIVE THE LESSONS!

I return now to the premise upon which *Living the Lessons* rests. Our efforts to teach our students to be People of Character, no matter how well-intentioned, will fail miserably if we, ourselves, fail to *live the lessons.* Our students grow to be People of Character only to the degree to which we model it before their discriminating eyes. When we fail to model the lessons with integrity, we must own the truth about our actions. With a humble, contrite heart we must take responsibility for our failures, and, if the occasion calls for it, publicly apologize and ask for forgiveness.

I enthusiastically invite my students to hold me accountable for my actions. We have Mother Teresa as our "Heart Smart" standard, so they will respectfully ask, "Ms. LaField, would Mother Teresa have said that?" Without fail, I honor the question with an answer, and, as you might have guessed, it is almost always a resounding, "No!" People who are serious about becoming People of Character,

I explain, must not only have role models to emulate and standards by which they can compare themselves; they must also have people in their lives who are invited and encouraged to hold them to those standards.

One solitary teacher committed to teaching his or her students to be virtuous People of Character, dedicated to meeting the needs of the Whole Child, learning to love each child unconditionally, and *living the lessons* with integrity can do much indeed. One solitary visionary who, in accord with Helen Keller, believes "What I can do and should do, by the grace of God I will do!" can instill in students a sense of personal dignity and self-respect. It can be done—one teacher at a time.

CALLING THEM TO GREATNESS

From the back wall of our classroom Dr. Martin Luther King boldly proclaims his truth: "Everyone can be great!" Early in the year my students learn that being great is about being the best we can be. It's about setting goals and persevering until we reach them. It's about "being fit for ourselves to know." They learn that being great is about becoming all that we were created to be, about not settling for "pretty good."

Recently, I taught my dear students a new chant:

> *Good, better, best—*
> *never let it rest*
> *'til your good is better,*
> *and your better is best!*

Our students are hungry for success. They loved it—as I knew they would. Did they love it because it was "catchy" or because we chanted it loudly with enthusiasm? That was part of it to be sure, the part they *enjoyed*. The part they *loved*—the part they immediately embraced—was the message: *I can be great!* They loved it because, despite their "at-riskness," their emotional issues, their F's, and their dismal educational experience thus far, they are hungry for greatness, hungry for the pats and the praise, hungry for approval. Our students are hungry for success. We can satisfy their hunger; it can be done.

I leave you with the important question: Are you one such teacher? Do you believe in the power of *one*? If with an unequivocal "Yes!" you do, then we are two! Both with the same heart—for the children. Both with the same vision—for the children. Both with the same purpose: to make the world a better place—for the children.

> ## My greatest goal victory...
>
> getting to know and trust my mother more. Hillary
>
> When I stopped talking back to my mom. Aween
>
> when I stoped fighting with my mom. Caitlin
>
> Respecting my mom♡ by Kathleen ♥
>
> When I began to care for my father. He had hurt my brother and I never forgave him for it then I met Mrs. Fafield and did. Christine
>
> I used to fight with my mother ALL the time! I was miserable at home! Now we're friends! Kolbi

Dear Alexia
Thur. 2-23-06

Yesterday was a **GREAT** day
I worked strongly ^ on my goal
to be RESPONSIBLE with everything
I do and say. So every time I
did somthing or said somthing I
alway thought before I jumped
right in. I got all my HW done!
cleaned my room and my backpack!
I am proud to see my self changin
in to a PERSON of CHARACTER.
It is not always easy to become
a person with Character! You
have to stand up for your self!
My next goal is to be KIND
to my brother!!!

CHAPTER 10

Thank You for the Truth

$\mathcal{A}$ few years ago I was invited to speak at a local teachers' conference on the topic of Caring Communities. Instead of my usual solo presentation, I decided to take some of my students along with me—sixteen all together. After a brief "big picture" explanation of Caring Communities, I introduced my students, who absolutely stole the show for the next two hours as they answered questions for which they had no preparation.

There was one moment in particular that I shall never forget. Someone asked about our Honor System. My little rebel, Caitlin, stepped confidently forward, and, looking boldly into the many eyes, announced matter-of-factly that she couldn't lie anymore since she "got into Ms. LaField's class."

Throughout the room were heard audible gasps of shock and disbelief followed by hushed whispers. Caitlin stood waiting until the silence was broken by one teacher, who raised her hand and asked politely if she had lied a lot before.

Knowing all too well Caitlin's reputation for being a notorious troublemaker, the other students exploded into uproarious laughter, and, wearing an ear-to-ear grin, Caitlin nodded her head and replied, "Oh, yeah!" More laughter followed. Then the teachers wanted to know how she learned not to lie. Caitlin responded: "We have this Truth Rock, and Ms. LaField talks about the truth all the time."

That was all she could tell them about how she had learned the importance of telling the truth. What she couldn't explain was that as she had received more revelation regarding "the truth about the truth," she had unconsciously come to embrace it and apply it to her life.

The teachers were more than impressed. I could have stood up in front of them for the entire two hours passionately advocating a stronger focus on the need for teaching our students to love the truth, and they would have shaken their heads in agreement. However, would they have been convinced that it is possible? I seriously doubt it. But they believed Caitlin. Her announcement was obviously unrehearsed. It was clear that she was not lying about learning not to lie.

100% DEDICATION

Did all the teachers go right back to their own classrooms with a wholehearted commitment to teach their own students to love the truth? I seriously doubt it. Why not? Good question.

Several possibilities come to mind. Perhaps some thought it was a great idea, and though they relished the idea of enjoying such results with their own students, in their minds they doubted their own ability to accomplish what for them seemed impossible. In short, they were too insecure to even try. Who loses? The kids.

Perhaps others thought it was a great idea and wanted to incorporate it into their curriculum, but their desire was weak. They didn't want it badly enough to do the work required. Who loses? The kids.

Still, others thought it was a great idea, and they fully intended to do it, but they were so preoccupied with other pressing matters that it was soon forgotten. Who loses? The kids.

Finally, there remains the strong possibility that some of the teachers, though certainly impressed by my students' commitment to the truth, were not themselves sufficiently devoted to the truth and would never, therefore, consider incorporating the idea into their curriculum. Who loses? The kids.

A teacher who incorporates the virtue of truth into his or her curriculum must, if determined to enjoy any degree of success, be 100% dedicated to it. Once in a while, I say something to the kids that is not the "microscopic" truth, as I call it. Immediately, I hear that gentle, yet convicting, voice urging me to come clean with the whole truth. In those moments, I stop whatever I am doing and say something like, "Kids, what I just said is not the entire truth." Then I go ahead and correct myself. Every time an opportunity like that arises in the classroom, I convince my students a little more that I am seriously committed to the truth.

Kids are amazed by adults who openly and honestly own the truth about their mistakes, failures, and inadequacies.

Kids are amazed by adults who openly and honestly own the truth about their mistakes, failures, and inadequacies. If you want to win your students' affection and respect, admit it when you are wrong and ask forgiveness. I say something like, "The truth is that I was wrong, and I am sorry. Can you please forgive me?" So often we hide the truth because we are worried about what our students will think of us. We aren't real with our students. My students would tell you: "Ms. LaField doesn't mind being wrong. She just doesn't want to be wrong about the truth."

Our students will be convinced only when they see us earnestly seeking the truth, humbly owning the truth, and wholeheartedly living the truth.

THANK YOU FOR THE TRUTH!

Modeling the truth comes first, but most of our students need much more. They need submersion. Here we must seek balance, for too little exposure will fail to achieve the desired results, while too much will breed overkill. It's a fine line that comes with experience and an open mind.

The submersion process begins for my students the first minutes of the first day of school when they hear me introduce myself and our Truth Rock. Now, of course, that does sound a little strange, especially considering that they don't even know me. Nevertheless, the point is well taken—if they remember only one point to share with their parents at the end of that day, it may likely be, "The truth is really important to Ms. LaField."

At some point in the first week of school, my students and I also have our initial discussion about lying. Somewhere in that discussion I bring up the topic of how students lie to teachers, and very quickly they are sharing examples of ways and reasons that students lie. I lead the discussion toward why kids lie when the teacher asks a specific question such as, "John, are you on task?" or, "John, are you listening?" Of course, they all agree that most lie to avoid trouble, but the main point of the discussion is to lead them to realize that quite often they lie out of *habit*. I help them see that when they automatically lie without thinking about it, they have a habit of lying. They're not bad. They just have a bad habit.

This is where I begin the process of teaching my students to respond to my questions. My job, I reassure them, is to lovingly and respectfully help them break the habit of lying and become people of honor and integrity, who can be trusted to tell the truth.

Next, I set up a pretend scenario where I actually show them what I mean. I ask two brave volunteers to come up front, where I have set up two desks. I give each a book and tell them to pretend they are reading for a few seconds, and then

I instruct them to start quietly whispering to one another. I instruct the first boy to lie when I ask him if he is on task. The class is watching with great interest as I casually approach the two whispering boys and ask if they are on task. The first boy lies as instructed.

At this point I look him in the eye and ask, "Is that the truth? Are you really on task?" I then indicate to him that he is to admit that he was not on task.

He will probably say something like, "No, I wasn't."

I make sure everyone is watching as I tell him exactly how I want him to answer. He is to say word for word, "No, Ms. LaField, the truth is I wasn't listening."

With this response, he is showing me respect by using my name, and when he adds the words "not listening," he is owning the truth about his precise behavior. He is telling me he knows exactly what he was doing.

He repeats it exactly as I asked, and I clap and laugh and maybe pat him on the back. In other words, I make the process fun.

Then I ask the other student if he was on task, and he knows just what to say. But we are not finished. I look directly at the boys and with respect, patience, and sincerity I say, "Thank you for the truth, Boys."

Because responding in this manner is new and somewhat uncomfortable, many students are initially reluctant. Helping them overcome their hesitancy is entirely up to us. We must, as I have learned through experience, make sure of several factors:

- ★ We must remain consistently patient.
- ★ We must never be confrontational.
- ★ We must speak in a normal, pleasant tone of voice.
- ★ We must address them with extraordinary respect.
- ★ We must be consistent; otherwise, they will revert to old ways.
- ★ We must coax, if need be, with a good sense of humor.
- ★ We must always respond with a sincere, "Thank you for the truth, (name)."
- ★ In the early stages of the training process, we must remember to praise the student's response.
- ★ We must not dwell on the interruption but must move on immediately.
- ★ We must be prepared to apologize when we fail at some point in the process.

With all these factors in motion, given time, you can expect all of your students to respond as long as you are devoted to building relationships with your students. If relationship building is your focus, the fruit of your efforts will manifest in the way your students perceive your actions and motives. They will know you care. They will value and regard you as a person of integrity. You will have earned their respect, and as a result, they will want to act appropriately.

Here are some student reflections on respect and owning the truth:

"It is so nice to be in an environment where you don't get yelled at for talking. Instead, Ms. LaField respects us as we respect her. She politely asks us if we were on task and trusts us to be honest in response. That's what it's all about—trust and respect. Last year I had a teacher that demanded respect and sent me out of the classroom for talking. I hardly learned anything that year. Now that I'm in a class with a teacher that freely respects me, I'm learning more than ever, and I'm slowly overcoming my problem of blurting out because she cares."

"When I came into Ms. LaField's core class, I would have lied to any teacher about anything, especially about being on task. And when she told our class to respond rather than react, to say yes, Ms. LaField, I am, or no, I'm not, I thought she was a teacher who wanted us to treat her like royalty. But now I realize that she just wants to teach us how to be respectful to others. And when she told us about the Truth Rock, I honestly thought she had gone insane! But now I realize that even a rock can teach you not to lie. Now I hate to lie. When I do, I feel low and worthless, like I'm a criminal. She wants us to know how to do things the right way. If you are reading this book, try some of these things. You won't regret it. I hated school. I would play sick just to not have to come. This year I have to miss one day of school a month for an appointment, and I whine when that day comes all because of the little things Ms. LaField does to brighten our days."

"In the past years when I was asked if I was on task, I would say I was even if I wasn't. I would never say I was sorry for being off task. I would just react instead of actually responding. Reacting is just an answer that doesn't make you think. A response is when you think about telling the truth and then answer truthfully. Ms. LaField has taught us to respond. She has taught us how to think about owning the truth."

THE HONOR SYSTEM

As we know, truth and trust are inseparable twins; we cannot teach one without teaching the other. Our Honor System further submerses my students in the truth by providing ample opportunities for them to prove that they can be trusted. Along with letting them grade their own tests, I sometimes leave the room for a moment during a test on the Honor System. Students who were absent and need to make up a test are often allowed to take it home on the Honor System. These are my ways of providing my students with opportunities to choose between honesty and dishonesty.

I realize that many disagree with the Honor System, contending that it sets kids up to cheat, that it tempts them beyond their capacity to resist. Although a few of my students certainly cheat, the vast majority would tell you they are learning that being trustworthy is more important to them than a grade. They would tell you that, where before they could cheat without compunction, they now feel convicted. They would tell you that they are learning to be People of Character.

Just as my students so often hear me say, "Thank you for the truth," they also hear me say, "I love the Honor System." When first introducing it, we discuss in depth the ease by which we can cheat our way through life. Without preaching, I launch an undaunted, year-long attempt at helping them see how their choices to deceive others actually hurt themselves—not by telling them, but by showing them. They have been told not to cheat all their lives, just as I was told not to lie. To what avail? They know that it is wrong in their heads, but their behavior does not change because the truth of how it hurts them has not yet pierced their hearts.

Only understanding the positive consequences of truth can teach children to love the truth.

Compassion is the key ingredient in successfully showing my students that cheating hurts them. When compassion speaks, it comes from a place of care and concern. It says, "Please listen because I want the best for you. I want you to be happy!" Fear, intimidation, and punitive measures never teach children to love the truth. A thousand "You should not's" will *never* teach children to love the truth. Pleading, begging, and crying do not teach children to love the truth. Only understanding the positive consequences of truth can teach children to love the truth.

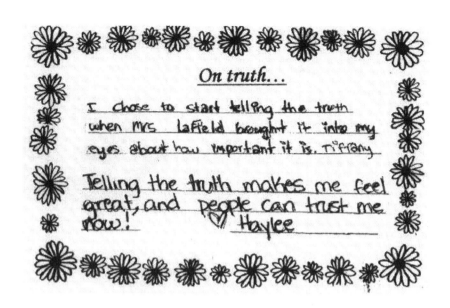

On truth...

I chose to start telling the truth when mrs laField brought it into my eyes about how important it is. Tiffany

Telling the truth makes me feel great, and people can trust me now! ♥ Haylee

On truth...

Mrs LaField taught me to own the truth. It helped me to make more friends. Eliza ♥

a while back I used to cheat, but knowing Miss Lafield trusts us with the Honor System, I have stopped. Hillary

"Stealing, cheating, and lying was the "Old Me." The "New Me" loves the truth! Lilly

Last year I never told the truth, but ever since I came into Mrs. La Fiell's class I have told the truth. Tyler

CHAPTER 11

Teaching Work Ethic
part one

*O*ne sweltering summer day, while digging clover from my flower garden, I chanced upon an ingenious approach to teaching my students a strong work ethic. Down on my knees in the dirt, with the sweat literally dripping off the tip of my nose and nearing exhaustion, I suddenly leaped to my feet and surprised myself by announcing, "I am the Little Red Hen!" For those unfamiliar with the classic children's story, its age-old message is the merit of *hard work.*

That night I read the story and found myself back on mother's lap hearing those familiar words, "Not I, said the Dog!" Sensing that the story would impact the lives of my students, I went to work on a plan for incorporating its message into my Character Education focus. That plan has become a classic story all by itself.

I AM ALL ABOUT HARD WORK

On the first day of school, my new students are greeted with a red cloud of helium balloons floating across the ceiling of my classroom. Stapled above the entrance and hanging loosely from red ribbons is a line of red discs, each decorated on both sides with a clip art red hen. And who stands at the door waiting to welcome my new students? Who else but their Little Red Hen teacher—dressed in red from head to toe.

It is a dramatic anticipatory set—with one major difference: the typical set introduces a lesson; this one introduces the entire year. By the end of that first day, my students are well-acquainted with the story of the Little Red Hen and leave with an unmistakable understanding: their new teacher is all about hard work!

For the next one hundred and seventy nine days—with the exception of the days I'm absent—not a day passes without mention of the Little Red Hen.

When working with the Little Red Hen concept, however, there is one primary non-negotiable: a compassionate approach. I don't nag my students, raise my voice, or guilt trip them. I don't jam the Little Red Hen down their throats, which would be an easy line to cross. And I don't *tell* my students that they should work hard; I *show* them why they should work hard. From time to time, I mention the Dog, the Cat, and the Mouse in the story, all of whom lazily refused to help the Little Red Hen tend the wheat.

Each time she asked, "Who will help me?" they replied "Not I!" So when her cake was ready to eat, the Little Red Hen enjoyed it all by herself because she did all the work. The Dog, the Cat, and the Mouse got nothing.

All year long I talk about "the cake." My students learn early on that the cake is the prize, the reward for our hard work. Before a big test I may ask, "Who's going to get the cake today?" I help them make the connection. Those who make the top grades are not necessarily the smartest in the class but the ones who work the hardest.

Another way I show my students a strong work ethic is by example. They learn through my modeling that their teacher works hard. Every morning I ask, "Who am I, Class?" and they respond in unison, "You are the Little Red Hen, Ms. LaField!" Throughout the year I tell them inspiring stories about the obstacles I faced and overcame to be their teacher. They see firsthand how hard I work on everything I do for them.

ONE-ON-ONE ENCOURAGEMENT

Imparting a strong work ethic would fail if I did not build strong relationships with my students. I inspire my students to work hard by encouraging my students to do their best individually. Their appetites are often whetted by a first taste of success, and it's my responsibility to make sure they get that taste. Different students require different methods of encouragement. I may invite a student to a study hall with me. I may ask a peer to tutor, or be tutored, during lunch. Sometimes a simple encouraging word can engage a student. Whatever the case, I strive to speak to the student in the encouragement-language that works best for them.

Once a student has that first breakthrough, I make sure to do two things. First, I make sure they receive praise. Some have never enjoyed enthusiastic approval. Sometimes I ask a trustworthy student to praise them privately. I make sure their parents hear about it. I may even share the victory with our principal, who will then come to our room and personally congratulate the student.

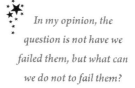

In my opinion, the question is not have we failed them, but what can we do not to fail them?

Second, I talk to the student about their victory— how good it feels inside, how proud they feel, and how "the prize was worth the price." We joke about being the Little Red Hen, but I make sure they get the point: They worked hard, so they got the cake. Most importantly, we talk about the next test. I assure them that they are smart and can do it again.

What about students who don't get the cake? What about those who don't "wake up" despite our efforts? Have we failed them? In my opinion, the question is not have we failed them, but what can we do *not* to fail them? We must never underestimate the power of high expectations to help our students get the cake. Today I push my students so hard that I continually ask myself, "Am I pushing them too hard?" My tough love may not feel like love; in fact, it often looks harsh. But deep inside, my students are convinced I want the best for them. And deep inside, they want it for themselves. My best continues to get better, so it only makes sense that every year, without exception, I have more Little Red Hens than the previous year.

By sometime in November, I always have a few Little Red Hens. At the time of this writing, I have five. They are my early "success stories." Before Christmas we will celebrate with a Little Red Hen party. I will secretly invite parents and the principal. The room will be red from top to bottom. There will be a table set up in the front of the room with five chairs, five Little Red Hen storybooks, five settings of red plastic ware, and, you guessed it, five red cakes.

Now please take a moment to imagine the scene—with all its tears, cheers, and congratulations. Imagine those five children looking around at the smiles of their parents and peers and relishing their applause. What you see are the glowing faces of children whose lives will be changed forever because of a teacher who loved them well enough to help them get the cake. We hear it said that it takes only one committed adult to change the life of a child forever. How true!

Now imagine another scene—this one bathed with cheers and congratulations as well. Your principal calls you into the office and enthusiastically shares your test results, which have considerably improved. Now who gets the cake? You do!

ONE DAY THEY WILL GET IT...HOPEFULLY!

Sadly, every year I have more students who have never been pushed hard by anyone. No one has ever pushed hard enough to help them reach their full potential, hard enough to help them become Little Red Hens. On the other hand, I have students whose parents do have high expectations, but no matter what these parents do, their children just don't seem to care. Worse yet, they rebel, and neither the home nor the school has any control over their choices. Regardless of the reasons why, every year I have had a few students, who, despite my best efforts never "get the cake." I stick with them until that last bell of the year, but for whatever reason, they didn't care enough to listen. They didn't care enough to work hard. I can only hope that someday they will realize what all the pushing was about. I know I did not fail these students.

One day, I glanced into the Commons and saw the familiar faces of two high school students who, when they were my students, had given me nothing but disappointment for an entire year. I had poured out my best for nine long months, and when they walked out the door on the last day of school, I was sad for them. But when I saw them looking at me expectantly through the glass, I knew why they were there. I recognized the softness in their eyes and their anxious smiles, and I couldn't get to them fast enough. They had come to say they were sorry. They had come because they finally understood: I had pushed them because I cared. And then their anxious smiles melted into smiles of joy and thankfulness when they saw that I had never stopped caring. Looking into their eyes, I saw hope, and as we parted I quietly thanked God that I still cared.

WHAT'S BEST?

When faced with a difficult decision regarding one of my students, I invariably ask myself: What's best for the student? If you are a teacher, you understand that extreme difficulties will arise, and often those issues will involve parties other than a student and yourself. Such was the case with Kyle, an extremely bright, though equally apathetic, student. Kyle convinced his father to remove him from my class because it was too hard—in other words, because he would be required to work.

I was trying to teach him a strong work ethic, to inspire him to strive for his full potential in my class. Sadly for Kyle, his father's choice was the "easy way out for his son." He was robbing his son of a chance to rise to his full potential and training him for a life of mediocrity. In such cases, the easy way out for the teacher is to yield to opposition. Why fight him? To those dedicated to my standard, the answer is clear: The easy way was not best for Kyle. My student's future was at stake. It was worth a fight.

I went to my principal who offered his full support. He agreed that transferring Kyle would not be an option. We gave the father two choices: He could allow Kyle to remain in my class or move him to another school. The father relented.

Though Kyle lost the battle, he ended up a winner. He seemed to know that my struggle to keep him was because I cared. Nothing else could explain the great lengths I went to make sure that he stayed in my classroom.

In the days to come, Kyle began joining his peers on the risers. He started participating. He started smiling. And then came the real breakthrough: He started doing his homework and caring about his grades. Was it worth the fight? You bet it was!

CHAPTER 12

Teaching Work Ethic
part two

*O*ne major vehicle for imparting a strong work ethic was inspired at a summer workshop where our district's teachers met with local businesses to hear their opinions on the employability of students in our community. The results, to the surprise of no one, were entirely dismal.

Listening attentively to the dialogue, I wondered what I could possibly do to help my students prepare for the work world. How could I help my students meet the challenges they will face in the future? How can I help them not merely earn a living, but excel at whatever employment they might pursue? The answers to these questions arrived the next morning in the form of a plan I deemed *You're Hired*. Along with imparting a strong work ethic, it has five additional bonus elements:

- ★ It meets the needs of the Whole Child.
- ★ It supports our school rules.
- ★ It supports and enhances my classroom management system.
- ★ It supports and enhances my Character Education emphasis.
- ★ It acts as an unparalleled incentives-based reward system.

THE PLAN'S SYSTEM OF LEVELS

The plan is a system of graduating, cumulative levels. Each level incorporates strict standards that must be clearly and consistently met before students can proceed to the next level. Similar to the demands of the real-life work world, students do not win the reward of moving to the next level; they work for the reward! Earning their promotions through diligence and dedication, they work their way to the top of the ladder, one step at a time.

Below are the specific graduating levels of the plan and the requirements for each. A student who consistently and faithfully fulfills all of the standards with a high degree of excellence earns the distinguished title of Valued Employee.

LEVEL 1: You're Hired!
★ On time
★ Dressed appropriately
★ Positive attitude
★ Follow all procedures

LEVEL 2: First Promotion!
★ All of the above
★ Hard worker
★ Obey with a Right Heart
★ Respectful
★ Courteous

LEVEL 3: Second Promotion!
★ All of the above
★ Help others get promoted

LEVEL 4: Valued Employee!!!
★ All of the above
★ A continued commitment to excellence
★ Completely trustworthy

GETTING HIRED

To be hired, students must prove that they arrive punctually to class and come to school dressed appropriately. The dress code at our school is progressively more difficult to enforce; nevertheless, once my students see how rigidly I enforce this particular standard, they are willing to comply. Finally, they must respect my standard for how they enter the room and how loudly they are allowed to talk in class.

By the end of the first two weeks of school, almost all of my students prove themselves worthy of being hired, and it's a joy to hire each one.

FIRST PROMOTION

My students have to work much harder to earn their first promotion than to merely get hired. To be promoted to LEVEL 2, students must show a high degree of respect and courtesy, work hard, and display a positive attitude. They understand what I mean by hard work, but teaching them my expectations about respect, a positive attitude and courtesy is an ongoing journey, especially considering my extremely high standards. My students are not merely required to treat others with respect, but with *extraordinary* respect. For example, when they ask for a word to be repeated in a spelling test, I require that they begin with a "Please" and end with a "Thank you." I also add the element of "Yes, Ma'am" and "No, Ma'am," which I convince them would cause an employer to fall over backwards with shock and delight.

Imagine the joy of hearing your students address you with such courtesy and respect because they want to and not because they have to. With all due candor, I would never have dreamed it could "get so good." Visitors are shocked as my students greet them with a level of courtesy now seldom seen in America. When students display these attributes, in addition to maintaining the requirements for being hired, they earn their first promotion.

Visitors are shocked as my students greet them with a level of courtesy now seldom seen in America.

SECOND PROMOTION

To be promoted for the second time, students must prove that they are helping others. They must be team players, who watch out for each other. As students build community in their groups, they naturally help each other and work together, so this requirement for promotion is easily accomplished and readily assessed by the Task Managers in each group. In our weekly meetings, Task Managers will often suggest that they believe a certain member of their community has qualified for his or her second promotion. This helps me with my decision because it is impossible to see all that goes on in the classroom.

THE PATH TO VALUED EMPLOYEE!

For a student to earn the coveted honor of Valued Employee, they must prove to me that they are completely trustworthy. Using a real "work world" example, I explain that if I am their employer and I leave money in the cash register, I must be able to leave them alone with the money and trust that every penny will still be there when I return. I must be totally convinced that they will always perform exactly as expected. In other words, my students must prove to be people of integrity.

Furthermore, they have to prove that their integrity is not restricted to our class; they must display it everywhere they go. Before my students rise to the level of Valued Employee, their parents, as well as every one of their teachers, must confirm their integrity by signing a check-off sheet that includes all the stringent requirements of becoming a Valued Employee. As you can well imagine, parents and teachers are impressed by this list. To date, no one has ever regarded the checklist casually; if anything, I have needed to remind an occasional parent that we must never expect perfection.

The system creates a climate of positive enthusiasm and a strong desire to conform to class standards.

I hold up the "prize" of Valued Employee on the very first day of school. Many of my students decide on that first day that they are going to be Valued Employees. Explaining the system is quite simple with the help of a bulletin board that covers a broad space on the back wall and clearly delineates each level. With my new students turned around facing me, I begin with Level 1: the path to getting hired. Introducing the program on that first day of school greatly facilitates the process of explaining my classroom expectations. The system creates a climate of positive enthusiasm and a strong desire to conform to class standards.

On a nearby wall space, I created an attractive spot for two posters that include my students' names and a record of their progress. The student names are listed vertically, and the four promotion levels horizontally at the top. Every Friday after Storytime the kids excitedly gather around the posters as I announce promotions. Beginning with the first name at the top of the list, I proceed down in alphabetical order. Having already determined in advance who will be promoted that day, I stop at the name of a student who has earned a promotion to the next level, and with tremendous enthusiasm ask, "(Student name), do you think you have earned your first promotion?" In most cases the student emphatically agrees, and with great animation I put a sticker in the correct box as the kids chant, "We are proud of you!"

From time to time, the student hesitates and publicly admits the need for improvement in some area or another. Everyone is impressed by his or her truthfulness, and together we cheer for the student. Such moments are prime opportunities for hailing a student's high level of honor, integrity, and respect for the truth. At such times I compliment the student heartily on their development as a Person of Character.

In this way, one Friday at a time, my students advance through the levels on their way toward the big one: Valued Employee. On the Friday I announce that a particular student is qualified for Valued Employee, they receive the checklist papers that have to be signed by their parents and teachers. Though some students fly through the qualification process effortlessly, others must work diligently to improve in one or more areas.

Last year one of my students had all of her papers signed by Christmas—except for one category that her father would not check: respect. Finally, in early May she met me at the door with the final check. It was quite a journey for her, but she persevered because she wanted to be a Valued Employee. That Friday she told the whole class that after all those months of effort, she and her father finally had a mutually happy relationship—for the first time.

My students come to me often asking what they still need to do to be promoted. Imagine that: students wanting to know how they can improve in your class and cheerfully working on whatever you suggest. One day I told Cody, who is often quite sullen, that he needed to sit closer to me during our English lessons and participate more with a Right Heart. What a happy surprise it was the next day when he voluntarily did exactly that—for the first time!

My students are so eager to be Valued Employees, not only for the prestige, but particularly for privileges, freedom, trust, and independence. Once students become trusted Valued Employees in our class, they are no longer required to ask permission to use the phone or go to the bathroom. They can use a computer without asking permission or go into the Commons to work. They can actually go to the library and work on their math homework or help a classmate with an essay, completely unsupervised by me.

THE COVETED GOLD MEDALS

Until a couple of years ago, I made each of my Valued Employees a very elaborate "gold" medal to wear around his or her neck. Using gold spray-painted Kerr jar lids, a ribbon of their color choice and a hot glue gun, I meticulously formed a complicated ribbon border and carefully glued it around the edges of the inside of one lid. Before gluing the two lids together, I glued in the "necklace" ribbon—

the one that went around the student's neck. Simply put, they wore a "ribbon/ medal" around their necks with the words Valued Employee on one side and their names on the other. My students cherished those medals.

Now my Valued Employees wear fabulous medals that were specially designed for us by a local trophy shop. They are fairly expensive; however, they are so incredibly impressive that my students are happy to split the cost with me, and most of them choose to have theirs engraved for two dollars more. One would think they were Olympic gold medals by the way my students so proudly wear them.

Our wonderful librarian, who has welcomed my Valued Employees into our library for several years, has this to say about the program:

"My experience with Valued Employee students has been very positive. I am impressed with how proudly they wear their medals and how important it is to live up to the high standards of a Valued Employee. Not only do they wear their medals with pride, but they aspire to become more responsible which, as a result, places them directly into a leadership role. The program builds confidence, self-esteem, and a sense of accomplishment!"

PROTECTING THE INTEGRITY OF THE PROGRAM

Because the integrity of the program must be fiercely protected, especially outside the parameters of our classroom, my Valued Employees are required to hold each other accountable using the Honor System. If, for example, one Valued Employee sees another Valued Employee obviously off-task outside the classroom, the first must return immediately to me and report the problem. If I learn that he or she failed to uphold the Honor System, both are in jeopardy of losing their titles.

At first, some find the Honor System uncomfortable; they feel like they are "tattling" on their peers. As I help them understand the vital importance of maintaining extraordinarily high standards of trust, they soon take pride in maintaining that level. They see that if we compromise our standards, the prestige of being a Valued Employee diminishes—even if only one person fails to uphold those standards with integrity.

Just as in the real world, Valued Employees can be fired. During one particular year, two students were disrespectful to a substitute teacher and immediately lost their titles. I shall never forget how those boys cried and begged for a second chance. I was not even tempted to compromise. You can be sure that it made quite an impression on the others: Ms. LaField doesn't "mess around" with disrespectful behavior.

Probation is a different matter. Every year, two or three of the kids "slack off" academically and immediately lose all privileges until their grades improve. It remains a personal issue between the student and me. To date I have not even conferred with parents about the problem. Being on probation is fairly humiliating in and of itself. The point is not to punish but to motivate the student to higher levels of achievement. From the inception of the program to the present, no student has ever failed to earn back his or her title.

Another reason a Valued Employee may be put on probation is for a lack of respectful, self-disciplined behavior during my lessons. I must be able to trust that they are focused on the task at hand with extraordinary attention. I don't expect perfection, but they must be willing to rise to my standards of excellence if they expect to remain active Valued Employees.

I have no specific time frame for how long a student remains on probation. When they believe they are prepared to live the lessons of a Valued Employee with integrity, they come to me and tell me. Almost without exception, I return their medal. I have never had a problem with a student repeatedly going on probation.

VALUED EMPLOYEES REFLECT ON THEIR HONOR

In June we host a gala dessert banquet in the library, where the parents and I honor their "valued" children. I wrote a fun play with which we impress the crowd every year, but the real highlight of the evening is the "open mic" after the play. All the kids sit down on the risers and one by one, on a completely voluntary basis, they come forward and share their hearts. Tears flow freely as my students praise and thank their parents for a lifetime of love and support. Much of the appreciation goes to me as I sit on the rug in front of them and do my best to hold myself together. It is a very emotional time for us all.

The following student reflections express the power of the Valued Employee program to meet the needs of the Whole Child:

"There are many benefits to being a Valued Employee. I like the freedom I earned from being trusted, and being a Valued Employee puts me on a whole new level of maturity and responsibility. Now I know I have the qualities to

get a good job. I am now the material to be a Valued Employee in the job world. Now I will become a man of honor, integrity, and trustworthiness. There is a shortage of these qualities in the world today, and my fellow Valued Employees and I will try to work to ensure a better, more honest job world."

"Valued Employees gain great amounts of trust and respect from teachers and students. The teachers all know we will stay on task and do exactly what we are expected to do. This responsibility gives me a sense of self-satisfaction knowing that the teachers trust me."

The following two pages are excerpts from the journal of Mack, a young man who was so shy at the beginning of the year his father actually paid him to talk to people! The 9/30/05 entry is his first journal entry of the year. Notice his focus from the start was a desire to become a Valued Employee. In the next entry he shares his unrepressed jubilation at having earned his medal. Comparing that first entry to the second, you see a little boy transitioning into a young man virtually overnight. Mack's committed decision to become a Valued Employee was one of the keys that opened the door to allowing his friendly, funny, fun-loving side to burst forth. Any teacher who decides to incorporate the program could share Mack's entries as a way of conveying the dramatic impact the award can have on the life of any student so fervently committed to change.

Friday 9/30/05

Dear journal, this year I am really looking forward to dedicating myself to becoming a Valued Employee. Valued Employee is where you go through 3 stages. The three stages are You are hired, First promotion and then Second promotion. After you get through all of the stages you are a Valued Employee! You are Completely trustworthy when you are a Valued Employee. I think It is so awesome to be blessed with being a Valued Employee.

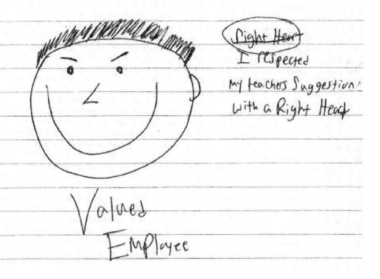

Right Heart
I respected
my teachers suggestion
with a Right Heart

Valued
Employee

2-15-06

Dear Journal, I Finally got my Valued Employee medal today! Miss LaField gave us our awards so I got to go up on the risers and say, "I'm a Valued Employee!" It was just like how I pictured it. It has my name on the back of it. My medal is hanging on the center of my desk so everytime I look at it I can think that Miss LaField helped me get that. I am proud that I worked so hard to get it. It was definetely worth it. I hope that I start working for what I want as hard as I worked for that medal.

Happy

I am happy that I finally got my medal!

CHAPTER 13
Choose to Care

*M*y class adopted the motto, "Choose to Care," one year after I read them a magazine article about the skyrocketing escalation of the homeless population in America. The article's picture revealed a man and woman sitting on a bed in a cheap motel room somewhere in America, staring glumly into the camera. Surrounding them on the bed were three children, all equally forlorn. What most astounded my students was the fact that both parents were employed—though with minimum wage jobs. The article went on to explain that because of the rise in the cost of housing, many families can no longer afford to rent, much less own their own home, even if both parents work.

I used the family's pathetic plight to drive home my point that unless they choose to care about their grades and their futures, they too could wake up one dismal morning in a dreary motel room—homeless. For most of them, I'm quite sure it was the first time in their lives they had ever seriously entertained the possibility that they could someday join the growing ranks of the homeless. Shocked and nearly speechless, the reality of the possibility struck them to the core and led them to coin our "Choose to Care "motto.

THE CHOOSE TO CARE MOVEMENT FOR EVAN

One memorable Friday, I stood, with a Sharpie and award stickers in hand, by the posters that record my students' Valued Employee progress. Just in front of the posters, which hang inside our sliding glass doors, is a group of six desks. Evan Taylor was sitting in one of the desks and all around him were squeezed together thirty-plus of his peers—all vying for a closer look at the posters. I cannot recollect at the moment why I spontaneously called his name that day, though it surely was not to put him on the spot or to embarrass him in front of his peers. Up to that point, Evan was little more than a C average student in my morning Core, who sat as far away as possible from me, and contributed rarely. He sat on the floor, hunkered down against a bookshelf, head bowed and literally hiding behind his hair. I had not figured Evan out yet. When I called his name, everyone looked down at him and the room grew absolutely quiet awaiting his response.

I don't remember if he even looked up at me. All I remember is the voice and the answer: "Ms. LaField, I really don't care if I'm a Valued Employee." Time stood still in our class for a moment.

It was a first, and it left me dumbstruck. How dare he not care? Everyone wanted to be a Valued Employee! Looking down at his head for a long moment and trying to gather my thoughts, all I managed to put together was, "Oh, really?" It was then I did something so utterly out of character for me that the class gasped in unison: I took my Sharpie and very slowly, very methodically, I drew a heavy black line through Evan's name. I actually crossed him off the list in retaliation. I took his apathy personally! Once again, it was all about pride.

That was it. Nothing more. No one said another word, and I continued down the list as if nothing unusual had happened. But as I was calling other students' names, I remember thinking, "I can't believe I just did that. I actually crossed his name off! Now what am I going to do?"

"EVAN HAS DECIDED TO CARE!"

I have to admit that I forgot about that experience until one day a couple weeks later, Kris came running into the room during lunchtime study hall. He was one excited boy. "Ms. LaField, Evan has decided to care! He's decided that he wants to be a Valued Employee!" Kris, who was himself a Valued Employee, had been talking to Evan about not caring, and, as true friends often will, Evan had listened. It was the beginning of the Choose to Care Movement for Evan, and he would never be the same.

It was one of the most exciting moments of my life. One of my students had made a conscious choice to care about his life!

I had about five minutes before the end of lunch to put Evan's name back on that poster. Flying into the Commons where I keep my fluorescent paper, I found the orange paper, cut it into just the right width and length, and glued it over that thick black line. I don't think I took a breath in those five minutes. It was one of the most exciting moments of my life. One of my students had made a conscious choice to care about his life!

The next morning when I met Evan at the door, we had our first genuine handshake. Our eyes met. He smiled. From that day forward, he sat up front, and his hand was in the air every day for the rest of the year. If he arrived a little late for class and the desks were already lined up in the front, everybody squeezed together to fit his desk in between the others. It was a given: Evan Taylor sits in the front. I will let him tell you the story:

"My name is Evan Taylor. I was in Ms. LaField's core class with Richard Stevenson and Matt McCartin. Because of the help from my peers and Ms. LaField, I was able to change my attitude, my grades and my LIFE!

Starting my seventh grade year off, I was not a caring student. Lazy and bored, I sat in the back not listening. By not caring I never made the honor roll. I got a 2.5 GPA the first quarter. Ms. LaField kept pushing me to care, but I didn't listen. To tell you the truth, I had never really cared about school. Last year I tried to make everyone laugh instead of listen. I was a complete goof off. I was tricking myself into believing I was stupid.

But this year I met Ms. LaField, and all that changed. Annoying but great, she kept on practically stabbing us with saying, "Choose to care!" Ms. LaField kept on pushing me to care, but I didn't listen. Then in the second quarter Ms. LaField asked me if I wanted to be a Valued Employee and I told her that I didn't care. Consequently, she took my name off the chart to become a Valued Employee.

Later, my friend Kris Konry heard about the news. Kris is my really good friend that I have known for a long time because of sports. So Kris came up to me and asked why I didn't care. Being the great friend that he is, he encouraged me to care and want to change. With the help from Kris, I walked up to Ms. LaField and told her I wanted to care. You could say I found my true self that day. She had already put my name back on the list, so I was back on the road to becoming a Valued Employee. The next day I sat in the front for the first time in my life!

I started to participate and listen to what Ms. LaField had to say about school and what she had to say about life. Surprisingly, I started to actually write in my journal and set magnificent goals. Finally, after my hard work and caring, I got my second promotion. Then I was ready to get my papers signed by all my other teachers so I could be a Valued Employee.

It felt like I was smart and that I could do anything in the world.

I got every paper signed except for one teacher who said I didn't participate enough and I wrote messy. Crying, I went to Ms. LaField showing her that I didn't get it signed. She comforted me and told me that I'd still be a Valued Employee that day if I promised to do what the teacher wanted.

When I became a Valued Employee, it wasn't just some small thing. It was like winning the lottery! It felt like I was smart and that I could do anything in the world. So I set a huge goal to make straight A's. Everyone thought I would fail except Ms. LaField, Kris and Richard, my best friends for my whole life. But I worked my hardest, and when grades came out, I had a 4.0!!! I could never have done that without Ms. LaField and my friends.

My journal had a big part to do with me changing my life. It was full of goals that I set over the year. For example, it helped me change my life with my family because I could talk to it and tell it things I couldn't tell my friends. I love my journal. I'm not going to quit doing goals ever.

Choosing to care CHANGED MY LIFE! Now I'm a 4.0 student, and I love myself because I'm not stupid. I just had to care first, then I could become my true self. Ms. LaField isn't a teacher that lets a kid fail. She chooses to care about kids and that's what turned me around—a teacher that really cared about me and my grades, but most importantly, the person I am."

CHAPTER 14
A Right Heart

*T*he Right Heart story began in the summer of 2003. The Friday before the first day of school I was in my room busy with some last minute redecorating and my attention was drawn to the expansive Valued Employee bulletin board on the back wall. With no particular purpose in mind, I was studying the different attributes that my students must display before earning the title of Valued Employee, when suddenly I realized that I had left a gaping hole in the prerequisites: obedience.

How could I have possibly missed the critical prerequisite of obedience for two whole years? After all, a Valued Employee always obeys those in authority. With utter disbelief, my mind meditated on the omission, and I realized there was even more to the revelation, something even bigger. I realized that the Valued Employee program was supposed to do much more than simply teach my students to obey. I was supposed to teach my students to obey with Right Heart attitudes.

With not a moment to waste, I went to work and created a new sign that fit neatly into the Valued Employee bulletin board under "Second Promotion." I shall never forget the moment when I stood back to admire my handiwork. Thoughtfully scrutinizing the words on that new sign—Obedience with a Right Heart—the thought suddenly struck me: How in the world do I teach my students what a Right Heart is?

I grabbed a piece of paper, sat down in the nearest desk and prayed for guidance. In a matter of a few minutes I scrawled a list of words on that paper. Specifically, the list included: a forgiving heart, a humble heart, a servant's heart, a loving heart, a giving heart, a brave heart, a happy heart, a compassionate heart, a grateful heart, and an obedient heart. I remember meditating over the list and remembering that it felt right. Certainly there are other words I might have added, but I didn't want the list to be too long. Much like the Seven Attributes of a True Community, they were the Ten Attributes of Right Heart.

IMPARTING THE RIGHT HEART MESSAGE

My next logical step was to devise a method of transmitting the words to my students. Instinctively looking around the room at the minimal wall space that remained, I decided to remove the sign from the narrow strip of space high above the sliding glass doors. About one foot high and twelve feet across, its shape alone determined the design of what soon became known as the Right Heart wall.

From pink fluorescent poster board I cut a perfectly shaped heart just big enough to squeeze into the space, and on it I neatly stenciled Right Heart. Then I cut ten smaller hearts and on each one I stenciled one of the words from my list. In the center of the strip I stapled the one big heart and then around it added the ten smaller hearts, five on either side. If you think I stood back and admired my new creation with satisfaction, you are right! Alone in my classroom, I grinned and giggled with childish delight.

In the same way that community evolved one day at a time with no pre-conceived notions or prior experience from which to draw, Right Heart just sort of "happened." A more precise explanation would be that I let it happen—until one day the first inspired idea came: a "staged" moment in class designed to show my students by example what I meant by obedience with a Right Heart attitude.

I took a trustworthy boy aside and prepped him for a pre-arranged performance in front of the entire class in which I would ask him to do something no student would be interested in doing, and he would jump right up out of his seat with a smile and respectfully answer with an enthusiastic, "Yes, Ma'am!"

As I expected, he was nothing less than brilliantly convincing. Every one of his peers dropped what they were doing and eyed him with amazement. To plant the moment securely in their minds, I beckoned my co-conspirator to join me in the front of the class, thanked him with a tone of heartfelt sincerity, and turned to the class with an obviously serious demeanor.

"What you just saw," I told them, "was a perfect example of obedience with a Right Heart attitude. And that," I continued, "is how you become a Valued Employee!"

USING TEACHABLE MOMENTS TO IMPART THE MESSAGE

Continuing to teach Right Heart is much like teaching my students to be People of Character—opportunities spontaneously arise in the form of "teachable moments." Case in point: One day, after introducing the topic of Task Managers and explaining my strict expectations, I invited all those who wanted to be chosen for first quarter Task Managers to raise their hands. As I recorded their names, I came to four students who were "less than equipped" for the responsibilities of a Task Manager. In front of all their peers, I told each one as I came to their raised hand that they were not yet ready to be Task Managers. By the fourth one, that internal voice was anything but still and small; in fact, it was screaming with reprisals.

I stopped everything and asked the class if they were uncomfortable with the way I was recording their names.

Almost all raised their hands. I should not have announced that a few students were not ready to be Task Managers in front of their peers. Without hesitation, I admitted my guilt and asked for the forgiveness of the four. You can just bet that they were stunned by my admission. It was a prime opportunity for turning my mess into a Right Heart teachable moment message.

"What you just saw," I explained, "is an example of how people with a Right Heart behave when they hurt others. What if everyone did that when they hurt someone?" I asked. Then, as always, came the personal application challenge and a sincere request for them to hold me accountable the next time it happened.

Never underestimate the power of teachable moments to not only change our students' lives but also to create a classroom with a Right Heart.

Never underestimate the power of teachable moments to not only change our students' lives but also to create a classroom with a Right Heart. For example, last year Anthony, a student with obvious rejection issues, isolated himself as we gathered around the risers for our Task Manager lesson. Immediately upon seeing him "outside the circle," I stopped everything we were doing and lovingly but sternly insisted that he join us, which of course is exactly what he was hoping I would do.

Katie, a sweetheart destined for the role of Task Manager, like a doting mother to her pouting son, lovingly admonished Anthony.

"You can't do that, Anthony. We're a family and you're one of us!" Anthony's shy grin elicited immediate applause from the whole class, and I used Katie's kind words to illustrate the obvious: A Right Heart is kind.

As I recount the story, I am humbled, grateful, and excited because I got to be their teacher. Katie's loving comment was a sure sign: We were going to have an awesome year. But you must remember that Katie's comment did not happen by chance. In twelve short days of school, the ground had been carefully cultivated with the seeds of Right Heart attitudes. In the safe, inclusive environment of Right Heart, Anthony would flourish.

USING STORYTIME TO IMPART THE RIGHT HEART MESSAGE

Another way I introduce my students to the Right Heart concepts is Storytime. To teach my students a servant's heart, for example, I read a story about a little girl who goes happily about helping and serving others. Rather than explaining that she had a servant's heart, I illustrate my point in a way they are not likely to forget. I bring a silver serving tray to school, load it with yummy chocolate treats, and as I slowly wind my way around my students graciously offering them each a piece of chocolate, they are guessing which Right Heart word I am illustrating. Never yet have they guessed servant first, but once we talk about what they observed, they understand the concept.

No method of impartation surpasses the power of the positive role model.

Next, I purposefully use the word. For example, every time my students begin to work on their independent writing, I announce, "I'm here to serve you if you need help." Other times I say, "How can I serve you?" rather than asking how I can help them. In so doing, I repeatedly model the Right Heart attribute of a servant, and my students begin to emulate my example. No method of impartation surpasses the power of the positive role model.

USING GOALS TO IMPART THE RIGHT HEART MESSAGE

An additional means of teaching my students the attributes of a Right Heart is through personal goal setting. Although I have thoroughly covered my approach to teaching my students how to set and reach goals in other chapters, I would be remiss in not including the topic of goals here. I do not believe that my students would ever cultivate Right Hearts to the degree they do if it were not for a strong commitment to reaching their goals.

Without their journals, they would, like most adults, forget their goals altogether.

To further ensure their Right Heart development, I added an element that hastened their progress even more quickly than before. In the past, my students have always set two or three personal, school, and family goals—at least six all together. I expanded that list to include at least two, preferably three, Right Heart goals. In the same way we have class discussions which help my students determine their personal, school, and family goals, we discuss the meaning of each of the Right Heart words, and they choose two or three on which to focus all year long, especially through their journaling. Without their journals, they would, like most adults, forget their goals altogether.

CLASSROOM APPLICATION FOR ALL TO SEE

Once my students understand the concept of Right Heart, they begin to notice examples of how it is displayed in our class. For example, David, a new student with a strong stubborn streak and a short attention span, was resistant to my early requests that he join me on the risers. I knew from experience that the best way to remediate David's problem was with a little special attention.

Within a couple of short days, we witnessed with delight a dramatic moment when David, once again off task, jumped right up and came immediately to my side—wearing a smile! Amazed and impressed, somebody made the connection and responded with, "Wow, David! You did that with a Right Heart attitude."

Spontaneously, we all congratulated him with our "We are proud of you!" chant.

David has not been the same since. It doesn't take much to touch and win a child's heart. I could so easily have ordered him to come down immediately (classroom fear management) and, yes, he would have obeyed. And then I would have predictably become another teacher who has impatiently demanded that David obey. Would David have resisted my authority for the remainder of the year if I had continued to control him with classroom fear management? Absolutely! Students like David thrive in an atmosphere of unconditional acceptance.

THANK THEM FOR THEIR RIGHT HEARTS

Now for one last example of a simple, yet powerful way to integrate the concept of a Right Heart. One week, my students and I enjoyed a truly wonderful week. It occurred to me to convey my appreciation in the form of a "mini-letter" on the overhead. In the absolute quiet of the darkened room, one by one, they stood in front of the bright screen and thoughtfully read the words that expressed my gratitude and the honor of being their teacher. I thanked them for their Right Hearts. Capitalizing on the words Right Hearts, I wrote them in a different color so that they would stand out. Essentially, the message conveyed one point: Their Right Hearts were the reason for my appreciation.

"ATTITUDE" VS. RIGHT HEART

The negative connotation implied by the word attitude can be summed up in one word: problem.

In my earlier teaching days, students who somehow resisted my authority had "attitudes." The negative connotation implied by the word attitude can be summed up in one word: problem. When I bluntly informed my "rebels" that they had an attitude problem, I was saying that they were a problem. But they already knew that because they had been hearing it for years—they were simply living up to their labels.

Approaching behavior issues from a Right Heart perspective creates an altogether positive, conciliatory atmosphere. Whereas before I accused troublesome students of having an attitude problem, now I talk to them, without judgment or shame-based reproof, about not having a Right Heart. Bad attitude vs. Right Heart—a profoundly radical difference. One labels, judges, and condemns; the other non-accusatorily encourages self-examination. One generally shuts the door to owning the truth and taking personal responsibility; the other opens wide the door to the possibility of learning and growing from mistakes. Only one is respectful.

"WALKING THE TALK"

Those of us who earnestly embrace the vision and zealously seek guidance for the creation of a safe, warm, and accepting Right Heart classroom—one that feels like home—must never forget the one factor without which the house is predestined to crumble: a positive example. We must be certain to consistently display the attributes of a Right Heart with uncompromising integrity. Otherwise, we will self-righteously "talk the walk" but miserably fail to "walk the talk."

And when we fail—as indeed we will—we must be certain to display a humble, contrite Right Heart as we seek forgiveness. We must, in other words, live the lessons before the discriminating eyes of our students. As they observe our behavior and accurately assess the genuine condition of our hearts, may we cling assiduously to the transcendent wisdom of St. Augustine who exhorted us long ago, "Let us sing a new song—not with our lips but with our lives!"

Wensday March 1, 2006
Dear Stumpy.....

Yesterday I was some
what respectfull to my mom also
I did the dishes because it
was my chore and it was farley
easy. I was nice to my sisters
the goals I have completed
are don't yell at my brother, Be
nice to my sisters, Pay more
atenttion to my teachers, and
Last but not Least Take resporsbilety
for my actions

Respect

I showed respect to
my hole family last
night I did not yell or get mad at the

★ INTELLECTUAL ★

CHAPTER 15
Intellectual Needs

I am going to start with a confession from my past so that you do not make the same mistake I did. In the first few years when I was making the transition from the traditional authoritarian, teacher-centered classroom to the student-centered, interactive Whole Child classroom, I lost "balance." I did what many people do when they fall in love: I lost perspective. I was so consumed by this whole new way of being that it became my entire focus. Doesn't that sound like falling in love? What is probably the most common piece of advice for new lovers? Slow down! Since I am a born zealot, my enthusiasm has helped me conquer the mountains in my life, but it has also buried me under them.

What did losing balance look like? I focused too much on the social, emotional, and moral needs of the Whole Child and not enough on the intellectual needs. For example, until the last several years, I never gave homework on the first day of school because I was committed to making sure my students enjoyed their first day of school. Unfortunately, the underlying message that I gave my students was, "Ms. LaField's class is easy."

To make matters worse, I ruthlessly judged another teacher with a reputation for giving too much homework on the first day. She inevitably had students go home complaining about being in her class. But you see, we were both out of balance. I did not give enough homework, and she gave too much.

Do I assign homework on the first day of school now? You bet I do. Part of that homework is a letter they must give to their parents that first night, which, among other things, informs the parents that their child has homework every night of the week unless the Homework Hotline states otherwise. My message to my students now is that they will work hard in my class and learn a lot, but at the same time they will enjoy the learning process. That is balance.

COMING FROM A PLACE OF FEAR

Last year, my students and I worked harder than all my previous years in the classroom; as a result, I enjoyed the most academically rewarding experience of my career. Did I maintain balance? Absolutely. Not surprisingly, however, I came close to losing balance in early spring as I prepared my students for state tests. Extremely determined, I intended to prove my theory that the intellectual needs of our students are met in significantly higher degrees when their other needs are addressed as well. As the testing dates drew closer, my natural tendency was to charge harder. Thankfully, I caught myself.

My red flag was that I started feeling "uptight." If you have been teaching for any time at all, you know what that feels like. I caught myself tightening my grip 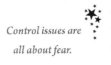 on the control button, and my kids felt the difference. I *Control issues are* was not the relaxed, patient, good-natured Ms. LaField *all about fear.* they knew and loved. I was coming from a place of fear, not a place of love. Control issues are all about fear. The irony, of course, is that the more we push that control button, the more we lose control.

I hope you are wondering, "Okay, Olivia, what did you do then?" The answer? I stopped in the middle of the lesson, turned off the overhead projector, and told my kids what they already knew: I was pushing too hard. It was time to give an apology, talk about why, and about what to do. In a few minutes, we were back on track with a plan. They were to hold me accountable every time they felt me fearfully use the control button, and they kept their word.

Did my students continue to work hard until the very last minute before testing day arrived? Yes, and with positive attitudes too. They gave it their best because they *wanted* to, not because they *had* to. From the first moment they walked into my class I had devoted every day to creating strong, mutually respectful relationships with every single one of them. I had valued them "beyond a galaxy of stars." The happy result? Their test results shyrocketed!

THE PERFECT COMBINATION

Effective classroom management is essential for meeting the *intellectual needs* of the Whole Child. I realize that in expounding on the importance of meeting the emotional needs of our students with *unconditional love*, you may have gotten the impression that I am "sugar and spice and everything nice." Not so! My students would tell you emphatically: "Ms. LaField doesn't let us get away with anything!" They would tell you that I am strict, but in a nice way.

"Strict but nice" is a good point of reference. That is how you want your students to describe you. That is the balance for which you must aim. It is possible to be too nice. Children take advantage of too nice. Too nice does not command respect when the situation calls for it. Children cannot learn unless the teacher can make them sit down, be quiet, and listen.

The student teachers from our local university know that my room has an "open door" policy. They are welcome to join us unannounced, which they often do. And what do they see? They see *mutually* respectful interaction. They see a teacher who is effectively meeting the intellectual needs of her students because she has created an environment where her students pay attention to her lessons, stay on task, and respond respectfully to her requests. They see a teacher using "strict but nice" methods for making sure her students are taking full advantage of the lesson. They see a classroom where—on most days—optimal learning occurs.

However, they won't see that the first week of school—or the second or the third or maybe even the fourth. The mutually respectful, interactive classroom takes time to create! And the process begins long before the kids walk in the door that first day of school. I know in exact detail how I want that first day to go. Day one is when the student training begins.

THE PRIZE IS WORTH THE PRICE!

Any discussion of meeting the intellectual needs of the Whole Child would be incomplete without a thorough examination of the role of the teacher's expectations. Once again, it's confession time. Until the last five years, my academic expectation level was low—comparatively speaking. Every year for the past several years I have pushed my students to higher and higher levels of academic performance, and every year they have risen to my expectations. Consequently, every year their test scores have improved.

Last year I pushed my seventh graders to unprecedented levels of writing proficiency. For example, to help them avoid the standard boring subject-verb sentence pattern, I taught them a sophisticated approach to constructing sentences using a variety of sentence patterns. They learned to create sentences that began with or included present and past participles, infinitives, appositives, dependent clauses, and adjective, adverb and prepositional phrase openers.

Along with the patterns, they learned advanced punctuation skills that transformed their writing, and I took my accelerated students even further with parallel construction, verb tense agreement, concise language, use of figurative language, and much more. Day after day different student teachers observed our English lessons and shared their amazement at not having learned such advanced writing skills until college, much less seventh grade!

I brought my own writing to school, put it on overhead transparencies, and challenged them to identify the various structures. Our English lessons grew exciting, challenging, and fun. Then when they applied their new knowledge to their essays, they were awed by the difference, indeed, many brought their writing to me with shocked expressions of, "Ms. LaField, I actually wrote this!"

"Yes," I would say, and "was the prize worth the price?"

They were learning that hard work was worth the reward of feeling such personal pride. They were becoming Little Red Hens in the truest sense. They were earning the cake, and they loved the taste.

They revised their goals essays until I knew many of them by heart. They were going for the coveted gold seal, and I would allow them to settle for nothing less. I agreed that I would stick with them no matter how long it took. When I passed back the "golds," everyone cheered for the recipient, and each time a student finally made it, they told the class how many times they had to revise their essay before it was perfect. Every single one of them eventually earned the seal with the A+ next to it, including Nick, who revised his essay eight times! At Open House we displayed those essays with intense pride. By the end of the evening, my jaw was sore from smiling.

LOWERING THE BAR BUT EXPECTING THEIR BEST

Perhaps you are wondering if I had students who struggled with the complexity of creating infinitive and participial sentence patterns. Of course I did. Every teacher in America teaches to a conglomerate of ability levels—all in the same room. It is a formidable challenge to say the least. My approach to meeting the intellectual needs of all my students, regardless of their ability level, has evolved radically over the years and is inextricably connected with my rising levels of expectation. I am convinced that in order to effectively meet the intellectual needs of the Whole Child, *we must set high expectations. We must expect their best.*

I am convinced that in order to effectively meet the intellectual needs of the Whole Child, we must set high expectations. We must expect their best.

In years past I would never have even considered teaching my students to write structurally complex sentences. Why not? My choice was a simple matter of underestimating not only my students' abilities to perform at such advanced levels but also their motivation even to try. There was the problem of what to do with those students who could not even write in complete sentences, much less complex sentences. I was satisfied to teach my students the basics, but in so doing, I failed to meet the intellectual needs of my more advanced students. Never again.

Right now you are surely wondering how I meet the intellectual needs of my strugglers. I modify. I lower the bar for those students whose needs fall below basic. Because I work with my students individually on their essays, I can privately conference with each one to explain my expectations. No one walks away feeling "stupid." Everyone is proud of their gold essay, even if it fails to incorporate even a single sentence pattern. They can be proud because they are learning to write complete sentences.

Did raising my expectations create more work for me? The answer is yes. Revising my students' essays takes time. But I can tell you this: I do not waste a minute on an essay that has obviously been thrown together. I am murder on apathy! I hand it back with an NYB: Not Your Best. I expect their best, and it takes only one essay to get that point across. After I have drilled it in enough times, it begins to penetrate.

On the other hand, those who pour their hearts into their revisions and give me their best are rewarded with my best. I make sure they know that I love helping them, that it is not a burden to grade their essay when I could be playing in my garden—as long as I am grading their best. I make sure, too, that they show their *A hard-working teacher plus an appreciative student make a great combination.* appreciation, that they thank me sincerely, realizing what a precious gift of my time they are receiving. When they really begin to recognize their growth, they make the connection: I couldn't have done this without my teacher. A hard-working teacher plus an appreciative student make a great combination.

CHAPTER 16
First Days

I have always loved the first days of a new school year. It's a fresh start, a new chance to get it right. There is so much of "This year I'm going to…" And each year, for most of us, it does get better. We fine-tune our program, improve our curriculum, and upgrade our rules, requirements, and expectations. Hopefully, we learn from past mistakes. Hopefully, we are one year wiser, not one year "wearier." Hopefully, we are ready.

Every year I spend an inordinate amount of time in my classroom preparing for that first day. Committed to designing a warm, inviting space for my students, I have successfully created an environment that looks and feels appealing to teenagers, while at the same time one that stimulates their imagination.

HONORED GUESTS

More than the color or the overall appeal of the room environment, my students are always most impressed by the warm reception they receive as they enter the room that first day. I welcome each of them at the door as I would an honored guest. And after completing roll, I profusely express the joy, honor, and blessing of being their teacher.

In their first week's reflections, they often describe feelings of genuine acceptance, which happily alleviated their anxieties. Whereas younger students would be less conscious of this unusually warm, personal reception, my students are elated because they invariably anticipate the usual "get down to business" approach to the first days. They *feel* the difference, and the difference feels good. And because it feels good, they are open and ready to receive whatever comes next.

INTRODUCTIONS

That first day I spend a few minutes sharing my multi-faceted personality. Beginning with *Learner*, I explain my passionate commitment to learning and growing, to reaching my full potential and becoming all I was created to be. I introduce our class theme of "We are here to learn" and I tell them about how I spend my time immersed in books and writing as opposed to television and the Internet. In short, I convey my effusive enthusiasm for learning.

I aim to convince my students that it is possible for a teacher to be strict without being "mean."

Next, I introduce myself as *Teacher*. When I am the *Teacher*, I explain, I have very high expectations for creating and maintaining an environment conducive to optimal learning. They can expect me to be strict but fair. We talk about their past experiences, frustrations, and hopes for this year, and I aim to convince my students that it is possible for a teacher to be strict without being "mean."

We also discuss the fact that students' lack of self-discipline forces teachers to strictly control those who have not yet learned to control themselves. It is truly surprising how many students have never made that connection. I emphasize the point that in the coming year, I will strive to teach them to control themselves so that I am not being forced to. My desire, I assure them, is to teach, not discipline.

After introducing myself as *Teacher*, I share the *Friend* part of my personality. Be infinitely aware that a fine line exists between friend and buddy! Never cross that line. I explain that the *Friend* in me cares very much about their feelings, their problems, their pain. The friend in me wants to help. The friend in me hopes they will open up and share. The friend in me can be trusted.

And then finally I tell them about the *Kid* in me, the part of me that loves to laugh and joke and be silly and sometimes even foolish. The kid in me, I tell them, *can* emerge only if they are mature enough to laugh with me and then, if the situation calls for it, get right back on task without delay. Repeatedly, I emphasize that learning always comes first but I believe strongly that learning should be fun. No argument from the students there.

WELL-DEFINED FIRST DAY GOALS

My goals for the first day are very clear in my mind:

★   I want my students to feel warmly welcomed and immediately accepted.

- ★ I want them to be impressed by and pleased with the appearance of the room.
- ★ I want them to feel safe and comfortable.
- ★ I want to impart a sense of who I am.
- ★ I want to give them a preview of what they can expect of me in the days to come.
- ★ I want to engage them in at least one interactive exchange of ideas.
- ★ I want them to feel safe enough to participate.
- ★ I want them to feel hopeful of achieving success.
- ★ I want to make it crystal clear that I will expect them to work very hard.
- ★ I want them to know that I believe learning should be enjoyable.
- ★ I want them to feel happy about their new class.
- ★ I want them to be excited about returning the next day.
- ★ I want them to tell their parents they had a great first day!

Naturally, there is the business of passing out informational parent/school handouts, learning names, assigning homework, etc.; but tasks become effortless when my overarching goals are well-defined.

BE PREPARED

Because the first day is so important, I want to help you make yours successful. I encourage you to try some of my approaches if you feel comfortable doing so, but more importantly, please do as the Boy Scouts say, "Be prepared!" Don't wait until a few days before school starts. You need plenty of stress-free time to create your classroom environment. Never be satisfied to just staple some ready-made, "pre-fab," store-bought pictures to cover your walls. That is not to say you should not use any, but they must not dominate your environment.

Make sure that you reserve ample space for displaying student work. Last year I found a picture of the cutest frog dancing on his hind legs and looking like he had just crossed the first place finish line. I knew the minute I saw him that I just had to use him somewhere. I enlarged him to about four feet tall, painted him with vibrant greens and golds, laminated him and made a sign that I posted above him with the words, "Worth Croakin' About!" I reserved a big space for him on the back wall of my new room, and my students'

When you are thoughtful about preparing your room, both your students and you will benefit.

163

first poems were displayed all around him. When you are thoughtful about preparing your room, both your students and you will benefit. Don't forget: A sufficient time investment before the school year begins results in fewer challenges during the coming year.

Be prepared by meticulously planning for the outcomes you hope to achieve. I teach seventh and eighth graders, so obviously my desired outcomes will vary greatly from the primary teacher. Whereas my students can sit still and quietly listen for fairly long periods of time, younger students have a much shorter attention span. Those who seriously plan for success know the general abilities and limitations of the age group they are teaching. If your expectations exceed their behavioral, emotional, and social maturity level, you will be unsuccessful. As I have endeavored to outline in this chapter, plan your goals to the "nth" detail. I always prepare *more* than we can possibly accomplish—just in case.

Be prepared physically. Get plenty of rest. Don't be in your class that last Sunday before the first day. Relax and do something you enjoy. But most critical, be prepared in your mind and heart. Constantly envision that first day in your mind's eye exactly as you intend it to unfold. See yourself welcoming your children. See yourself moving about the classroom as you successfully accomplish each and every goal. See yourself looking into your children's eyes and smiling warmly. See them returning your smiles.

If fears arise, do not entertain them. Immediately replace negative self-talk with positive affirmations. Use your marvelous imagination to envision a calm, organized, happy, self-congratulatory day. Believe for the best. Believe in the power of love to accomplish miracles. Above all, believe that "the value of a single child surpasses that of a galaxy of stars."

Yes, it seems like so much. And it is—even for a thirty-seven year veteran. But be encouraged! It does get easier. So much easier, in fact, that someday you may hopefully look forward with eager anticipation to that first day. Our PE teacher has been kidding me for more than twenty years about the first day being my favorite of the whole year. We'll definitely all laugh about it at my retirement party.

We must never forget that children are very perceptive. They watch and they wait—not to see if we have sufficiently mastered the fine art of the perfectly planned lesson that leads them logically from "anticipatory set to closure," but to see if we care. Children are very forgiving. When they

Don't try to be perfect. Be yourself!

164

know we care, they will readily overlook our foibles and failures. Keep that in mind as that first day approaches. Let it quell any fears that may rob you of sleep. Don't try to be perfect. Be yourself!

FIRST DAY IMPRESSIONS

One year I asked my students to share their impressions of the first week.

"When I walked into my core class, I knew that I was going to have a good year because after the first day with Ms. LaField I had confidence in myself."

"On the first day of school she didn't do the, 'OK, I'm here to teach you, so just sit down and shut-up act, or the rules, rules, rules type of thing.' She let us be us."

"Many teachers start school by telling you the rules and lots of other stuff and it's like BLAH, BLAH, BLAH, yeah, whatever. Ms. LaField started our school year by getting to know us and us getting to know her."

"It was like when I first walked into the classroom I just had to smile and be happy because I felt like everyone there was going to be my friend. She just made me feel like I wanted to come back every day."

"The first day I walked into my new class I was very nervous. I had enough butterflies in my stomach to fill an entire field, but as soon as I walked into Ms. LaField's classroom, I felt a sense of calmness come over me. I think it was the first impression Ms. LaField gave me that made me calm."

"I've never really wanted to come to school so on the first day I was really bummed. I had to go back to that dreadful prison called school. But my thoughts shifted once I stepped into Ms. LaField's classroom. MY GOSH! I had never seen so many colors! I had never felt so content in an actual classroom. For the first time in my life, I was happy about school."

"When I stepped into Ms. LaField's core class I had mixed feelings. I talked nervously with some of my friends. When the bell rang, I thought here we go. I have a Mohawk, and the first thing Ms. LaField did was say, 'I really like your Mohawk. Can anyone tell me why I like it?' Brooke raised her hand and said, 'Because he is unique.' And at that moment I felt good in Ms. LaField's class. I felt it was okay to be me."

BEGIN WITH A SMILE!

I have often heard it said that teachers shouldn't smile until Thanksgiving. The dictatorial "You'd better respect me because I'm the boss" mentality works for the Marine Corps, but in my opinion, it has no place in education. Teachers who use these tactics in the classroom do so from a sense of insecurity, from the fear of losing control of their students. Their first day invariably begins with a plethora of rules, regulations, and restrictions. Ironically, the tighter their grip, the more likely their students are incited to rebel, thus creating an even greater control nightmare.

In this chapter, more than anything else, I have attempted to convey a first-day emphasis on *creating relationships*. The rest of the year entirely depends on the degree to which I have learned to love my students—even before I meet them! For many long years I have dedicated my life to learning to love on deeper levels, for "Where there is great love, there are miracles!"

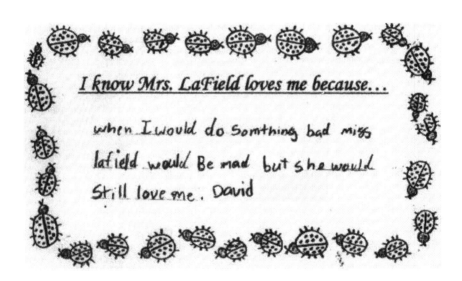

I know Mrs. LaField loves me because...

when I would do something bad miss lafield would Be mad but she would Still love me. David

Thank You Miss LaField

I am so thankful that you have taught me so much on this essay and if it wasn't for you I would not be the great writer you say I am. Someday I will write a book, and it will be on the New York Times Bestseller List because of you, and on the dedication page it will be dedicated:

To Miss LaField, the wonderful teacher who in 7th grade taught me how to succeed, how to become popular for the right reasons, how to become a better person, and most importantly, how to be the writer I am today! Thank You Miss LaField!!!

— Tim

CHAPTER 17
Remediation

*M*eeting the intellectual needs of our steadily increasing numbers of below-grade level students is virtually impossible without some form of remediation. Recently, I hit the jackpot—thanks to the "Choose to Care" peer remediation movement.

For the past several years I have offered a study hall every day in my room during lunch. Yes, I give up my lunchtime. I am not advising you to do the same, but it works well for me for several reasons. I do not want to end up like the *Giving Tree*—with nothing left for myself. All day long, every moment, non-stop, I strive to give my students my best. By the time that last blessed bell rings, I am ready to leave. I cannot give my best to my students in an after-school study hall. Mornings do not work for me either, so that leaves lunchtime. Also, many students who cannot come before or after school have no excuse during the lunch period. In addition, my lunchtime study hall has always provided a safe haven for a few "loners," who would otherwise sit by themselves every day.

One year, my lunchtime study hall evolved into a "see it to believe it" affair. Founded upon the principle of selfless giving, it blossomed into a living example of the foundation upon which the life of Mother Teresa was built: servanthood.

EVAN AND RICHARD: TWO BOYS WHO CARED!

In January, Evan and Richard started coming in at lunch to help David, an at-risk boy in their group. David's troubles in school grew serious in third grade when he threw a chair at the teacher. From then on he was expelled from every school he attended. He joined us in late fall.

Taking Richard and Evan aside, I implored them to step in and reach out to this deeply troubled boy. If anybody could help David, those boys could. I asked them to come to study hall every day and help David with his work. It was a monumental request for two boys who love nothing more than to burn up the basketball court during their lunch free-time, but they agreed without even blinking. We shook on it, and I knew they would keep their word because they were learning to be young men of honor and integrity.

Just as they promised, they marched into study hall the next day with purpose all over their faces. Nobody could believe it. With their heads huddled together, they poured over David's assignments as they gobbled up their lunches. The kids whispered. Nobody wanted to disturb the miracle. Surely, it would not last. But it did last, and other athletes joined the boys.

After a week or so, I sensed there was more to unfold. I envisioned a study hall where kids would come to receive help from fellow classmates who volunteered to give up their lunch period to help others because *they cared*. I created a formal plan for a daily tutorial program where students could come for one-on-one remediation from their peers.

First, I had to recruit my tutors. After revealing my vision to both classes, I shared a passionate plea for committed tutors, people of integrity, who could be depended upon to faithfully honor their promise. I was believing for ten. Fourteen signed on, and the "Choose to Care" peer remediation movement was officially launched.

Next was a plea to those who needed remediation. I drew up a list of their names and invited them to join me in the Commons for a private moment of decision. What I said to them was nothing short of begging them to care about their lives. Fourteen signed on.

That was on a Friday. By Sunday night I had created a full-sized bulletin board with the title "We Choose to Care" emblazoned across the top in bold fluorescent poster paper. Each tutor had a "name plate" which I stapled around the title, and above each name were the words: Selfless Servant. I wanted to give them public recognition for their involvement as well as remind them of their commitment. Under the title across the center, I posted a fitting quote by Confucius, a favorite from our unit on China: "If you want to find yourself, lose yourself in the service of others." The rest of the board was covered with rows of 10x12 blank fluorescent poster paper upon which to display outstanding student work.

In addition to the bulletin board, I rearranged a long countertop in a strategic location and taped seven metal file trays together side by side in a long row. Organization, I knew, would play a critical factor in the success of the venture; my tutors would need to be well-furnished with hand-outs and worksheets galore—all at their fingertips. Knowing my students would hastily return the papers to the wrong files when the lunch bell rang for their next class, I even labeled each file so they could be easily reorganized.

Until we finished with state testing in late April, our servant-centered study hall never lost momentum. I did have to keep pushing a few of the at-risk boys who were dragging their feet, but a few calls to their parents took care of the problem. On a few occasions, I had to gently but firmly remind Evan and Richard of the importance of standing by their promise to help David every day. As always, they received my reminder with Right Hearts and remained true to their promises.

For the purposes of sharing this story with you, I wish I had kept a record of the "before and after state test scores" for the students being "served" by their selfless peers. Suffice it to say, our study hall met and exceeded the *intellectual* needs of those students receiving remediation. But equally important, all who played a part in our "We Choose to Care" study hall that began with Richard and Evan had their *social* and *emotional* needs supremely met as well.

SCHOOL GOALS

Still another way I meet the intellectual needs of my students is by helping them set and reach school goals. Along with the personal and family goals in their journals, my students choose at least three school goals on which to focus throughout the year.

During the third or fourth week of school, my students join me in a lively discussion of their past educational experiences. By this time they have already started creating their journals and clearly understand our goals focus. This discussion is one of our most intense of the year, for I have learned

I pour heart and soul into impressing my students with the life-changing potential of goals.

that without intensity, my students often miss the profound importance of the message. Before they begin formulating their school goals, I pour heart and soul into impressing my students with the life-changing potential of goals. First, I invite them to consider their problems from past years, especially those weak areas that spelled disaster and gloom. As my students volunteer their problems, I

For most, their academic failure in the past is due overwhelmingly to issues unrelated to the intellectual domain.

write them on an overheard transparency for all to view. We laugh together good-naturedly, and I allow a few "elaborations" but always keep the discussion on target.

Significantly, the vast majority of the problems that our students face originate in the realm of the social, emotional, and moral. For most, their academic failure in the past is due overwhelmingly to issues unrelated to the intellectual domain. We Whole Child proponents believe that as we nourish the *social, emotional, physical,* and *moral* needs of our students, we are "clearing out the clutter" to make room for enhanced *intellectual* development. We must somehow help our students get down to the core issues that haunt them and hold them back.

If you decide to adopt a goals-oriented approach to meeting the needs of the Whole Child in your classroom, you must teach your students the difference between long-range and short-range goals. My students invariably want one of their school goals to be that they make the honor roll every quarter. That's wonderful, of course, but we have to help them see that it is a long-range goal, and they need short-range goals to get there. I go into great lengths to make sure they understand the concept. They must add to the long-range goals the short-range goals that will help them achieve the big ones.

For example:

This year I will make the honor roll all four quarters...

1. By sitting in the front of the class and listening to my teachers.
2. By doing my homework before I watch TV.
3. By treating all my teachers with respect.

Invariably, I have students with an enviable problem: They always make straight A's. This is the point in the discussion where we stop and talk about our imperfect world. We can always get better. We must never be satisfied! Yes, we feel proud of our straight-A report card, but we still look at those little obstacles that inhibit reaching our maximum potential.

Through this discussion, my students also understand that their teacher has lofty long-range goals for herself, and that every day she works diligently on the short-range goals that will help accomplish the larger ones. Most importantly, they learn that I am imperfect and that I will make mistakes along the way. They will see my passion to keep learning and pursuing my goals, and it will inspire them.

Their homework that night is to discuss their school goals with their parents and come back the next day with goals finalized and signed by their parents. I collect and revise until I am satisfied. Their final copies must be in perfect form—no spelling errors, etc.

CHAPTER 18

Personal Responsibility Plans: Pinkies!

*P*erhaps you, along with legions of us in education today, are feverishly searching for answers, for ideas that elicit nothing less than your students' best. There is an answer to the growing epidemic of student apathy: Pinkies!

We've all heard the proverbial, "Necessity is the mother of invention." Trite but true, it illustrates how Pinkies (Personal Responsibility Plans) came to be. It was necessary that I invent a solution to the dismal numbers of F's in my grade book. I was losing kids, and the life rafts were in short supply. Tired of waiting for the next ship to come along, I resolved to build my own.

When I contemplated my options, one factor loomed altogether obvious: Any life raft I might toss out to my "under-achievers" would surely sink without strong parental support. Parents don't like to see their children fail! Unfortunately, many are at a loss when it comes to turning their child's failure into success. In their minds, they have "tried everything."

Along with the necessity of reliable parental support, a further glaring prerequisite quickly surfaced: the student accountability factor. Any idea for improving academic performance was destined for the dregs if the students failed to assume personal responsibility for his or her actions.

From experience, I knew the new enterprise would have to be "incentives-based." Intrinsically, the incentive of higher grades would motivate student involvement. However, in addition to the reward of seeing and sharing A's instead of F's, extrinsic enticements would need to be an added element of student "buy-in." Whatever I came up with would have to exude appeal. So with the indispensable prerequisites of parental involvement, student accountability and enticing incentives clearly in mind, I sat expectantly at my computer, poised to "invent" a well-delineated, comprehensive, practical, albeit appealing approach to the formidable task of replacing student apathy with student empowerment. Daunting would be a shallow word for the task set before me.

LOCK, STOCK, AND BARREL

Happily, a plan was conceived that felt right. The student would have a daily accounting (Pinkie) that he or she would be required to show their parent. The parent (or guardian) would be encouraged to review the Pinkie each week-night. They would also be encouraged to devise a personalized reward/consequence plan for the student. If the student came home with an approved Pinkie for five consecutive days, the parent would reward him or her with a previously agreed-upon reward. For example, the student would be allowed to play video games. On the other hand, if the student did not earn a Pinky that day, the video games would be denied.

Instinctively, I was certain it would work. Pinkies—as I dubbed the system after deciding to print them on bright pink paper—has proven to be the most innovative, transformational remediation plan I have personally conceived. Here's why:

* ★ The parents love it because they feel empowered to help their children succeed.
* ★ My students are excited because Pinkies are positive, productive, and help them improve day-by-day.
* ★ Through the support of their parents and teacher, my students learn to care about their grades.
* ★ Students who thought they weren't smart enough to make honor roll grades are realizing that it's about hard work, not I.Q.

What are the incremental steps for integrating Pinkies into your classroom? First, you must get parent "buy-in." I targeted key students and invited their parents and them to a meeting in our room. I made sure the letter of invitation was enthusiastic so they couldn't refuse.

It was an "intimate" roundtable discussion among parents with one concern in common: Their son or daughter was in trouble, and they were searching for answers. Our counselor joined us as well, which turned out to be an integral component of the overall success of that initial meeting.

Important to note here is that prior to that meeting I had soundly established two irrefutable realities: My students trusted me, and their parents knew I was a teacher who cared. Nobody questioned my sincerity, my excitement, nor my intentions. They bought in "lock, stock, and barrel" because I had already established the indispensable groundwork—solid relationships.

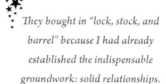

They bought in "lock, stock, and barrel" because I had already established the indispensable groundwork: solid relationships.

As I explain the details of the plan, please refer to the following pages, which I have included for your convenience. Use my ideas, adapt them, or create a whole new format. Undoubtedly, my methods can be improved.

INTRODUCING PINKIES TO PARENTS

Using the overhead, I begin the meetings with a quick overview of the whole process. Then I begin with the activity entitled "Let's Play to Win!"

Under the heading of TEACHER'S/PARENTS' responsibilities, I play the role of the passionate coach in the locker room, who, faced with a dismal losing streak, must convince his or her players that this game is too important to lose. What's really wonderful is that I truly believe my words.

Under STUDENT'S responsibilities, I unveil the game plan in detail, beginning with a focus on the importance of ON-TASK behavior. Aside from the task of convincing apathetic students to care, this can be our most daunting challenge. Next on the list, they learn that their student is required to attend study hall. They must bring lunch and focus on remediation as they eat.

Next under "Let's Play Ball to Win," STUDENT'S responsibilities are to "Evaluate their performance to determine if he or she has earned a Pinkie." Here is where the fun—or the frustration—begins. Using the "I earn a Pinkie when I" list (see next pages), they check their daily performance and determine for themselves whether they earned a Pinkie—or not.

At first, they approach me with the question: "Did I earn a Pinkie today, Ms. LaField?" Repeatedly, I must remind them to look at the list on the wall and determine for themselves. The look on my face and the tone of my voice often indicates the answer, but often, if a student has enjoyed an exceptional day, I will "fool them" into insisting that they earned a Pinkie—despite my look. Then, of course, I break out into a smile.

Eventually, they stop coming to me at the end of the day with a Pinkie and Sharpie in their hand. They know better. They are learning to hold themselves

Talk about a splendid opportunity to teach children on a daily basis the sometimes painful lesson that every choice we make has a consequence.

accountable. Until that time, I must explain to them why they did not earn a Pinkie. Here is another chance for teaching accountability, another opportunity to impart a "truth" lesson. It's another chance for them to utter those blessed words, "Ms. LaField, the truth is I didn't earn a Pinkie because I…" and then they name the specific reason(s).

At first, they try to convince me to change my mind. They know their parents are waiting for that Pinkie when they go home. Talk about a splendid opportunity to teach children on a daily basis the sometimes painful lesson that every choice we make has a consequence.

The parents' responsibilities are just as important. Every day they meet with their child to discuss why they did or did not earn a Pinkie. This meeting, I strongly advise the parents, must be a very calm, matter-of-fact discussion if the child comes home empty-handed. The "fear factor" will sabotage the success of the system every time.

Finally, the meeting ends with the "win or lose" requisite: THEY MUST NOT DROP THE BALL! They must plaster in their minds that no matter how daunting the task, no matter how tired or how exasperated, they must stick with me until we win the game. The moment either they or I give up, their child will lose faith and walk off the field. I zealously concur with the great Vince Lombardi: "Losing is not an option!"

THE HEART AND SOUL OF THE MATTER

In closing, I must emphasize once more that the most powerful factor in helping kids perform exceptionally on the standards is not classroom management, but our depth ofcaring. Student apathy is the real enemy of the standards. Many of our students don't care to listen, do their homework, or excel academically because they do not have an adult in their life who believes in them, an adult who views education as a critical key to success. They have no one at home who expects their best, who pushes them to reach their full potential. Why should they care about those F's on their report card if no one in their life cares enough to encourage and support them? And why, of all things, should they care about the "almighty" state standards?

We can be the one adult in their life who truly cares, the one motivating factor that makes all the difference in the life of a child. How? By believing in them, by refusing to give up on them despite extreme resistance, by giving them the sweet taste of success. Not only *can* we be that adult; we *must* be! In truth, it is our high calling as teachers.

LET'S PLAY TO WIN!

TEACHER'S/PARENTS' responsibilities:

* ★ 100% dedication and nothing less
* ★ Teamwork
* ★ Encourage and praise at every opportunity
* ★ Use TOUGH LOVE when it's called for
* ★ Settle for nothing less than the student's best

STUDENT'S responsibilities:

* ★ On task! On task! On task!
* ★ Study Hall (lunchtime) Monday-Thursday
* ★ Get grades from math and science
* ★ "Winner on the Way" weekly progress update/goals (in Study Hall)
* ★ Evaluate his/her performance, determine if he/she earned a Pinkie, and report to teacher

It's all about: PERSONAL ACCOUNTABILITY!!!

PARENTS' responsibilities:

* ★ Expect a Pinkie daily
* ★ Maintain consequence/reward agreements
* ★ Check "Homework for the Week" on Monday
* ★ Check "Weekly Progress Report" on Monday
* ★ Sign nightly Reading Log
* ★ Help student with assignments
* ★ Check Aeries often
* ★ Stay in close contact with the teacher

DON'T DROP THE BALL or everyone loses!!!

I EARN A PINKIE WHEN I:

1. Obey the teacher's procedures.
2. Get on task right away.
3. Stay on task almost all the time.
4. Sit up front and respect the teacher.
5. Come to study hall and work.
6. Respond with a Right Heart.
7. Behave maturely.

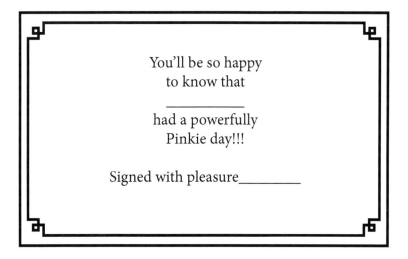

You'll be so happy
to know that

_____

had a powerfully
Pinkie day!!!

Signed with pleasure_____

CHAPTER 19
The Standards

I remember the day I was introduced to the standards as well as I remember the day President Kennedy died. Only the day I met the standards, I felt as if I had taken the bullet! My principal at the time pulled the trigger when I heard her blithely say: "All those wonderful, fun, creative lessons that you've loved so much over the years…Well, you can just throw them away if they do not fit in with the standards."

Incredulously, I sat there in the library with my peers and became sick to my stomach as jolt after jolt of nightmarish forebodings ran through me. Disgusted yet fiercely determined, I left that library the proverbial "queen of denial." It would be years before I reluctantly relinquished my crown.

I spent the greater part of the next three years pretending like the standards nightmare was a very bad dream from which I would eventually awaken—except on Wednesdays. Oh, how I dreaded those early morning teachers' meetings, which never seemed to conclude without reference to the standards. On those brief occasions, reality momentarily interrupted my fond illusions, forcing me to remove my crown and look briefly into the monster's eyes. The instant those meetings ended, I recovered my crown, and resumed business as usual—my way.

But eventually, entire meetings were devoted to discussing the standards, and it grew increasingly difficult to pretend that they would go away and leave me alone. One fateful morning, the crown finally came off for good, and I moved into that stage we know as acceptance. This was definitely a healthy choice on my part—though not yet a happy one.

Clearly my principal had been right. Many of those precious lessons of the past had to go. But one thing I knew I would never surrender: my fierce allegiance to the Whole Child philosophy. Much to my chagrin, the standards—at least on a middle school level—do not in any way support my uncompromising belief that we must strive diligently, whenever and wherever possible, to meet the intellectual *as well as the social, emotional, and moral needs of our students.*

A zealot with a cause, I determined early on to "go down fighting" before ever abandoning what I had come to recognize as the best hope for education. When it became all too clear that the standards were an obvious threat to the Whole Child philosophy, I geared up not only to defend my cause, but to prove that students, whose needs are met on all levels can and do score higher on the state tests than those students in classrooms where the sole focus is on meeting the intellectual needs of the child.

...every teacher fervently committed to meeting the needs of the Whole Child can find a way.

For the sake of those of you who are or will be teaching a single subject, particularly math and science, the Whole Child approach obviously poses formidable challenges. Rigid time constraints, as well as the very nature of the subject matter, allow little room for any focus other than that of effectively meeting academic objectives. Of course, the older the student, the more exacting the academic focus, especially in the case of honor students competing for entrance into their college of choice. Nevertheless, every teacher fervently committed to meeting the needs of the Whole Child can find a way.

The strong focus on the standards forced me to become a better teacher. I began in earnest to look for ways to improve my program.

EVERY MINUTE COUNTS!

As I first began to consider the need for positive change, I knew instinctively that the first and possibly foremost area to address was *time*. I realized I would need to become a time efficiency expert if I ever hoped to include the broad spectrum of standards as well as the indispensable bricks that, when firmly cemented together, form the foundation of The Whole Child Philosophy. Two bricks in particular draw time and attention away from purely academic on-task activities: our strong community focus and building personal relationships. The Valued Employees brick requires only about ten minutes every Friday, and the other bricks—the goals focus, Character Education and Right Heart—are integrated neatly into the academic curriculum. Somewhere I needed to create more time devoted exclusively to the focus on standards.

To accomplish that feat, I began analyzing my every move. From those few precious minutes before the first bell to the last second of the final bell, I started paying acute attention to the moment-by-moment progression of activity in a typical day. With that conscious awareness ever in the forefront of my mind, I quickly recognized spaces in my program that devoured minutes of time, especially transition time.

STREAMLINING MANAGEMENT TECHNIQUES

Challenging myself to make every minute count, I streamlined my classroom management techniques and "tightened my management belt." Since my time-management revolution came in the middle of the school year, I knew I had to prepare my students for change in a positive manner. Not only did students deserve an explanation for the changes; they would more than likely resist without one. I gathered them around me and explained the situation. I had prepared a visual: a newly laminated poster emblazoned with the words "Nothing Less." I made it about us instead of about me. The general idea was that we would accept nothing less than our best in our endeavor to save precious minutes.

I made it about us instead of about me.

To further enlist their support and make it about us, I invited their ideas for specific ways to save time. We laughed together as we talked about silly and realistic ways to "split moments." By the time the discussion ended, we were all headed for the championships.

Wouldn't life in the classroom be the ultimate mountaintop experience if we could, like Olympian coaches, enthusiastically infuse our students with "go for the gold" mentalities and then stand back and applaud as each one triumphantly accepts their medal? Yes, one by one, on different days and in different ways, I watch my students choose to be champions. It is why I am a teacher. But I have been teaching long enough to know that the course of a classroom does not change with one discussion. Unrealistic expectations inevitably invite defeat. I went into "Nothing Less" with my eyes wide open. I resolutely raised the bar knowing the goal was attainable, but that it would not happen overnight. I was very clear about one truth: If my kids were going to win the championships, I had better be an amazing coach.

LET THE GAMES BEGIN!

So, there we were. I was intent on saving every possible second, and they had verbally agreed to play along. It was time to let the games begin.

I had already determined beforehand what needed fixing, so I discreetly drew my ideas out, thus making the kids feel like my ideas were also theirs.

One of the strategies I used was: Streamline transition times. As promised, I gathered the kids and asked for input. How and where could we save precious minutes as we move from one activity to the next? Of course, I had already determined beforehand what needed fixing, so I discreetly drew my ideas out, thus making the kids feel like my ideas were also theirs. As it turned out, we decided that what we already had in place simply needed some fine-tuning.

We had our entrance and behavior standards, but everyone agreed they could be more tightly enforced. As we talked about how that would be achieved, I constantly reminded them of their part as well as my own. We agreed that the Task Managers would need to enforce the policy more strictly with their groups. We also agreed that no enforcement would be necessary if everyone managed him or her self. I reminded them of a vital point: I did not want to control them.

Next, we talked at length about the amount of time wasted before, after, and between lessons—transitions. Everyone agreed good-naturedly that those were the times when they talked most, when they didn't know what to do because they weren't listening, when they could not find or did not have what they needed, or when they moved at a snail's pace. As we discussed each idea, I asked for honest self-evaluation.

Ultimately, we agreed on three standards:

1) The Task Managers, if necessary, would encourage the kids in their group to cooperate with our commitment to more efficient transitioning.
2) They would listen with all eyes on me and no movement whatsoever until my verbal signal: Immediately upon hearing the signal, they agreed to follow the specified directions both quickly and quietly.
3) To make the effort as positive as possible, those who wholeheartedly committed to becoming time efficiency experts would be rewarded with academic bonus points.

THE MAGIC OF QUICK & QUIET

To help them keep track of their bonus points, I created a clever score sheet dubbed Quick & Quiet. In the center of the paper, I put a cartoon picture of a lady in combat boots and covered the rest of the sheet with twenty sets of the words Quick & Quiet. If they moved through the transition both quickly and quietly, they would circle one of the words and receive one extra credit point—all on the Honor System. Once all twenty sets were circled, they could turn their paper in for forty points and receive a new sheet.

This idea worked like magic for two reasons. It saved precious minutes that could be devoted to the standards, and it created a *sublime* atmosphere—more smoothly flowing and organized than I had ever experienced.

Motivational extra credit incentives like Quick & Quiet make kids feel good about themselves. They make school a positive place to be. They help kids achieve success. The more kids taste success, the more they are going to learn, and the higher their state standards test scores are sure to be.

Quick & Quiet works simply because my students respect me and, as a natural consequence, work diligently to meet my expectations.

Quick & Quiet works simply because my students respect me and, as a natural consequence, work diligently to meet my expectations. That includes performing their best on the state tests.

CHAPTER 20

Parent Relationships

*N*o consideration of methods for meeting the needs of the Whole Child would be complete without mention of the integral role that parents play. Even though I have to expend great effort and determination to create that partnership, for the past several years I have actually enjoyed stronger, more supportive parent relationships than ever before. Thankfully, despite the rising numbers of single working mothers, incarcerated fathers, homeless families, grandparent care-givers, students in foster care, etc., the great majority of my students still have someone who loves them. Last year every single one of my students had someone with whom I could communicate on his or her behalf.

I believe there are three key ingredients to developing successful parent/teacher relationships. First, parents must know we care. I realize that sounds ridiculously obvious, but it is a crucial component to parent buy-in. Second, we have to show them we care from the moment their child enters our door. Third, we have to show them often.

Before I even meet my students on that first day, I have already shown their parents that Ms. LaField cares. I get my students' names and phone numbers, and I call their parents the weekend before school starts. That one phone call establishes an immediate and positive connection. Parents are amazed by a two-minute, friendly, "Hello! I'm Ms. LaField, and I am so happy to be your child's teacher this year." They breathe more freely from a sense that their children are going to have a wonderful year with a caring teacher. Teachers with 100-200 students will undoubtedly find this far too time consuming, but a friendly, sincere letter can go a long way in establishing an immediate, positive rapport.

I make the calls short and to the point, and voicemail works wonders when you have sixty plus calls to make. If I am unable to reach the parents, I call back

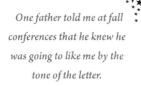

One father told me at fall conferences that he knew he was going to like me by the tone of the letter.

during the week until we finally talk. Yes, it does take time and effort, but it will undoubtedly save me time and energy in the long run. When I have to make the next phone call to a parent, which might be negative, I already have a tremendous advantage: Parents will know they are talking to a committed teacher who cares about their child. I have already established that fact by my preemptive actions.

The next time the parents hear from me is on the first day of school when my students go home with an informative but friendly letter of introduction. One father told me at fall conferences that he knew he was going to like me by the tone of the letter. Upbeat and enthusiastic, it conveys the heart of a teacher who loves what she does. It says for the second time, "I am so happy to be your child's teacher."

In addition to the letter, they receive a questionnaire about their child, which they are asked to thoughtfully complete and return by Friday. Included are questions like: How can I best help your child? What are you most concerned about this year? What are your child's greatest strengths? Weaknesses? Most parents have never been asked those questions, especially on the first day of school. Once again they receive the message: This teacher cares about my child.

During the first couple of weeks, I read those questionnaires over and over until I can remember certain notations I have made on each one. As I read them, I remind myself, "I need to remember that," so I mark it. Most important are the questions regarding concerns. For example, the parent may be worried because their child is a new student to the school and has no friends. A valid concern! For a couple of weeks I observe how their child is doing, and when I have an assessment, I call them to discuss that particular concern.

The third notification the parents receive is an announcement about Back to School Night. Without exception, it is the most important night of the school year, and I treat it as such. I actually ask for a signed commitment that they will attend. One of my students' five-paragraph expository essays is a letter imploring their parents to attend. By the time the big night arrives, they have received five announcements. I aim for 100% attendance. I want my room overflowing with parents. I want them to be impressed with my professionalism and witness my superior program.

By mid-September I have successfully built strong parent connections by proving that I care and by proving it often. For the remainder of the year, I continue connecting with my parents in several ways. I am a believer in positive parent phone calls, especially on behalf of those students who are improving somehow. Anytime we face difficulties with our students and enlist parental support, we must diligently report back to the parent regarding progress.

One unusual way I connect with parents is by creating special focus lessons that require my students and their parents to spend time together discussing a particular topic. The first such lesson covers the story of a homeless family in a motel. Essentially, the student reads the story and then a directed discussion ensues based upon specific points that the student must cover. The parents must sign at the bottom of the activity sheet and write comments, a requirement for credit. If given a broad enough time span in which to complete the assignment, parents rave about this activity, and most of my students enjoy communicating with their parents.

Establishing positive relationships with parents plays an integral role in insuring my students' success. When my students know their parents and I are working closely together on their behalf, they are more inclined to stay engaged in the classroom.

CHAPTER 21
Classroom Management

I spent the first fifteen years of my career managing my classes with the opposite of love: fear. Classroom fear management creates an environment where kids *have* to follow procedures. The underlying tone, unspoken though clearly recognizable, was "You had better obey me because I am the teacher in this classroom, and you will respect my authority!" You don't have to go through the painful process of being a classroom dictator. I am so happy that I learned to manage with love—and so are my students, who now obey with Right Heart attitudes because they *want* to. That is where Classroom LTL (Living the Lessons) Management wants to take you—from *have to, to want to*.

THE CLASS THAT LOVE BUILT

Before I share some of my tried and true managerial methods, it is important that you understand what Classroom LTL Management is and what it is not. It is neither gushy and sentimental nor fearful and insecure. It is not overly concerned that a student might resent fair but firm discipline. It never intimidates with threats and ultimatums, and it is never stubborn and inflexible. Most importantly, Classroom LTL Management, love is never conditional.

Classroom LTL Management is and must be patient. It chooses patience when it wants to scream; it closes its mouth when it knows it will be sorry. It listens to the voice that guides with wisdom. It bends when necessary, and it always admits wrong and quickly makes restitution.

Classroom LTL Management does not raise its voice. It speaks firmly when necessary and commands respect without demanding it. It uses a good sense of humor, and it smiles often. It overflows with thank-you's and effusive praise for students who "sit up and pay attention," and it gently encourages those who do not.

Through Classroom LTL Management, my students and I have created what I call "The Class That Love Built."

TRAINING THE TROOPS

Just because my students obey because they want to does not mean they never "mess up." What it does mean is that they are more willing to "go along with my program," and because of that willingness, they transgress less often as the days go by. Kids are all different, and that means they learn at different rates and to different degrees of consistency. Classroom LTL Management is patient with the managerial challenges but never compromises its standards. Each year, I have fewer management problems.

My student behavior expectations are extremely high. On a one-to-ten scale, I am a ten all the way. I know some teachers can tolerate much higher levels of noise and activity than I can and still teach with absolute mastery. Personally, I cannot tolerate anything that resembles confusion. I must have order. I want my kids to walk in, sit down, and get right to work.

The fine art of getting our students' attention must begin on that infamous first day of school. Usually it is easier to get their attention that first day because they are either too nervous, too overwhelmed or just too plain tired to do anything but enter quietly, sit down immediately, and at least pretend they are listening. Assuming that they walked in whispering quietly, found a seat, and sat down right away, I use their orderly entrance that first day to my advantage.

After I greet my students warmly and introduce myself, I begin "training the troops." I commend them on their entrance, telling them exactly what pleased me and why, using words like respect, self-discipline, and self-control. Younger children will need a simplified version, but the objective is the same no matter the age: I am teaching them exactly how to enter the classroom so that the moment they pass through the doors they have "left the playground outside" and are poised to pay attention and learn. I am intent on leaving a strong impression: "Ms. LaField expects us to walk in quietly, and she is going to make sure that we do." I do not tell my students that I *want* them to enter in a quiet, orderly fashion; I tell them, with a pleasant tone of voice, that they *will* enter according to my standards. "Want" and "will" are entirely different messages. One is declarative, the other imperative.

This is very important. Your students will be sizing you up that first day. You want them to walk away feeling like they have a new teacher with the take-charge confidence, poise, experience and expertise to control the class. And you can accomplish that with a smile. Yes, I smile on the first day, the last day and every day in between. A smile tells your students that you are relaxed, prepared, confident in your ability, enthusiastic, and happy to be their teacher.

If by chance you do have a problem with a student that first day, call home that very night, talk to other teachers, find out as much as you can about the student, and then make a commitment to his or her success. Any student who shows their "true colors" on the first day of school is a student who desperately needs all the compassion you can give. Never forget: The kids who are the most trouble are the kids who are the most troubled.

A word of warning here. As you are training the troops that first day, be careful not to belabor your points. Make your point strongly—i.e. walking in quietly—then move on. Reinforce it with a review at the end of the day. Knowing who listened that first day tells you volumes about your students. The sooner you assess the troops, the sooner you can determine your approach to training.

> *Never forget: The kids who are the most trouble are the kids who are the most troubled.*

Cardinal Rule #1:

As much as possible, manage your students proactively. If, for example, the class failed to meet your entrance standards that first day, tighten the reins the next day and explain why. Or, perhaps, share your standards the second day—with a firm but tender voice—and tell them you will be watching tomorrow.

Cardinal Rule #2:

Follow through. Say what you mean and mean what you say. Tread carefully, because Classroom LTL Management never threatens; it firmly states its case. If you tell your class you will be watching their entrance the next day, make sure your body language speaks loudly enough to reassure them that their teacher means business.

Cardinal Rule #3:

Be consistent. Every day, without exception, consistently enforce your entrance policies.

Cardinal Rule #4:

Reinforce positive behavior. Acknowledge, thank, and praise them when they remember and obey your instructions. When your students forget, which they will, gently and lovingly remind them that they can do better. Even if it seems like the entire class forgot, there will always be a few who remembered. Ask those students to raise their hands so you can see who they are, and thank them personally.

FOUNDATION PRINCIPLES

No matter how masterful our classroom control methods may be, they will fall to pieces if we fail to build them on a solid foundation. "The Class that Love Built" rests securely on five foundations, beginning with:

Foundation Principle #1: Mutual Respect.

As I treat my students with extraordinary respect from the first bell to the last, I earn their respect and their Right Heart willingness to fully cooperate with my requests.

Notice my use of the word "earn." Classroom fear management demands respect; Classroom LTL Management earns it. In the classroom where the mutual respect foundation is firmly in place, the teacher does not control the students; the students control themselves. If you are frustrated because your students are not cooperating as well as you would like, examine yourself. Are you treating your students with extraordinary respect—otherwise known as unconditional love?

Foundation Principle #2: The Golden Rule.

I am not big on rules. You will not find a list of rules on our wall. Kids don't like those lists either. Very few—if any—ever look at that list of rules on a regular basis and ask themselves how they are doing. By the time my students get to seventh grade, they are downright sick of the lists that have been staring at them for the last seven years.

When my kids walk into our class that first day of school, one of the first things they see is a big beautiful sign hanging from the ceiling in the middle of the room. It is impossible to miss, and it sums up my "rules" in five words: "One rule: The Golden Rule."

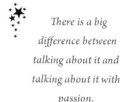

There is a big difference between talking about it and talking about it with passion.

How do I teach The Golden Rule? I talk about it with passion. There is a big difference between talking about it and talking about it with passion. I believe in it; I don't just "kind of" believe in it. It's passion that gets my students to begin examining their lives. It's passion that makes my exhortations come alive and take root in my students' hearts. And once the seed of The Golden Rule has been planted in their hearts, it needs lots of nurturing.

After we complete our unit on goal-setting the first month of school, I challenge my students to consider The Golden Rule as they determine their personal goals. I invite them to share their victories when they consciously apply it to their lives and to enthusiastically celebrate each other's successes with our "We are proud of you!" chant.

When I ask an offender, "How would you feel if someone did that to you?" it is not a rhetorical question based on condemnation. I am not putting the emphasis on the word "you" in the question. It is on the word "feel." That's what I want them to do—to feel the pain of others. It is never intended to shame them into making empathetic choices. Shame makes kids think they are bad. No one wants to listen to someone who is essentially saying they are bad. I ask the question softly—from my heart—and I wait for an answer.

Foundation Principle #3: We are here to learn.

On the very first day of school, I draw my students' attention to this, the most prominent of all the messages on the walls and ask them what they think it means. Naturally, they think it is about learning reading and English and history—academics. Yes, I tell them, it is about schoolwork, but it is about so much more. I explain that the word "we" refers to all the people in the world—not just to those of us in our room. The word "here" is about here on Earth, not just here in our room.

The "to learn" part is a little difficult to explain to twelve-year-olds, so I try to keep it basic by using key phrases that I have typed on small signs and hold up one at a time. Here are a few examples: We are here to learn from our mistakes, to be the best that we can possibly be, to love each other, to forgive, to love the truth, to obey The Golden Rule, to live with purpose, to be givers, to be People of Character, to have Right Hearts, to make the world a better place, to examine our lives, to care. That initial lesson introduces them to their first "big picture" view of what our class is all about.

On the first day, they learn that I want to prepare them for life. We are embarking on a nine-month journey, I tell them, and on the last day of school they will be different people—not because of what they learned out of our books, but because of our life lessons. It's new and different, to be sure, and most of it goes right over their heads, but that's okay. I refer back to this lesson throughout the year, and it incrementally changes the way they view their lives.

On the second day of school I teach my students how we will greet each other for the rest of the year. I begin very enthusiastically with, "Good morning, Class!" and they reply, "Good morning, Ms. LaField!" Then I say, "Happy Monday!" and they answer, "Happy Monday, Ms. LaField!" On that second day I ask, "Why are we here, Class?" and I teach them to respond enthusiastically with, "We are here to learn!"

For classroom management problems that involve some sort of behavioral issue, I use one phrase in particular: "We are here to learn to grow from our mistakes." For example, I observe that a student is cheating, lying, or stealing. Classroom fear management goes straight to punishment, leaving the child feeling ashamed, angry, resentful, and bereft of dignity.

In contrast, Classroom LTL Management compassionately takes children aside at an appropriate time and turns their self-deprecating choice into a character-enhancing lesson. It gently coaxes children to open their hearts to wisdom and advice. It talks non-judgmentally about self-respect, honesty, integrity and trust. It helps children see how their choice to cheat seriously hurts *them*. Without fail, it addresses the choice and not the child.

Classroom LTL Management succeeds in helping children realize that they can never be proud of themselves, never love themselves, and never be trusted by others if they choose dishonesty. Classroom LTL Management ends by asking children what they can learn from their mistake. It leaves them feeling unconditionally accepted and loved, with a desire to learn and grow from their mistakes. Classroom LTL Management takes a mess and turns it into a message.

It leaves them feeling unconditionally accepted and loved, with a desire to learn and grow from their mistakes.

Foundation Principle #4: Choose to Care!

As my students arrive that first day, they are greeted by seven "Choose to Care!" signs hanging from the ceiling that express the foundation of "The Class that Love Built." Over the course of the year, my students will read those signs literally hundreds of times. I want them to see those words in their sleep. I want them to unconsciously stare at them. I want them, like the words "We are here to learn!" and "One Rule: The Golden Rule," to get inside them and begin to change the way they look at their lives.

Foundation Principle #5: The Truth.

It is indeed possible to teach children the value of truth, and is not difficult. But as with the other foundations, it must be taught with passion. How many times as a child I heard, "You'd better tell the truth!" How my life would have been different if a caring adult had—from a gentle place of concern—taught me to treasure the truth. You and I can be that caring adult.

CAPTURING THEIR ATTENTION—NOW!

The next part of Classroom LTL Management is capturing the attention of the *whole class*. The purpose of this section is to give you some ready-made, on-the-spot "tools" to help you on your path toward mastering the fine art of capturing your students' attention—now! I want your students to sit up straight and pay attention the moment you request their cooperation. I want your principal to walk into your class unexpectedly and be impressed.

Let's begin with the two attention-getting devices that I teach my students on the very first day of school. For the first, which I call "Everybody go…" I created a visual that serves as a reminder in the days to come and helps with the training process. It is a bulletin board that I display up front where I do most of my teaching. In the middle is a big picture of a pretty lady with her index finger pressed to her lips, conveying an unmistakable message: Be quiet! Above the picture are the words, "Everybody go…." Under the picture is a very long "Shhhhhh!"

On that first day, I draw my students' attention to the picture and explain that when they hear me say, "Everybody gooooo….," they are all supposed to say "Shhhhhh!" immediately. After we practice a couple times, I ask what they think it is about, and then I share a little about the high standards that make our class so special. I emphasize that one of the high standards is about them giving me their attention immediately. Before they go home, I make sure we practice it a couple more times using a 1 to 10 scale.

The 1 to 10 scale is a little device I instituted years ago that helps me convey my standard of excellence for whatever I happen to be teaching them. For example, the "Everybody go..." attention-getter has three basic ingredients that all work together to make it one of the most effective devices I have used: I want everyone's attention, I want it with Right Heart attitudes, and I want it now. When they are too slow, I say something like, "That was a 7. Who can tell me why?" Someone will say that they were too slow. Then we talk for a minute about our high standards and why nothing less than a 10 is acceptable. I respectfully "drill into them" that they will give me their attention immediately.

Every class is different, so I can never predict how long we will have to practice before I can finally stop using the 1 to 10 scale, but I use the device until we are earning almost straight 10's. I make it clear that we should set high standards for our lives and never settle for less. The cheerleader in me makes earning a 10 a personal challenge for all of us.

If they are not learning fast enough to satisfy my standards, they start getting some classroom "tough love" management. I begin to target individual students—holding them a minute after the bell, or sitting them down for a serious talk about how I do not want to control them, but they are making the decision for me to use discipline with them.

BODY LANGUAGE

Hand-in-hand with the "Shhh" signal is the effective use of body language as an attention-getting device. When I want my students' attention, I stand straight and stiff like a soldier at attention, clasp my hands tightly in front of me and look up at the ceiling or close my eyes tightly—any combination works. Those students sitting right in front of me can obviously see me before those further away, so I teach those in the front to quickly spread the word: "Shhh! Ms. LaField wants our attention!" As soon as it is quiet—usually in a matter of seconds—I scan the room very quickly to make sure that every single one of my students is looking at me.

I am not satisfied until *all* of my students are giving me their attention promptly after I ask for it. I don't settle for *most* of my students. Although it may take a moment longer for those one or two who are engaged elsewhere to look up at me, I insist on 100% respect. Any compromise in this area of classroom management will be a clear signal to my students: Some of us can get by with not paying attention. I resolutely "hold that line" and refuse the temptation to move ahead when I have *almost* everyone's attention.

Capturing and keeping our students' attention begins on the first day of school and ends at the final bell on the last day. Undoubtedly, it is one of our most daunting challenges. But we must never forget the power of positive relationships to ease the task. Students who love and respect their teacher are infinitely more inclined to cooperate.

Still another way I use body language is to cover up my ears, close my eyes, and drop my head, which is one indication to my students that I cannot and will not listen to them all at once. I generally use this sign when I have several students gathered around me, who want my attention simultaneously. It is amazing how quickly that signal quiets the students, and equally important, it is so much easier on me. I don't have to raise my voice and demand that they be quiet. I merely drop my head, and it is almost instantly silent. It is simply impossible to try to talk to someone who has nodded off!

From time to time, especially if I am frustrated, I will completely turn my back to the class as if to say, "That's it!" But instead of expressing my displeasure with a verbal outburst—an indication to my students that I am losing control— it is much more effective to let my body do the talking for me.

Once I sense that all is calm and my students are focused once again, I turn around and, in a slow and deliberate manner, communicate the thoughts that may be troubling me. Remember, we can be firm and clear without using the threat of impending doom. Students never respect the teacher who loses control out of desperation and lack of competence and then threatens with ultimatums and extreme punishment.

Students never respect the teacher who loses control out of desperation and lack of competence and then threatens with ultimatums and extreme punishment.

Another attention-getter I often use is effective when the noise level is high and the kids are spread out. In my normal voice I say to the students close by, "If you can hear me, clap once." Then when those students and I clap together, a few a little farther away join in when I say, "If you can hear me, clap twice." By the time we've clapped to four, everyone is usually poised to listen. The kids enjoy the activity, and it works.

And we must not ever forget the magic of counting backwards. A few times each year when I want to really get the kids moving fast, I will begin to count backwards from ten. Though I use a loud, stern voice, I am always chuckling inside as they scramble to beat the countdown. And more often than not I reward the students who were first to give me their attention. Some things seem to work for every generation.

DON'T FORGET THE BELL

I cannot end a chapter on getting my students' attention without mentioning my bells. The first is a dainty little silver bell given to me as a gift many years ago. Though it has a soft, melodious sound, it captures their attention immediately. I merely tell them at the beginning of the year that when they hear the bell, they are to stop and look at me.

The other bell is a replica of an old antique school bell that is loud enough to scare my students into a state of rapt attention. I can recall using it only once last year. I was very tired, they were very loud, and I rang it out of impatience and irritability, but you would have thought I had dropped a bomb by the way they virtually flew to their desks. They grabbed their seats and looked around at each other and at me with shocked expressions and huge expectant eyes, and for several seconds everyone just sat there waiting for the axe to fall. Suddenly, we all realized at the same moment how comical it was, and we burst into laughter.

Why did that bell work so well? First, it was extremely loud, so it startled them. Next, it was the first time I had ever rung it, which added to the element of surprise. But most importantly, it was very much out of character for me to capture their attention in such a dramatic way, so they thought something terrible was happening! Every teacher should have an extreme attention-getting device, if for no other reason than emergency situations.

THE MISSING PIECE

Now, let's pretend for a moment. You decide that you are going to adopt all the attention-getters I have shared. You buy your bells, make your Shhh! bulletin board, and begin to practice your body language. You begin to dream about that utopian classroom where you are respected by every single one of your students.

Everything is in place, but it is just not working the way you had envisioned it. What could be wrong? You are learning to respect your kids more each day. They are beginning to respect you. Why are you so often frustrated? Why do you catch yourself raising your voice? What is the missing piece?

Let's see if you can guess the answer. It's a two-syllable word that begins with a P. No, it isn't practice. You have had plenty of practice. No, it isn't punish. You do not need to punish the kids for your frustration. It is *patience*.

Without patience, some days would leave our classroom resembling a war zone. Those are the days when my students behave as if they have forgotten everything I have worked so hard and so long to teach them. It is almost as if some wild, contagious force temporarily possesses their entire beings, causing them to act out in ways that shock even their peers. Usually it seems to be triggered by some deviation from the regular daily routine. Factors such as a drastic change in the weather, a rampant sugar-high epidemic (during Halloween), excitement over an upcoming event, or the imminent approach of the last day of school often lead to such behavioral deviations.

It would be much easier if these alterations in personality were predictable. And therein lies their destructive power. We are never quite prepared for them, which is precisely why they are the true test of our capacity for patience.

My formerly teacher-directed classroom was strictly controlled, extremely quiet and, though the tension level seldom escalated, it was downright dead! In such a controlled environment, I experienced very few of "those days." Through inspired direction, I progressed from that stifled, restrictive climate to an enthusiastic, interactive, student-centered environment, one that encourages the free flow of ideas. Such an environment provides fertile ground for the development of self-control; however, for those students who are neither prepared nor equipped to handle the greater degrees of freedom that such a classroom affords, the teacher must act as controller and enforcer. And that demands extraordinary degrees of patience—without which such an interactive classroom would not be possible.

PATIENCE WITH THE OFFENDER AND IMPATIENCE WITH THE OFFENSE

I want to be very clear about when I am and should be patient and when I should not be patient. I am not patient with the inappropriate behavior itself. For example, when my students do not give me their attention as quickly as I expect, I will not patiently allow that to continue. I will, with patience, immediately draw their attention to the problem. In other words, without yelling or accusing or otherwise pitching a fit, I simply state, in a non-threatening yet *very firm* tone of voice, my dissatisfaction with their behavior.

Please note that it is my students' behavior that I am addressing, not them personally. The focus must always be on their behavior; otherwise, our students will recognize that we are loving them *conditionally*. In other words, I focus on their "do" and not their "who."

I practice this every single day. In an interactive classroom such as ours, the motion is so constant that I expect to deal with management issues. If I become impatient with the numerous daily minor irritations, our classroom could never be a place that feels like home. If I had not developed patience, I would still be stuck back in the Dark Ages. Patience is not an option. It is a must!

Dear Summer,

I am so excited to finally get to write in you for the first time. I am going to work so hard in school and especially on my goals. I love Miss Lafields classroom! It's so colorful, and I love all the words off encouragement all around the walls. I also like all the wonderful quotes. I love Miss LaField, she cares so much and she's so nice. ← That over there is Miss LaField. I asked Miss LaField for that picture because in 20 years or so I want to be able to look back and remember exactly who she was and all she taught me!

CHAPTER 22

Teaching Responsibility

Longfellow once said, "Discipline is like a bridled horse with the reigns held lightly." The key is finding the balance between lightly and tightly. Classroom LTL Management always holds the reigns as lightly as possible with the intent of allowing sufficient freedom for students to learn to control themselves. My students learn that they must *earn* their freedom in our class. But more importantly, they learn that with freedom comes responsibility. I teach them that when they are not responsible with their freedom, there are consequences.

In the real world, I tell them, the consequences can be very serious, the ultimate consequences being prison and even the death of oneself or others. I help them see that the older they grow, the more serious the consequences become. We talk about learning to be responsible now, so they are ready for the real world.

"Tightening the reins" does not necessitate nor justify any deviation from the application of Classroom LTL Management. When we are angry with our students, they perceive the consequences as punishment rather than natural consequences for their own lack of self-discipline. When this is the case, they are much less inclined to take personal responsibility for their behavior and choose to learn from the experience. Our challenge is to consistently and respectfully enforce consequences and be careful not to exaggerate the consequences. A fine line separates fair from unfair, and our students have a very keen sense of where fair ends and unfair begins. My first impulse is often too harsh, but once I see that shocked look on a face or two, I am quick to reflect and consider whether I have been too reactive.

I once read somewhere that the consequences we choose must include the 3 R's: Respectful, Reasonable, and Related. I remember them now because they made so much sense at the time. I believe that any time and every time we choose the consequences, we must do our best to incorporate and reflect the 3 R's.

Sometimes when my students display an exceptionally respectful and obedient Right Heart upon hearing their consequences, I reward them by decreasing or even dropping the consequences. On the other hand, anyone who displays a negative attitude can expect to have his or her consequences escalate.

Because kids are kids, I have good days and not-so-good days. On good days, I let the kids know how wonderful they are and how much I enjoyed being their teacher. On the not-so-good days, I patiently tell them how wonderful they are but that I did not enjoy being their teacher. Then I prepare to come back the next day with tighter reins and a new plan for enforcing the policy they failed to respect. But whatever that new plan or the consequence may be, I make certain to enforce it consistently and with LTL tough love.

ONCE UPON A NOT-SO-HAPPY TIME

Quite a few years ago I had what is sometimes referred to by exasperated, end-of-their-rope teachers as "the class from hell." They were not bad kids. I would say that the kids in this particular class were a combination of a few troubled kids, some very "social" kids, and some uncommonly hyperactive kids. I loved them dearly, but they would also admit that they pushed me into a corner and I came out fighting. And it was one fight, I can tell you, that I was not about to lose.

For four full months I used every tool in my tool belt. On a particular Friday in January, my student teacher, poor thing, was scheduled to teach her first solo lesson. Though she knew her lesson backwards and forwards, and had probably practiced all night in her dreams, nothing could have been perfect enough to have held their attention for more than ten minutes. But the kids really liked her, and I was hopeful—too hopeful as it turned out.

When I left the room that day, it was definitely not with a lot of peace; in fact, I remember walking out very slowly backwards, making eye contact with every one of them who dared look my way. If ever a look threatened merciless retribution or prophesied impending doom, mine that day should have been enough to jolt them into humble submission.

I will never forget the look of frantic desperation on my student teacher's face when I unexpectedly returned to the classroom ten minutes later, nor the looks on my students' faces when they saw the look on my face after seeing the look on hers. My students froze as if paralyzed. Time stood still as my spirit commanded: *Do not open your mouth. Do not take over. Do not say or do anything for which you will be sorry.* By sheer grace alone, I didn't. Never dropping my gaze from those transfixed stares, with deliberate self-control and purposeful movement, I backed out slowly, closed the sliding glass door behind me, and this time I did not return until after the final bell.

Thank goodness it was a Friday! I had two days to figure out how to turn around a class that had spiraled out of control. One thing I knew for certain: Nothing short of a miracle would do. I prayed passionately, and by Sunday afternoon, a plan was beginning to unfold.

WHO'S IS IN CONTROL?

I knew I needed to present consequences that would not be construed as punishment but would help my students recognize the error of their ways and take personal responsibility for their actions. Whatever the plan might include, it must not act as a temporary band-aide but as a permanent change agent. They had to accept the plan as my effort to help them, not hurt them. To accomplish all of this, they had to accept the plan with Right Heart attitudes.

The first revelation that came to me was a reminder that the majority of the problems in that class all centered around one issue: lack of self-control. Since the first day of school, I had emphasized the importance of self-discipline. Over the course of the previous four months, I had asked offenders "Who's in control?" so many times that it had lost its power. They simply could not handle any freedom that required them to be responsible for their own behavior.

I decided that weekend, as a consequence for their behavior, they would lose all freedom they had previously enjoyed. I would become the controller, the enforcer, the rigid disciplinarian of the old days. The principle, I would explain, was as old as the hills: When

When we abuse freedom in the real world, we lose it. When we lose it, we have to work to get it back.

we abuse freedom in the real world, we lose it. When we lose it, we have to work to get it back. If we are not willing to work, we will never get it back. It was simple. It was their choice.

Questions I would use for a discussion with my students began coming to me in meaningful sequence. Each question addressed an intention, an objective I hoped to achieve. By the time I finished late that evening, I was exhausted but happy. The final product, which I entitled "Who's in Control?" included thirty-five questions, which I was confident addressed all of my aspirations (included at the end of this chapter).

THE TEN-STEP BEHAVIOR RESOLUTION PROCESS

The next morning I invited my students to join me on the rug. They were sober, serious and expectant. Nobody was talking. I sensed their dread of impending doom as they waited anxiously for their punishment. Knowing instinctively that the outcome of the plan rested on the success of the forthcoming discussion, I proceeded with Step 1 of a Ten-Step Behavior Resolution Process that I had previously developed for situations that necessitate a radical change in behavior.

STEP 1:
Check my emotional state. My students needed to know first that I was not angry, for in their minds, anger precedes punishment. If the plan was to work, it must not be construed as a penalty for "being bad."

STEP 2:
Check the emotional state of the party(ies) involved. My students were clearly open and receptive. I sensed no defensiveness or defiance whatsoever. Had they been even a little resistant, I would have had to reassess how to proceed with the following steps.

STEP 3:
Calmly and without prejudgment ask, "What happened?" Here the discussion began in earnest. I asked for their interpretations of what had happened with the student teacher on Friday. I had already established a hard-and-fast policy to allow the offender(s) to speak first. We discussed why it happened, how they felt about what happened, and what should have happened. When kids are not backed up against a wall by an intimidating adult, they generally drop their defenses and admit to the truth, and that is exactly what happened that particular morning on the rug.

STEP 4:
Encourage them to own their behavior. Nobody was casting blame, denying the truth, justifying their behavior, or minimizing the problem. They were, without exception, assuming complete responsibility for their actions. Often, kids refuse to look at the truth and get "stuck" in denial, where it is

difficult, if not impossible, to help them. I lavishly praised my students for their honest, forthright acceptance of personal responsibility for the problem. At this point in the discussion we all relaxed, and it was clear to me that we were rapidly approaching the heart of the plan.

STEP 5:

Ask, "What can you learn from this problem?" Their part in this step was easy. They already knew the answer because we had been talking about it for almost five months. But obviously, I had not gotten through. I had talked to them about respect, responsibility, and self-discipline until I had begun sounding like a nag. Not good! But it was time to take my students deeper. I wanted them to learn that how we regard the issues of respect, personal responsibility, and self-discipline has everything to do with who we are and what we become.

This is the ideal place to use the problem as an opportunity to enhance our students' emotional and social intelligence by infusing the conversation with the attributes of People of Character with Right Hearts. It is the perfect place for The Golden Rule. But a word of warning here: Be careful not to push too hard.

STEP 6:

Ask, "How will you benefit from learning this?" Since they were with me for an hour and a half in the morning, we had plenty of time to spend on the benefits of learning to control themselves. Obviously, they all wanted freedom, success, happiness, healthy relationships, financial security, and a rewarding life imbued with meaning and purpose—not to mention parents and teachers who trusted them, a car at sixteen, and a job to pay for gas and insurance. Nobody wanted to work at McDonald's forever.

STEP 7:

Ask, "Are you willing to do what it takes to change your behavior?" Most kids will answer yes to the question without any idea of how hard the work will be, so the best I can hope for is a strong, "Yes." As I told them, this is where their level of emotional intelligence comes in. We talked about the choice to give up or to persevere when the life lessons get tough. On a surface level they had wanted to learn the lessons I had been trying unsuccessfully to teach them for four months, but they had not been willing to get serious about the work. Now they were ready, or so they adamantly professed.

STEP 8:

Ask, "Can you think of a way to solve this problem?" At this step of the
process, I always ask the student(s) involved for their input. As my students
pondered the question, I waited for the hands to go up, but not even a single
student offered an idea. After all, hadn't we already tried everything? At this
point in Step 8, if the student(s) cannot think of a workable solution, I
propose a plan.

STEP 9:

Introduce and implement the plan. Wisely, I chose to lead up to the
announcement of the plan with thought-provoking questions. My intent
was to lead them to see, understand, and accept its practical logic.
"What happens," I asked, "when you get caught driving while intoxicated?"
You lose your license.
"What happens," I continued, "when you arrive home two hours after
curfew?"
You lose your freedom to stay out late.
"What happens when your report card doesn't reflect your best efforts?"
You lose privileges.
"And what," I finally asked them, "do all these actions have in common?"
You lose something for not acting responsibly.
As we talked, I helped them truly see that with freedom comes responsibility.
I further explained that when people do not act responsibly, they invariably
lose freedom in some capacity, and that to regain freedom, they must prove
that they can once again be trusted to act responsibly. I was helping my
students make the obvious connections that would lead them to willingly
accept the drastic consequences of my plan.

ZERO HOUR

It was zero hour, with five minutes before the final bell. I had to capture the
moment. The room was quiet. They seemed to know what was coming. And
then I said it: They had lost their freedom in Core because they had not learned
to be responsible.

What I had thought might descend upon them like a bomb, created only a
quiet stirring in the room. Loss of freedom was the worst possible consequence.
Since the first day of school they had enjoyed more freedom than they had been

offered in any other classroom. They could get up, walk around, and work outside the room. I had begun the year by treating them as responsible, trustworthy "adults," not as little children required to ask permission to sharpen their pencils or throw away trash. They finally had choices, power, and trust, and they relished it.

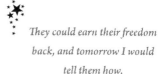

They could earn their freedom back, and tomorrow I would tell them how.

I waited for the impact of their loss to sink in. They had heard the bad news, and before the bell, I had just enough time left to give them the good news: They could earn their freedom back, and tomorrow I would tell them how. Thankfully, they were leaving on a positive note.

We had gone further and deeper than I could have ever hoped. They had listened intently, owned the truth, made all the connections, and humbly accepted the consequences without any apparent resistance. The Ten Step Process had worked flawlessly because they were open and willing to look at the truth and because I had approached the subject with an attitude of non-judgmental, non-threatening, unconditional compassion.

Never forget: So often we blame our students for a defensive, defiant attitude when in fact we generated their hostility. We do this by reacting to their behavior with our own hostility rather than by responding with self-control and patient tough love. In other words, we fail to display emotional intelligence. We are supposed to be the "adult," but so often we act so like the children we are admonishing. Why should they listen? Why should they respond with respectful compliance? Why should they welcome the truth and seek to learn from their mistakes?

CONTROL WITH RESPECT

The following morning we were right back on the rug, and once again my students were poised to listen. I began with a quick review and then proceeded to explain that until they earned back their freedom, our class would be a very different place. What had once been an open, free environment would now be restrictive, controlled, and very quiet because I was taking control as the traditional authority figure.

On the board I wrote the words: "Extreme control with extreme respect." In a sense, they would be soldiers in boot camp with a respectful drill sergeant who would control their every move. My promise to them was that no matter what happened in the days to come, they would always be treated with the highest degree of respect.

With all systems green for go, it was time to introduce the actual plan itself. They could not have been more ready, and I sensed something wonderful was about to unfold. I directed the kids to move all the desks into one big circle, and each received a copy of "Who's in Control?" (See handout at the end of this chapter.) Woven into the thirty-five questions were the key concepts that I believed must be addressed in order for my students to change their attitudes and behavior.

In the weeks to come, we would be discussing the questions and concepts included in "Who's In Control?" The questions would guide our classroom management education, and they would help my students (and me) internalize the characteristics necessary to manage ourselves.

THE MAGICAL MISSING PIECE

I incorporated a powerful tool that would help them accept the new restrictions. After all, if they fought "the system," they would not learn the lessons and the plan would fail. This tool turned out to be the "magical missing piece" I had finally discovered after more than twenty years of searching. This tool is *modeling* the difference between responding and reacting.

Sitting in our circle the next day, we discussed the concepts of responding vs. reacting. To make sure they clearly understood the difference, we acted out short impromptu scenes. Everyone was well-acquainted with the defensive *reactions* that always precipitate even more trouble, and I encouraged them to share some of their stories. Then we talked about what might have happened had they wisely chosen to *respond*—another clear connection. They would definitely have avoided a scene and might quite possibly have even "gotten their way" by acting responsibly.

On the board I wrote: "Responsible > able to respond." We analyzed the word until it took on a whole new meaning.

Since my greatest frustration in the past few months had been their excessive talking which kept them off-task, I made sure we enacted scenes around talking that were sure to arise in the future. In this way, I began to teach my students how to respond to my control. In one scene I asked, "Andy, are you talking?" and instead of answering with a lie, or blame, or excuses, I taught them to answer in a whole new way. "Yes, (own the truth) Ms. LaField, the truth is I was talking (take personal responsibility), but I'll stop right now" (make a wise choice), after which I respectfully responded (modeling the behavior) with, "Thank you, Andy, for the truth."

At first we all laughed; it was so new that it sounded ridiculously contrived. But like a new language, they would practice it so often in the days and weeks to come that it eventually became second nature. By learning to respond in this new manner, I had given them a tool to own their behavior with extraordinary respect.

Little did I know at the time that this new technique for helping my students respond would not only revolutionize my approach to teaching the character traits of respect, responsibility, and honesty, but would also create a mutually respectful environment where I no longer struggled with disruptions in a controlling, traditionally authoritative manner. The tone in our classroom changed from negative to positive.

The true beauty of this tool was not only that it worked in our classroom, but that it worked so well they began responding positively to their parents at home! Many of them set family goals to practice being responders, and their parents were thrilled, which naturally made me popular—an unexpected bonus. They were making real-life connections that they applied to relationships outside of our classroom. The results were dramatic.

THE REASON BEHIND THE "RULE"

My students agreed that the main behavior problems pertained to respect, responsibility, and self-discipline, beginning with the most obvious: off-task behavior. I made absolutely certain that they not only understood clearly *which* behaviors would no longer be tolerated, but also *why* they would no longer be tolerated. When our students understand the reason behind the standard— when we can answer their why with reasonable, rational logic—they are much more inclined to accept and respect our decisions.

To prepare them for the days to come, I reminded them that they could expect me to enforce the standards—I do not call them rules—with extreme control and extreme respect. I also reminded them that the sooner they lived the lessons and controlled themselves, the sooner I would relax my extreme control.

ADDRESSING THE CONSEQUENCES

After we had thoroughly covered the basic standards, it was time to address the consequences for failing to respect the standards. We focused initially on examples of natural consequences that could be applied to their own lives outside the classroom. What might be the consequences if they chose to associate with friends who were always in trouble? What about if they chose not to do their homework?

Once again I was trying to help them see that if they did not become conscious thinkers who controlled themselves, their unwise choices would eventually lead to natural consequences that could spell disaster for their lives. Of course, every one of them saw the logic. It was the real world we were talking about, and they could all relate.

This discussion naturally led to the next topic: the natural consequences in Core for failing to respect the standards. I assured my students that I would hold them personally accountable for every infraction; however, if they owned the truth about their behavior and consciously chose to respectfully respond instead of react, the penalty would be reduced. In this way, I would reward them for practicing the lessons. As it turned out in the weeks to come, this incentive of a reduced penalty proved to influence my students' willingness to accept my control. Each time they made a wise choice to own their behavior and respond accordingly, they were rewarded, and each time they practiced the lesson in this way, they grew more respectful, more personally responsible, and more self-disciplined.

PROBLEMS: OUR GREATEST TEACHERS

I wanted to teach them to face their problems with a mindset to learn from them.

We then analyzed the quote, "I am not a problem simply because I have a problem." This quote was included for two main reasons. First, it was important for them to understand that problems help us grow if we are willing to look for the lessons embedded. Problems, I told them, can be our greatest teachers. I wanted to teach them to face their problems with a mindset to learn from them. Here we discussed in depth the deep meaning of our class motto: "We are here to learn … from our problems."

Secondly, the quote was included to help them stop identifying with stigmas they may have acquired over the years based on their behavior. Because teachers so often label students as problems, and actually often call them a problem to their faces, students begin to accept the label as truth about themselves and enact it as a self-fulfilling prophesy. *Never forget: Every word from our mouth holds the power to hurt or to heal.* We must never think of our students as problems!

CHOOSING TO CARE: THE CLINCHER

"What do choosing to care and this activity have to do with you?" This question was the clincher! I wish you had been there for this one. Oh, the tales they told! Tales of never caring about their behavior, about their homework, about their grades. As the mood grew serious, I realized that I needed to give this question time. They needed to share. They needed to feel. They needed to hear their peers tell their similar stories.

This question united us on a more intimate personal level. Many cried and for the first time I could feel the stirrings of community. You can be sure that by the time we were ready to move on, they understood on a heart level that unless they truly cared about their lives, they would never grow up to be people with the power to make their dreams come true. This is the question that inspired them to see that Ms. LaField's "Who's in Control?" activity was much more than a mere attempt by a teacher to get her class under her control.

Although many were ready to share their decision publicly, I stopped them short. I did not want words. I wanted action. We talked of integrity, of being People of Character who prove who they are by their actions. They would be telling me of their decision in their final project, but I was much more interested in them showing me and their peers through their daily commitment to living the lessons.

We had successfully completed STEP 9 of the TEN STEP plan for changing student behavior: Ask the students if they agree to the requirements of the plan you have created to help them improve their behavior. After three days of talking, the real work would begin as I initiated

STEP 10:
Put the plan in motion and do everything in your power to help the students succeed.

THE FINAL OUTCOME

What followed that three-day discussion can be described as nothing less than a complete metamorphosis from the dark cocoon stage to the emergent butterfly. For my part, I consciously focused each moment on my intention to impose extreme control with extreme respect. For their part, they worked to make wise choices but owned their behavior and responded appropriately when they did not.

A week later I asked my students to evaluate that first week in a personal letter to me. I was stunned by their overwhelmingly positive responses. Every student in the class agreed, without exception, that although they missed their freedom, they were learning much more academically as well as personally. They agreed, too, that I had kept my promise to treat them with extraordinary respect.

Three weeks later, the first group earned back their freedom. It was a day of celebration for those students and a powerful motivator for the rest. Within five weeks all but one group followed suit.

WHY DID THE PLAN WORK?

Imagine what would have happened had I gathered them together on the rug that momentous Monday morning and announced suddenly, "Kids, I am taking away all of your freedom and as of today, we have a whole new set of rules which I intend to strictly enforce. And kids, things will be very different in this room from now on because I am now in complete control!" In all actuality, that is exactly what happened. They did lose their freedom, and I did take control, and yes, they would have rebelled. Why didn't they?

If we want our students to become proficient learners, we must give them opportunities in a safe place to practice their lessons.

Once we set the plan in motion, several key factors helped ensure its success. To begin with, it was a positive incentives approach, not a traditional discipline plan. Because the natural consequences in the plan were not construed as negative punishment, students were willing to own their behavior. They were highly motivated to earn their freedom, and respectful responses were rewarded by reductions in penalties. I called parents with the happy news, wrote encouraging notes, and praised students at every opportunity. Positive reinforcement is a powerful change agent.

Furthermore, the plan was successful because I included the element of practice. If we want our students to become proficient learners, we must give them opportunities in a safe place to practice their lessons. Each infraction was an opportunity to make a wise choice, own their behavior, and respond respectfully. They needed time to practice, and though they often fell, they picked themselves up and tried again.

Finally and most important to the success of the plan was my commitment to a promise: to treat my students with extreme respect. In a supreme effort to honor that promise, I consciously guarded not only the words I spoke, but their quality, tone, and volume as well. Mutual respect reached unprecedented levels that spring. I faithfully honored my promise because I modeled the behaviors I was asking of my students. This, of course, was asking of myself the impossible. I reminded my students that because we are human, we all make mistakes, and that although I would do my absolute best in the days to come, I would, nevertheless, need their help just as they would need mine. As I always do, I asked them to hold me accountable for each word, each action. I asked them to be my teachers and help me live the lessons as I tried to help them.

I shall never forget the day Travis raised his hand and said with respect, "Ms. LaField, I think you are picking on Kevin." I turned to the rest of the class, and they, too, agreed. And then I turned to Kevin, whose eyes confirmed it. My relationship with Kevin would never be the same after that day. After struggling with him for six long months, he opened his heart to me and finally chose to respond. Kevin, who would have remembered me as the teacher who picked on him, would now remember me as the teacher who lived the lessons.

What had begun as an experiment born of frustration, ultimately proved to be one of the most exciting, rewarding, and transformational adventures of my teaching experience. Though I cannot say that "the class from hell" evolved overnight into "the class from heaven," I can say that the change was miraculous.

WHO'S IN CONTROL?

1. Compare a robot to a thinking individual.
2. Are you more like a robot or a thinking individual? Explain.
3. Define conscious vs. unconscious.
4. In which of the above states are we able to make wise choices?
5. Examine your life in the light of the truth. Do you usually make wise choices? Explain your answer.
6. Now think! How do consciousness and wise choices relate to you? (When I am conscious I___, but when I am not conscious I___.)
7. What is the difference between responding and reacting?
8. What happens in relationships when the people are responsive?
9. What happens in relationships when the people are reactive?
10. Examine your life in the light of the truth. Are you generally responsive or reactive? Explain and offer examples.
11. What happens when you are reactive with your parents and teachers?
12. What happens when you are responsive with your parents and teachers?
13. How will being responsive help you in Core?

14. How will being responsive help you at home and in life?
15. What does the truth have to do with responding and reacting?
16. Is the truth important to you? Explain.
17. Now think! How do consciousness, wise choices, responding/reacting, and the truth relate to you? (When I…, but when I…)
18. What are consequences?
19. When are consequences positive?
20. When are consequences negative?
21. When do you most often enjoy positive consequences? Give examples.
22. When do you most often suffer from negative consequences?
23. Now think! How do consciousness, wise choices, and consequences relate to you? (When____, but when____.)
24. Describe people who are "in control" of themselves.
25. Describe people who have to be controlled by others.
26. Who's in control of your life? Explain.
27. Do I (Ms. LaField) want to control you? Explain.
28. Now think! How do consciousness, wise choices, responding/reacting, the truth, consequences, and control relate to you? (When____, but when____.)
29. What am I (Ms. LaField) hoping to teach you from this activity?
30. How can it help you all of the days of your life?
31. Explain the quote: "I am not a problem simply because I have a problem."
32. Relate this to your own life.
33. Why is this quote so important to remember your entire life?
34. What do choosing to care and you have to do with this activity?
35. Relate this activity to your life. Be thoughtful! Be serious!

CHOOSE TO CARE!

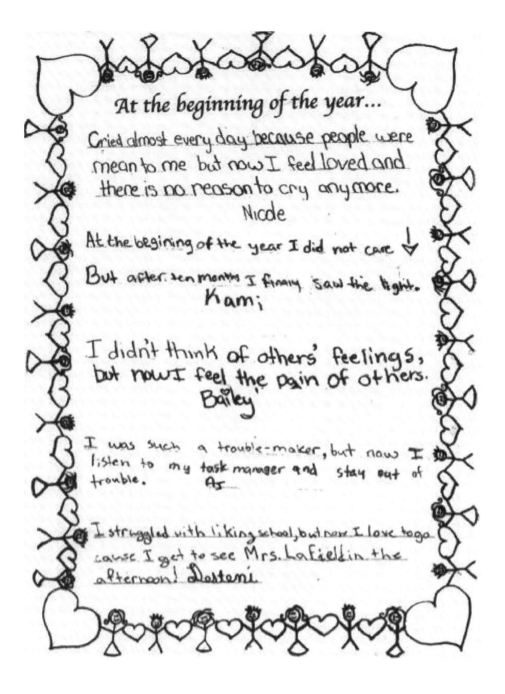

At the beginning of the year...

Cried almost every day because people were mean to me but now I feel loved and there is no reason to cry any more.
Nicole

At the begining of the year I did not care ↓

But after ten months I finany saw the light.
Kami

I didn't think of others' feelings, but now I feel the pain of others.
Bailey

I was such a trouble-maker, but now I listen to my task manager and stay out of trouble.
AJ

I struggled with liking school, but now I love to go cause I get to see Mrs. Lafield in the afternoon! Destoni

CHAPTER 23

Expect Better!

*I*t happens to us all when we least expect it—like the pop quiz that tests us on what we have not yet learned. It's the final exam of Classroom LTL Management, the one we all dread, that moment when we do not quite know what to do and are one breath away from losing it. It is what happens when the system breaks down. It is what happens when our students fail to live up to our standards in a painfully obvious way. It's what happened to me once upon a time, not long enough ago.

It happened on a field trip to our local junior college. My sixty-five students and I—along with two hundred or so other eighth graders from our school, plus several hundred from other schools—were being led by high school students on a tour of the college with the intent of introducing our students to the various career opportunities available on campus. That sounds innocuous enough, but add to the picture three hours outside in one-hundred-plus-degree weather, presenters who could neither be seen nor heard, exposure to careers for which my students had zero interest, blisters on their feet from zigzagging back and forth across campus, and parched throats from lack of water.

My students were more than miserable and did not care who knew it. They were, in my astute opinion, acting like spoiled, undisciplined, disrespectful children. "Brats" would be the more accurate terminology. As the temperature soared mercilessly well past the century mark, they were, before my bewildered eyes, rapidly mutating from Dr. Jekyll into the hideous Mr. Hyde.

Not all of the students underwent this radically uncharacteristic change— many rose to the occasion and stoically suffered in silence. Unfortunately, the "howling Hydes" invariably dominated the scene, thus casting everyone into the category of culprit. What had promised to be a pleasant day perusing the campus quickly dissolved into an organizational nightmare of epic proportions. My perpetual smile melted into a frown, then a scowl, then a reproachful glare of seething anger. It was better-watch-out time, and the malcontents were not even noticing.

TIME FOR THE SHOWDOWN

Minute by minute, I was losing control of the situation, and as I've mentioned previously, I am not one to lose control without a fight.

Minute by minute, I was losing control of the situation, and as I've mentioned previously, I am not one to lose control without a fight. At that point, I did not care who saw it—and watching nervously close by were at least ten apprehensive adults. It was showdown time. I had reached that climactic point in the classic Popeye cartoons when, exhausted and exasperated, he is willing to tolerate no more and with renewed determination howls, "That's all I can stands! I can't stands no more!"

But this was not just a simple case of ringing my little silver bell to get their attention. We were outside, surrounded by clamor and confusion, squeezed in between two other groups of students from other schools. I would estimate that within close proximity were at least one hundred and twenty students, most of whom were milling about chatting with friends and paying no attention whatsoever to the alleged speakers. How does one lone teacher capture the attention of sixty-five eighth graders under such formidable conditions? The only way I knew how: I paused for a deep breath, raised my voice above the din, and with body language that threatened nothing less than impending doom, barked very loudly and assertively at the top of my lungs. I did not say please, and I did not ask politely. I commanded my students to sit down on the grass in front of me…NOW! My entire demeanor was so out of character that my students, whose faces registered stunned disbelief, scrambled to "hit the dirt!"

Despite distractions all around us, I had sixty-five sets of eyes glued on me. Oh yes, I had their attention. It was time for Classroom Tough LTL Management. Despite the intensity of my feelings, I determined in those seconds to live the lessons. One very important lesson that I teach my students is to Stop! Think! and Choose Wisely! Thank goodness, that is exactly what I did. For all to see, and believe me, they were scrutinizing my every move, I stopped, closed my eyes, took another deep breath, and gave myself several seconds to regain my composure as the thoughts formed in my mind.

When I opened my mouth to express my feelings it was with a calm though stern, tone. I was in control of my feelings, of myself. And the words I chose after I stopped and thought, addressed their "do" and not their "who." Every word conveyed my disappointment—not with them personally but with their actions.

After "speaking my truth" we had only two more stations left before boarding the busses. During that time and including the bus ride back to school, I did not smile. My intention was to impact them with a strong impression of my disappointment. It was not an act because I was still feeling the residual after-effects of the strongest surge of anger I had felt in a long time. When the bus arrived at school, I intentionally waited until everyone unloaded before I stepped off the bus.

A TRUE KODAK MOMENT

As it turned out, it was very important that I waited because it gave my students time to reach our class ahead of me. When I walked through the door, I was blessed by one of those Kodak moments that you would give anything to have on camera. All sixty-five students were standing in the front of the room expectantly facing the door as I entered.

They were holding the "I'm Sorry" sign, and the humbled expressions on their faces told the whole story of how they were feeling. Somebody counted to three and in unison they pleaded, "Ms. LaField, we're sorry. We were wrong. Will you please forgive us?" Clearly, it was one of those precious moments that you want to savor for a few seconds because you know you will never forget it.

In those fleeting moments, as I stood motionless and our eyes met, they knew before I opened my mouth what the answer would be. Love forgives. I had already taught them that. We had just enough time before the bell rang for a huge group hug and my assurance that I loved each and every one of them. And then they were off to their next class—feeling affirmed. That was important. We would talk tomorrow.

QUESTIONS...

That night I meditated on the problem while gardening in my backyard after school. These are questions that came to me:

- ★ What was my part in creating the problem?
- ★ How well or how poorly did I handle the situation?
- ★ How could I have handled it differently?

* ★ What could I learn from it?
* ★ Why was I so upset by their behavior?
* ★ Was pride an issue?
* ★ What would I say to my students tomorrow?
* ★ How could I bring goodness out of it?
* ★ What role did my students play?

I am convinced that we create and perpetuate as many problems as our students do.

I mused over these questions from both a negative as well as a positive perspective. On the positive side, it was a difficult test that confirmed what I already knew: I had taken giant leaps in living the lessons. Remember, "Nothing is truly learned until it is lived." Whereas the year before I would have mixed their "who with their do," this year I effectively separated the act from the actor. I do not believe that there is any chance whatsoever that they would have stood waiting for me on the risers with the "I'm Sorry" sign if they had felt personally attacked.

I am convinced that we create and perpetuate as many problems as our students do. How? By the ways we unconsciously mistreat them. We actually limit our students' capacities to become People of Character because we ourselves are limited. When we do not freely give them the no-strings-attached commitment that every human being so desperately needs, we deny them the opportunity of reaching their full potential.

NEXT TIME...

Okay, so that was the plus side. But I cannot leave it there. I could have done better. Next time I would be proactive. I would *Be Prepared!* After thoughtfully considering what happened that sweltering day, I generated the following list of steps I could have taken to prevent the disaster:

* ★ I should not have waited for the pressure to build to the boiling point.
* ★ I should have come equipped with a whistle.
* ★ I could have brought a sign to hold up—a happy face on one side, a frown on the other.
* ★ I should have engaged more chaperones.
* ★ I should have divided the class into smaller groups.

224

★ I could have taken rewards to pass out for exemplary behavior.
★ I could have created a contest for the best-behaved group.

Once I had thoroughly scrutinized my part and recognized what I had done well, where I had failed, and how I could improve the next time by *living the lessons* I had learned, I was ready to look at my students' parts. That was easy. They had failed to rise to the occasion, to overcome adversity, to persevere. They had succumbed to a difficult situation with whining and disrespect.

The next day, rather than focusing first on their misdeeds, I virtually drenched them with praise. I was so proud that of the entire group of sixty-five, not one single student had displayed a stubborn, defensive attitude. I talked at great length about the life-altering significance of assuming personal responsibility for their behavior, which they had modeled so magnificently.

Many confessed that never before had they processed their behavior in such a mature, honest, responsible way. For as far back as they could remember, they had refused to admit to their wrongdoing, especially with their parents.

It was truly a teachable moment ripe with the power to change lives. I stressed that it would be a turning point in their lives if they would choose to live the lesson with the people closest to them. I tried to help them see that their future relationships were destined to fail should they choose to persist in stubborn refusal to accept responsibility for "their part." I boldly challenged them to choose the better way, the one that would lead them to a better life.

I boldly challenged them to choose the better way, the one that would lead them to a better life.

A CHARACTER-BUILDING TEACHABLE MOMENT

By the time they had almost drowned in my praise, they were poised to receive my straightforward, blunt assessment of their less-than-lovely behavior at the college. Because I use every opportunity possible to relate positive character traits to their real life experiences, I brought perseverance into the picture. Yes, it was hot, and they were thirsty and bored, but they had exacerbated their discomfort by giving the dismal conditions so much power. The more they focused on the heat, the hotter they got. We laughed together when I told them how I had seen Jared, a fellow classmate, looking like he was ready to keel over from heat exhaustion and how I had jokingly chided him to "Get tough!" whereby he had replied, "Where do I get it?"

I could have easily rationalized my students' poor behavior by blaming it on the adverse conditions. I am confident in asserting that many well-meaning adults, upon hearing about the day's dismal outcome, would ask, "Well, Olivia, what do you expect considering the conditions?" My answer? I expect better! Never will I give my students an excuse for unacceptable behavior. It is possible to take disasters and turn them into positive learning experiences, and I am committed to teaching my students to rise above the adversities life sends them.

★ THE TEACHER ★

CHAPTER 24

A Classroom That's Alive!

*E*very once in a while we happen upon a line in a book that shoots straight to the center of our being, leaving us somehow different—deeper, better. Recently I was profoundly touched by one such line in John Eldredge's *Journey of Desire*: "I continue to be stunned by the level of *deadness* that most people consider *normal* and seem to be *contented* to live with." [1]

Level of deadness…normal…content? In my spirit I knew immediately that I was supposed to do something with those words, though I had absolutely no idea what. My first thought was to type the quote on my computer and then print a copy. Easy, I thought. As I sat at my desk pondering the wisdom of the words, the next impression came: I was supposed to share the quote with my students. Not quite so easy. I remember wondering how I could possibly interest seventh graders in a quote about deadness. I knew I would have to sleep on it.

The next morning when I got to school, I wrote the quote on the whiteboard. Alone in my classroom, I stood back, read it once again and wondered what in the world I was supposed to do next. Then I walked away, trusting that guidance would come, as it always does. In this case, it wasn't long in coming. Less than an hour later, after my traditional morning greeting, I turned my students' attention to the whiteboard and asked everyone to thoughtfully read the quote to themselves. Once everyone had read it and was looking expectantly at me, I heard myself inviting anyone who was curious about the meaning of the quote to join me for lunch.

I would have predicted that perhaps two or three might join me at lunchtime. I watched with amazement as one by one, fifteen curious students marched into our room with cafeteria lunches in hand and eagerly helped me assemble the desks in a circle.

Once the laughter and excitement subsided, the kids naturally looked to me for direction, unaware that I too was still seeking direction. "What," I asked, "is 'deadness?'" I got up and drew a long line down the middle of the whiteboard, wrote "Deadness" on the left side "Aliveness" on the right and then challenged my students to look around our room and find something they could see that had the quality of "aliveness." One answer was the blinking Christmas lights. Another was the bright fluorescent colors. I wrote the opposite of their answers in the Deadness column. For example, bright lights and colors are alive; darkness and dull colors are dead. From that part of the discussion came the obvious conclusion: Judging by the environment, our classroom is definitely alive.

They clearly understood the concept of "aliveness" in terms of tangible objects, so I challenged them to go deeper—to think of examples of "aliveness" they could feel. We laughed together as they shared: snowboarding, skateboarding, and going to the movies with their boyfriend or girlfriend were all very much "alive." Lying on a couch for hours, glued to a television, fighting with their parents, and feeling bored in class were all "dead."

It was such fun that we were all disappointed when the bell rang, rudely interrupting our animated, lively flow of ideas. We unanimously agreed to meet the next Wednesday, dubbing our new group the Dream Team. As they hurriedly scattered in different directions, I challenged them to consciously look for examples of "deadness" and "aliveness" in the coming days.

From that first meeting until our last, the Dream Teamers and I enjoyed many happy moments. A true community, we shared a close common bond that not one of us will forget. Equally important, my students became "deadness" experts, who not only learned to recognize it when they saw it, but actually made a commitment to eliminate deadness from their lives.

One day the kids were sharing their victories in the "war against deadness." Dallas, who had struggled all year with dishonesty, candidly told us that he was lying and cheating less often—both of which are definitely dead behaviors. With spontaneous gusto, our "We are proud of you!" cheer erupted, leaving Dallas feeling affirmed for his candor and encouraged to persevere on his path to becoming a Person of Character.

THE JOY OF "ALIVE" ENTHUSIASM

My purpose for relating the Dream Team story is twofold. First, I want to inspire you to use spontaneity to build community. Second, and more importantly, teachers can create the joy of "alive" enthusiasm in their classrooms vs. the dread plague of "dead" boredom.

Do we want our students to look forward to our class and even occasionally moan when the bell rings? Certainly, if we are not genuinely enthusiastic about teaching, they will not be enthusiastic about learning.

For the sake of any who might be feeling a bit uncomfortable with the subject of "producing" enthusiasm in the classroom, please know that I am not promoting "canned" entertainment. Teachers are not stand-up comedians nor Academy Award-winning actors. The classroom is not a stage.

However, enthusiasm is neither characteristic of nor limited to certain personality types. Enthusiasm is the natural "by-product" of a heart that fervently believes in and is supremely committed to a cause. The outward expression of an inward disposition, enthusiasm manifests itself in a myriad of ways.

The outward expression of an inward disposition, enthusiasm manifests itself in a myriad of ways.

Consider, for example, the similarities of Mahatma Gandhi and Dr. Martin Luther King. Equally committed to a righteous cause, both gloriously lived and sacrificially died. Espousing the ideology of freedom and justice with equal verbal fervor, both stirred the hearts and minds of their countrymen to remarkable levels of social change. Yet their differences were stark. King was a young, robust Christian African American; Gandhi was an older, frail Hindu Indian. But even more stark than their racial, religious and physical differences were their differences in personality and style. King was the classic extrovert; Gandhi was a true introvert. Though we remember King as a humble servant, we cannot forget his charisma, or his public appeal. He enjoyed the spotlight and the crowds simply because he was a "people person." Gandhi spoke his truth softly but powerfully from behind the scenes. Shy and retiring, he preferred a private, less invasive world. Once again, it was who he was. King held a microphone; Gandhi held a staff. Yet both held the lasting attention of the world they so fiercely fought to change.

In the final analysis, it is not their methodologies but their ideologies that we remember best. It is not only what they said that we remember but the passion with which they said it. They commanded respect and spoke the truth with wisdom, authority, and enthusiasm. Each in his unique way inspired us to examine our lives. Each taught us so much more than just the facts. Their indelible life lessons left their imprints on us, making us better people for having listened and "obeyed."

WHAT'S INSIDE YOUR PACKAGE?

Do you relate to either King or Gandhi, or are you somewhere in between, as most people are? I am a "Kinger" all the way, but, of course, you already knew that. Great teachers come in a variety of packages, but it is not the package that is important—it is what is inside the package. If inside your "package" is a passionate enthusiasm for loving children unconditionally, you have the seeds of a great teacher. You can always work on improving the outside of the package. But if you lack passionate enthusiasm on the inside, perhaps you should consider another career.

If you can read the quote at the beginning of the chapter and honestly say that you are very much "alive" with an absolute aversion to any level of "deadness," then your students will not be bored in your class. If you are "alive" with enthusiasm, your students will listen and learn, and what is infinitely more wonderful, they will care for you—and listen to you—because you cared first. *Never forget: If you are a "dead" teacher, your students will be bored, bored, bored.*

What is important is that your classroom is plugged in and lit up with the electricity of life. Kids do not learn well in the dark.

For the remainder of this chapter, I will illustrate how my way of enthusiastic and "alive" love expresses itself in our classroom. As you read, remember that my way is not the right way or the only way; it is simply a manifestation of who I am. Perhaps my way will work for you, perhaps not. What is important is that you not settle until you find a way of expressing enthusiasm that feels comfortable with your unique personality. What is important is that you get serious about "the level of deadness" that you recognize in your own life. What is important is that your classroom is plugged in and lit up with the electricity of life. Kids do not learn well in the dark.

WHAT IS MY CAUSE?

But before addressing the "how to's" of my way of expressing enthusiasm in the classroom, let's start with the bottom-line question: Exactly what am I so enthusiastic about? What is the "big picture" cause I believe in? What is the driving force that fuels my enthusiasm? Quite simply, I am 100%—heart, soul, and mind—dedicated to learning to love children unconditionally.

Does the standard seem too high? A few years ago it seemed too high for me. In fact, it seemed impossible. Impatient and impulsive, I had not even remotely learned to love the unlovely in my classroom, nor did I even aspire to love them.

Nevertheless, I enthusiastically committed the rest of my life to answering that high call of valuing every single one of my students. It became and continues to be my cause.

On the last day of the 2004-05 school year, my students had completed their Emotional I.Q. Inventories for the last time, and we were gathered around the risers for what would be our final moments together. The kids were sharing the one area of personal growth about which they were most proud. For the first time, I asked them if they had noticed any positive personal growth in me. Cara, an unusually perceptive thirteen-year-old, commented that she noticed I had grown more patient over the course of the year, and everyone agreed.

Try to imagine how that felt. My entire morning Core class agreed that I loved them more on the last day of school than I did at the beginning of the year. Even though they may not be able to put the concept into words, kids know that love is patient. And because I learned patience on a deeper level that year, I grew closer than ever before to actually living Augustine's high standard.

UNCONDITIONAL LOVE

Christina was a sweet girl in my afternoon class whose life was dramatically impacted. Through an unhappy chain of events, Christina was transferred into my class in early February. Painfully shy and withdrawn, I knew in a matter of minutes that she was a deeply wounded child in desperate need of healing, and that it wouldn't be a "quick fix." I would first have to earn her trust, and for that I would need patience.

Careful not to push too hard or too fast, I drew her in one day at a time with heartfelt smiles and extra attention. Three entire months passed before there was any observable progress. Then in early May I sensed an almost imperceptible glimmer of light in her eyes. And one day, quite suddenly, Christina began to return my smile—not occasionally but often and always with a full-fledged, ear-to-ear smile from a happy heart. These enthusiastic smiles jet-propelled her from apathetic D's and F's to enthusiastic A's! She was Sleeping Beauty awakened by the kiss of unconditional love and acceptance.

MORE THAN THE STANDARD HANDSHAKE

How is valuing my students more than a galaxy of stars practically implemented? How does my enthusiasm for loving children unconditionally actually manifest itself? Quiet simply, our encounter at the beginning of class sets the tone for the rest of the day. I greet my students enthusiastically at the door before class begins, but not with the standard handshake and hello. These greetings change radically from the beginning of the year to the end of the year because once my students trust that I am happy to see them each day, they begin to return my enthusiasm. That's when our greetings get fun.

I initiate a completely different greeting for each one of my students. For Cameron, who is thoroughly enamored with the Japanese culture, I bowed one day and said hello in Japanese. He loved it, and from that day forward, we laughed as each of us competed to see who would bow lowest each day. Of course, Cameron always won.

Because I was determined to see David become a Valued Employee, I purposefully made up a "You can do it!" dialogue for our greeting. With a convincing smile and an intent look into his eyes, I said, "Good morning, David," to which he replied, "Good morning, Ms. LaField. What am I going to be?"

"You tell me."

Every single morning with a glowing smile, he enthusiastically answered, "A Valued Employee, Ms. LaField!"

Oh, don't you know that every time we said those words together, David believed them a little more?

My greeting for Whitley evolved over a period of time. Each day she took one soldierly step forward, stopped abruptly, looked expectantly into my eyes, and on the precise count of three, we both said matter-of-factly, "Hello," with exactly the same tone of voice. I smile now just thinking about it.

The extreme opposite, her triplet sister, Carley, burst forward with her face lit up like a Christmas tree, grabbed my hand with relish, swung it high into the air and, holding it there momentarily, chanted gaily, "Great afternoon, Ms. LaField!"

Then I returned the swing—but in the opposite direction—and parroted, "Great afternoon, Carley!" Such fun.

With shy, quiet Melissa I simply held her hand lovingly and said, "Good morning, Sunshine." Honestly, Melissa shone brighter every day.

Matt, on the other hand, stepped forward with intense gusto, grasped my hand firmly, and with furrowed brows looked directly into my eyes as he pronounced seriously, "Good morning, Ms. LaField," to which we both enthusiastically replied in unison, "No, GREAT morning!" as he revealed his smile and dimples.

My greeting with Richard came from our unit on Africa and a few words I taught my students in Swahili.

I began first with an enthusiastic, "Hamjambo, wanafunzi!" (Good morning, student.) and Richard replied, "Hatujambo, mwaleeemoo!" (Good morning, teacher.)

The best part of our greeting was how he dramatically emphasized the "mwa" syllable, making it smack like a kiss. To that sound he never failed to add a radiant smile. Richard's greeting was a gift to which I looked forward every day.

My greeting with Evan evolved as our relationship evolved—slowly but ever so surely. You saw in his testimony that as he chose to care about his life more each day, his enthusiasm grew more intense. With each passing day he looked more intently into my eyes, squeezed my hand a little longer and more firmly, smiled more genuinely and said, "Good morning, Ms. LaField!" One day, with no forethought whatsoever, I responded with, "Good morning, Superman!" It was perfect. Now, Evan will always be my Superman.

LOVE MAKES TIME

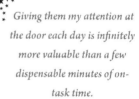

Before moving to the next topic, it occurs to me that you might wonder how I have the time to greet each of my students individually every day. I make time! Giving them my attention at the door each day is infinitely more valuable than a few dispensable minutes of on-task time. Never be in such a hurry that you forget what is most important. As you daily welcome your students with "alive" enthusiasm, they will feel your love, and they will welcome you into their hearts.

Giving them my attention at the door each day is infinitely more valuable than a few dispensable minutes of on-task time.

After I greet each student individually at the door, they are expected to go into the room, find their seats, get their journals out, and begin to write—all on The Skills of Independence. I occasionally have to interrupt my greetings to remind one or two students of these expectations, but on an ideal day, I finish my final hello and then follow that student into a quiet classroom where every student is fully engaged.

GREAT MORNING, CLASS!

About seven minutes later, after I have completed attendance and the kids are finished journaling, I greet my students as a class. Like the greeting at the door, it is a daily "ritual." Standing on the second step of the risers, I clap my hands sharply to capture my students' attention and wait until every student is looking up at me. Task Managers help me with this. When I have their complete attention, I say cheerfully, "Great morning, Class!" to which they reply, "Great morning, Ms. LaField!"

Next I say, "Happy Monday!" (or whatever day it is) and they respond with, "Happy Monday, Ms. LaField!" Sometimes they get a little carried away with their degree of enthusiasm, and I actually have to shush them so that we don't disturb the class next door.

This "group greeting" looks rather ordinary on paper. What sets it apart is the infusion of enthusiasm in every syllable. Embedded within those simple words is a deeper message: "It is a great day to be alive! I am so happy to be your teacher! I love each and every one of you!"

As I greet the whole class, I quickly scan the room from left to right hoping to look into every single one of their eyes. I want my students to feel that I have a personal relationship with them. And yes, I do have to teach them to look at me as well. Most kids are not used to a teacher who wants to connect with them as an individual, not merely as a student.

On low-energy days when my students don't respond to my greeting with their usual degree of enthusiasm, I good-naturedly insist that we repeat the greeting. If I can't *feel* their greeting, I explain, then it means nothing. At the beginning of the year when I am teaching them the many strange ways of Ms. LaField, some are a little reluctant to "up" their enthusiasm. But it doesn't take long at all until they see how much fun it is to be alive.

Whether we like it or not, we, their teachers, have a whole lot to do with whether our students want to be at school.

Learning should be an enjoyable experience. Whether we like it or not, we, their teachers, have a whole lot to do with whether our students want to be at school. Children can't enjoy going to school if their teachers don't enjoy being there with them. If we believe that "the mind is not a vessel to be filled but a fire to be lit," it is up to us to learn how to light their fires!

ANTICIPATORY PIZZAZZ!

So what exactly does my pizzazz look like in the "ideal" lesson? Let's start with anticipatory set. What does anticipatory imply? In my opinion, it means that ideally our students will anticipate—look forward to—our lesson if we begin with a little bait. But the "catch," as any good fisherman will tell you, is that you have to use the right bait. And the bait that keeps the fish biting in my pond is—you guessed it—enthusiasm.

Every one of us who learned English grammar the "dead" way knows the experience can be deadly boring. We must consider more contemporary and interactive approaches. Just recently, I came up with an idea that virtually doubled our enjoyment of three units in particular.

The first unit is a two-week, in-depth course on advanced punctuation. Not only are my students required to effectively punctuate their writing; they must also be able to identify the rule they used. My thought was to give the unit an actual name, something I could use as a part of my anticipatory set each day. "Power Punctuation" suddenly occurred to me. Now that doesn't necessarily sound amazing, but remember, it is all in how you say it. Before the first lesson, I introduced Power Punctuation as if it were the most important unit of my students' lives. They were going to learn valuable lessons that were going to help them succeed in the future. They were going to impress all of their high school and college instructors with their extraordinary command of the comma, semicolon, colon, and dash. They were, in fact, going to amaze themselves!

And then, for the first time ever, I taught my students to help me introduce the lesson each day. Every day I enthusiastically announced, "It's time for…." and they completed the sentence with a resounding, "Power Punctuation!" On that first day they had to repeat their part of it several times until I was satisfied with their degree of enthusiasm. But every day afterward our introduction seemed a little more alive. We actually had fun with what otherwise could have been a thoroughly lifeless, boring English unit. And the best part? My students learned advanced punctuation as never—and I do mean never—before. It is sheer bliss to teach a potentially hazardous unit to students who eagerly anticipate each lesson.

Next came a very intensive capitalization unit. With a little more difficulty I settled on "Killer Capitalization." No need for training. They knew exactly how important this unit would be. I dubbed the third unit "Partying with Possessives." Their line was a little different with this one. I said, "It's time to…" and they finished with, "party with possessives!" That last unit was the most alive unit of my English career.

I have been teaching a long time, and my students and I have undoubtedly missed out on many wonderful, even unforgettable, lessons because I never gave any thought whatsoever to anything so radical as a name for a unit. Now I often begin my lessons with something like, "Kids, this is going to be the best English lesson I have ever taught!" It is kind of a tradition, and the kids and I really have fun with it.

Someone will say, "Oh, Ms. LaField, you say that every time," and I will say, "Yes, but this one really is going to be even better!" and we all laugh.

Like my cheerful morning greeting, this, too, has a strong underlying message: Kids, we are going to have a great lesson today because I really love teaching you English, and you are going to learn a lot today that is going to make you a better writer! I would say it is a pretty non-traditional "hook," but it surely keeps those fish biting.

Do I begin every lesson in the same way? Not at all. Unlike the first lesson of the day when I have to wake them up with enthusiasm, history comes at the end of the day when the energy level is usually much lower. Sometimes I have to be especially creative and work harder to keep their attention—not only to command their waning attention, but also to keep my own engine revved up. With the exception of the days when I am introducing a new unit, our history time always begins with a review. The typical pre-lesson review doesn't usually get the fires blazing in any classroom, but a few years ago I discovered a better way, and now I can't imagine history without it.

I use a fast-paced question/answer platform that engages my students while providing ample opportunity for extra credit. I invite students to elaborate on answers by providing minor details, and students can earn points in a short amount of time. The kids enjoy because it's fun, but also because it's a great way to improve their history grades.

Often I will surprise them to keep them on their toes. For example, I ask a question and Tanner starts to answer. I can immediately see that he knows the correct response, so I interrupt him and say, "Stop! Give yourself a point!" (on the Honor System, of course). Then I say, "Who can add to that?" and Reed offers more detail, is also interrupted, and earns a point. Finally, when the answer has been fully explained or expressed in different ways, we move on. The next question may be a one-word answer, like a person's name, which requires no further explanation. It varies, of course, with the question. In addition, I often go back and repeat questions. One reason I like it so much is because we cover the answers so quickly, yet thoroughly. When several kids contribute to a full explanation, everyone benefits. Equally wonderful is that they have to listen to each other's answers to know what has or has not been said. I'm sure you can appreciate the beauty of a review where kids are actually listening to each other.

My students would tell you that one of the main reasons they enjoy our lessons is because Ms. LaField has a sense of humor, that we laugh much and often. But whatever our personality, we can—and should—have fun with our students during lessons. When we are tense, they are tense. It is contagious. Use a little energy to cultivate a great sense of humor. It's hard to have a dead lesson when everyone is laughing.

My students would tell you that one of the main reasons they enjoy our lessons is because Ms. LaField has a sense of humor, that we laugh much and often.

"CONTROLLED" ENTHUSIASM

Occasionally, I encourage my students' enthusiasm by giving extra credit points when I witness it. I call it "controlled" enthusiasm, and it's not for everyone; in fact, I've had student teachers actually question the level of enthusiasm during a lesson because they misconstrued my students' participation as being out of control. We're so used to the traditional classroom where kids are required to sit quietly in their desks and raise their hands politely that anything a little loud or out of the ordinary—and we must know by now how boring the ordinary can be—looks somewhat like chaos. So what exactly does controlled enthusiasm look like, and why do I encourage it?

If you were to witness controlled enthusiasm in our class, it would be during the question/answer portions of the lesson. You might see several kids waving their hands wildly—maybe right in my face—and hear loud voices begging me to call on them for the answer. Many teachers will not feel comfortable with allowing this level of activity in the classroom. In extreme controlled enthusiasm you might even see a couple of kids in the back jumping up and down and calling out my name above the rest. What would appear to be chaos would actually be extreme on-task behavior in a free-flowing, non-restrictive environment.

If you visited my classroom, you would see loud learning. You would see kids competing to share their answers. You would see an entire classroom of students and their teacher having a great time with a potentially dead topic— like punctuation. It's difficult to describe. I'm afraid you may see kids climbing the walls in your mind. Remember, it is controlled. I can stop it in an instant and often do.

Why do I encourage it? Because it's fun. Because kids love it. Because it's alive. Because they are learning.

A PASSION FOR THE SUBJECT MATTER

My sixth grade teacher, Miss Birch, had a passion for poetry. I still remember most of the poems we learned in her class. Edna St. Vincent Millay's "The Ballad of the Harp Weaver" was my favorite: "Son, said my mother when I was knee-high, you've need of clothes to cover you, and not a rag have I…"

Unfortunately, far too many of us with a passion for a particular subject matter are not free—for whatever reason—to express that passion in our classroom.

I loved that poem so much that I asked Miss Birch if I could borrow the book to write it down. (In those days there were no copy machines.) I memorized the whole thing and recite it to my students every year. I loved Miss Birch. She "lit my fire" with her passion. I am forever thankful to Miss Birch for penetrating my young soul with her passion. What a precious gift she gave when she "passed the torch" to me so that I could, likewise, pass it on to other young souls. A passion for our subject matter goes far in meeting the intellectual needs of our students.

Unfortunately, far too many of us with a passion for a particular subject matter are not free—for whatever reason—to express that passion in our classroom. We are also asked to teach subjects that we are not particularly passionate about. What do such teachers do to solve their problem? What solution can they employ that would best meet the needs of their students? I believe the answer lies in the difference between passion and enthusiasm.

One difference, I believe, is in a matter of degree. Passion is the more intense, forceful, and powerful; whereas, enthusiasm, though expressed in varying degrees of intensity, is less so. Another difference lies in their power to perform as "change agents." Whereas enthusiasm can definitely light our students' fires, passion can spark bonfires. And finally, whereas passion effortlessly springs forth from within, enthusiasm can be cultivated.

Where am I going with this line of reasoning? I believe the optimal solution for both the teacher who lacks a strong passion for his or her particular subject matter, as well as the teacher who teaches a subject matter outside of his or her preferred domain, is the same. If you desire to continue as an effective educator, you must lay aside your lack of passion and make a conscious choice to generate enthusiasm. Do it for the sake of your students—as well as for your own sake. Of course, the decisive word is *choice*. I fervently believe that if your desire is great enough, you can create a classroom that is "alive" with enthusiasm and "lights your students' fires."

Years ago in late May I was sitting at my computer checking my e-mail, and up popped a message from my principal: "Your assignment next year will be seventh grade Core." Out of the blue, with no explanation. Let me tell you, I looked at those words, and all I could think was, "This can't be true! This is not happening!" It was a professional nightmare. I loved eighth grade. I had spent twenty years developing a curriculum for which I was passionate. I returned her e-mail thusly: "I pray this is not so." It was so.

I spent three weeks that summer packing my things and moving to a new part of the country—again. I had moved the summer before, firmly believing it would be my final career move. But before I began to collect those first boxes for packing, I seriously renewed my vow of the previous summer: I would not utter one word of complaint. I chose to look ahead to what could be and never again behind to what used to be. And guess what? *I love seventh grade.*

I am enthusiastic about all the subjects I teach, but my passion is writing. This year I asked several of my students to express their impressions of my approach to teaching the subject about which I am most passionate. Amy wrote,

"Ms. LaField teaches the class so many important skills in writing like sentence patterns and Power Punctuation. Absolutely, I love the way she puts all of her lessons on the overhead projector and thoroughly explains them to us. Quickly and quietly, her students walk into the classroom ready for the next exciting lesson. The lessons are fun because Ms. LaField gets so excited about them. Telling stories, laughing, and even some tears, all the students are flooded with emotion during the lessons."

"I learned so much that I thought my head might explode. I found myself yelling to my mom, 'Mom, Mom, guess what I learned today?'"

"Prior to meeting Ms. LaField, writing was a skill that I had not yet mastered. Because of my involvement in her lessons and my level of enthusiasm, I now possess a lust for writing. Other teachers have given me a topic and told me to write without giving any instruction, whereas, Ms. LaField goes to great lengths to show us the full extent of writing. The topics of our essays invariably played a motivational role in shaping my newfound excitement for writing."

USING ENTHUSIASM TO TEACH MANNERLY RESPECT

I have a few tricks I use for teaching my students to be enthusiastic, while teaching them to use respectful manners. To begin with, I strive diligently to teach the kids to say "Thank you"—like they mean it. For example, after each lesson I say, "Thank you, Kids, for a great English lesson!" and they reply in unison, "No, thank *you*, Ms. LaField, for a great English lesson!" It is a positive way to end the lesson, and it is their signal that they can go back to their seats.

Another great trick that I suggest you use in your own classroom is what we call Quick Question. Over the years I have struggled with the problem of being surrounded by several students who all want to talk to me first. It simply doesn't work for me. For one thing, it can be very frustrating and confusing— for the kids and me. For another, some kids have only a quick question, while others need more time. Those with only a brief question waste time waiting for their turn, and wasting time means lost on-task learning time. So one day I got frustrated enough to do something about it.

I created a 6x9 inch sign that says "Quick Question" in big bold letters on one side, and says "Excuse me. Thank you. I appreciate your help," on the back. After my good friends at Kinko's copied several on pink fluorescent cardstock and laminated them, I pushed a ruler up inside to use as a handle and stapled around it to hold it securely in place.

Here's how Quick Question works. When it is obvious that two or more are in line for my attention, whoever has a quick question grabs the sign. We use it most during English lessons when I am helping students individually with their essays. The majority of the students will be quietly working on their essays at their desks. I sit up front in my beanbag on the middle step of the risers, while next to me is the student receiving my complete attention as I help him with his essay.

Lined up side by side directly in front of me are three chairs in which three students quietly sit as they wait patiently for their turn. As I finish with the student next to me on the beanbag, the next student in line—the one in the chair on the end closest to me—comes and takes his turn to receive my help. The two remaining kids in the chairs move over, and now a new student may sit in the empty chair. I begin helping the new student, but I see that one student is holding up the Quick Question sign. I stop helping the student next to me and look at the student with the sign, who says sincerely, "Excuse me, Ms. LaField." I acknowledge, he asks his quick question, I answer his question, and he says sincerely, "Thank you, Ms. LaField. I appreciate your help!" If he said it like he really meant it, I say, "You are welcome, [name of student]" and he puts the sign back and returns to his seat as I resume helping the student. If I don't feel the student was sincerely enthusiastic enough, I say, "Please say it like you mean it," and he repeats his thank you with greater sincerity. We both smile. The entire interchange takes only seconds, and the student, who would have otherwise waited in line, has lost no time getting back to work.

Another way I connect enthusiasm with manners is by teaching my students as a whole class to answer "Yes, Ma'm!" or "No, Ma'm!" For example, I ask the class if they would like to go to lunch on time. They respond in unison with, "Yes, Ma'm!" If it's not enthusiastic enough, I say good-naturedly, "Convince me!" and they repeat it. Once again, it's about training the troops—with a sense of humor.

WE ARE PROUD OF YOU!

One important way I inject enthusiasm into our class is by teaching my students to support each other's achievements with a chant. For example, Kris, who in the past made failing grades, earned a 3.8 GPA on his report card. I brought that achievement to the attention of the whole class, and they erupt in unison with, "We are proud of you, say we are proud of you!" They end the chant with a sort of loud grunt—sort of like the sound of someone getting punched in the stomach. They really like that part.

In the first few weeks I always start the chant, but I constantly encourage the kids to take the initiative because it means so much more when their own peers applaud them. That chant takes only seconds, and to a child who has never felt the support of an entire class, it can be life changing.

THE BEST PART!

Now for the best part of the chapter: my precious students' personal reflections on the topic of creativity and enthusiasm in our classroom. If I did not convince you, perhaps they will.

> *"When I came to Ms. LaField's class, I thought she was a weirdo because she was so enthusiastic. At the beginning of the year I was not enthusiastic. I sat in the back of the room and did not raise my hand. Then I started wanting to be more enthusiastic, so I started sitting in the very front of the class and*

raising my hand more than anyone! Now I'm enthusiastic every day and I love school better because of it."

"At the beginning of my seventh grade school year, I had the pleasure of having Ms. LaField as my Core teacher. In the same room I had the privilege of meeting Stephanie, who from then on became one of my dearest friends. This girl was probably one of the shyest girls I have ever met. For example, she was so shy that she couldn't even answer questions in class without fear and anxiety taking over her body. But because of Ms. LaField's enthusiasm, with the combination of care and love, my friend cracked out of her thick shell to live a life full of excitement! Now Stephanie is very bouncy, and to tell you the truth, she never stops talking."

"On the very first day of school I could feel her enthusiasm when she greeted us all at the door. When she shook my hand I could tell that she was sincere. Not that fake wannabe enthusiasm. She doesn't have that fake Barbie smile either. She is totally 100% sincere. What she does, is she uses her enthusiasm to make us want to learn. She uses passionate enthusiasm and phrases like 'Today is going to be the best English lesson ever!' I don't know why, but we just can't refuse her. She just has an aura of peace, kindness, cheer, and a bunch of other words. No—you know what? Words can't describe it."

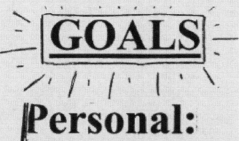

Personal:

#1. To start thinking of others rather than myself.

#2. To stop judging people by their outer appearance.

#3. To start solving all my conflicts easy without so much tension.

Family:

#1. To have a better relationship with every member of my family.

#2. To spend more time with all my family without conflicts.

#3 To be nicer to all my family so we can get along better.

School:

#1. To do my best with all my work and get it in on time. ★

#2. To become a Valued Employee and a Task Manager. ★

#3. To choose to care. ★

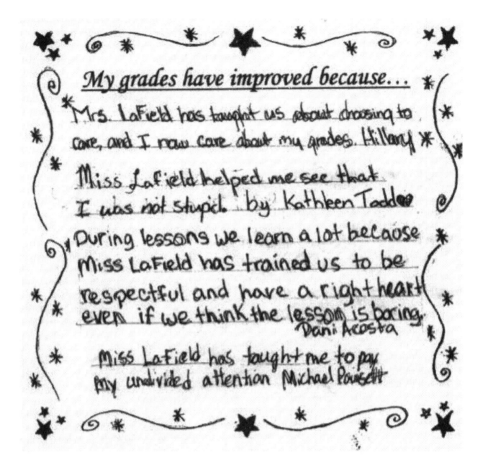

My grades have improved because...

Mrs. LaField has taught us about choosing to care, and I now care about my grades. Hillary

Miss LaField helped me see that I was not stupid. by Kathleen Todder

During lessons we learn a lot because Miss LaField has trained us to be respectful and have a right heart even if we think the lesson is boring. Dani Acosta

Miss LaField has taught me to pay my undivided attention. Michael Powell

CHAPTER 25

Love in Action

*H*is name was Josh P. The year he came to me, he had such a well-established reputation that when other teachers learned he was in my class—for three periods—they offered sincere condolences and good luck wishes.

We got off to a good start. He was happy to be in my class, especially because his best friend, Josh W., who had earned the second "highest" reputation, was also in the class. They were double trouble all right, yet with a definite degree of difference. Josh W. was like fine sandpaper, while Josh P. was the coarse variety. Both can grind you down, but the latter does it more quickly and efficiently.

It wasn't long before the Joshes dominated most of my attention in class. I tried to split them up—put one in my morning core and the other in my afternoon. That never happened. I could fill a page with the "I tried's" and really impress you with my creativity and level of tolerance. I did, in fact, impress myself. But the day finally came when I didn't like them any longer, especially Josh P.

I'll never forget the night I went home with such a heavy heart over my Joshes. Up to that point I had chosen to care for them, but I didn't feel like loving them any longer. I felt like it was time to bring out the heavy artillery, and that didn't feel good. I remembered what war felt like; it hadn't been that long since I used my heavy artillery daily.

That night I did something for the first time: I went to God in prayer and asked him for help. I asked him to put love in my heart for my Joshes, and then I just let it go. When I woke up the next morning, the boys never even crossed my mind. No frustration "hangover." Just nothing. I got in my car and drove to school as usual.

And then, as I was approaching the back door of my classroom, I saw Josh P. standing under one of the trees in the patio talking to his friends. What happened next was a miracle.

As I looked at Josh, I was suddenly flooded with a supernatural love for him. It was nothing I tried to muster up, nothing I did. It was just suddenly planted in my heart. I'll never forget the sense of peace I felt in that moment—like the battle was finally over. It was more like the warring sides had laid down their weapons and called a truce.

Josh, of course, had no idea what had happened to me in that moment; in fact, he hadn't even noticed me there. I simply went back into the room, hoping it would last. When the bell rang I was waiting for Josh at the door with a big smile. And from that very moment on, life got better in morning Core.

This is no Pollyanna story! Josh P. didn't surrender his guns that day and suddenly don a respectful, polite, submissive persona. We still had our moments, to be sure. He still grated on my nerves. But both Joshes stayed together in morning Core, and they would tell you to this day that I'm their favorite teacher.

LOVE IS PATIENT

At the beginning of each new year, I "target" the students who are most needy, the most demanding, the most exasperating; the ones who will test my limits. It is vitally important, therefore, that I make a conscious choice to regard them with compassion. I set my mind to it; I determine, in fact, to reserve for them an abundant supply of patience. As a result, I am prepared for the inevitable.

By focusing on what they are teaching us, instead of how they are affecting us, we can become better teachers and better people.

In addition, I view them as my teachers, for only the ones who test our limits can teach us the important life lessons. By focusing on what they are *teaching* us, instead of how they are *affecting* us, we can become better teachers and better people.

TIM, MY TEACHER

Tim taught me more about patience than any student who had come before him. Tim's irritating habits were constant, and in my earlier teaching years, he would have driven me to distraction. His relentless interruptions—though innocuous in nature—dominated our valuable time. And what is more, every student in the class viewed Tim in the same light. He was a pest.

I was losing the battle for patience, and I knew it. Everyone knew it. It was impossible to conceal my all-too-apparent aggravation, my obvious intolerance. And then one day, as if the veil were lifted, I saw the needy little love-starved boy inside him.

I was sitting in my beanbag with the kids gathered around me for a lesson. Tim was sprawled out on the floor in his usual place: right in front of me. Once again he had interrupted me with an irrelevant question. As I spurned him with a look of disapproval, his face dropped in anguish, and in that moment I finally recognized his pain.

Once again I had failed to care for him. I stopped everything, looked right into Tim's eyes and, with every eye and every ear upon us, asked him if he felt that I had been impatient with him. Meekly, he admitted that, yes, I had been impatient but that he hadn't noticed because he was so used to everyone being impatient with him. Nobody moved in the following moment of silence. It was as if they were all wondering what would happen next.

It was my turn for meekness. How many, I asked, had noticed my impatience with Tim? Every hand went up.

If it were possible with a remote control to press pause at those moments, we might have enough time. Time to deliberate. Time to meditate upon our options. Time to take a deep breath and wait for the answer. We could be that universal character in Robert Frost's "The Road Not Taken," who wistfully muses in retrospect, "Long I stood…" as he meditates upon the choice that altered his life forever. But, as we know, life does not come replete with pause buttons. As Omar Khayyam so poignantly expressed it, "The moving finger writes, and having writ moves on." Therein, to a great degree, lies the dilemma with patience: We have little time to think. Nevertheless, in that one compelling moment, I chose the road less traveled, and it has made all the difference. With Tim sitting right there in our midst, I confessed to my students my "lovelessness."

Humbly, I asked for Tim's forgiveness, which he happily conveyed, and with utter seriousness and deep emotion, I asked my students to hold me accountable if they suspected even a hint of impatience with Tim in the days to come. This was, for all of us, new territory.

After that day a remarkable thing began to happen: We all began to value Tim despite his irritating idiosyncrasies. We began loving him unconditionally. It was a class-wide phenomenon. My students began to report back to us about how they had protected Tim in another class, how they had befriended him openly. They were clearly excited and proud of themselves, and Tim was, for the first time in his life, the recipient of his peers' support and affirmation.

LOVE BELIEVES THE BEST

The more we think something, whether truth or lie, the more it becomes our reality.

A message of critical importance to my students— one of our "wall words"—is one that addresses the power of thoughts to affect the direction, events, and outcomes of our lives: "Thoughts lead to feelings, feelings lead to behavior, and behavior leads to consequences." The vast majority of people allow their minds to be programmed by the influences around them and spend their entire lives unconsciously controlled by these deeply ingrained messages. By and large, they are negative messages: I am stupid, I cannot do anything right, I am ugly, Nobody likes me, etc. I explain to my students that these negative thoughts have a powerful, self-fulfilling capability. The more we think something, whether truth or lie, the more it becomes our reality.

The subject is not difficult to understand, though it is challenging to put into practice because we are so dismally unaware of our thought patterns. We just roll merrily along like robots unless we, with a titanic effort, jerk back the reins of that wild, untamed mind of ours with a mighty "Whoa!" I tell my students there are three kinds of people: Those who make things happen, those who watch things happen, and those who ask, "What happened?" The people who make things happen have their thoughts under control.

I have very strong feelings about this topic and could easily go off on a tangent about this generation of students losing their brain cells to television, movies, computers, cell phones and video games. These days I actually give extra credit points for *thinking*. Plato's quote on our wall, "The unexamined life is not worth living," is especially pertinent when we are discussing the topic of using our brains for the purpose for which they were created. I make them analyze this quote, but they inevitably decipher the meaning: It is better to be dead than not be a thinking individual.

But I am not writing this to challenge your students to be thinkers. It is you whom I am hoping to challenge. Do you want to be in the category of people who make things happen? Of course you do, and I want to help you make good things happen with your students. My challenge to you is to begin to pay very close attention to your thoughts about your students. If they are anything less than positive, I am challenging you to consciously, with determined effort, change them! Another challenge, equally important, is to pay very close attention to the words you speak about your students. If they are anything less than positive, change them or say nothing at all. Every time we refuse to utter a harsh word, we are that much closer to victory over negative, destructive thinking.

LEARN TO TRANSFORM YOUR MIND

In simplest terms, the thoughts that we *think* about our students, affect the way that we *feel* about our students, which then determines the way we *treat* our students. Children are extremely intuitive. They don't have to be mind readers to know how we feel about them. Consider this: "Little Robert" really pushed your buttons today! He tested your limits and you failed Classroom LTL Management 101's lessons.

You go home muttering about him while at the same time trying to figure out how to deal with him the following day. You are going to blast him into submission! You are definitely *not* thinking positive thoughts about how you might be able to help him reach his full potential and become all he was created to be. Your mind is not free to think positive, creative thoughts that would help both you and Robert because it is too polluted with negativity.

So you go back to school the next day and Robert walks—no bursts—into the room behind sweet, innocent Valerie, who is howling because Robert just flipped her off and called her a nasty name. Are you ready to handle this situation wisely? Patiently? Impartially? Who is in control here? Who is walking in peace and coming from an empathetic place of compassion?

Hopefully, you are smiling as you are reading this commonplace description, but if it were really happening to you right now, and you were not ready, you would definitely *not* be smiling. Neither would Robert nor Valerie nor your other students nor even the principal if he or she just happened to be walking by. What then, is the answer? You have to learn to transform your mind.

Let's just carry this a little further. You go to the teachers' lounge for lunch and some blessed time away from little Robert, and all you do is rehash this morning's fiasco with anyone who will listen. Of course, it is all little Robert's fault. He *made* you so crazy you could just pinch his head between your thumbs. He *made* you lose control and make a spectacle of yourself in front of the other children. He *made* you momentarily forget why you ever wanted to become a teacher.

Now lunch is over, and you spent the whole time speaking less-than-kind words about little Robert. Now you are beyond irritated and upset. You are livid. And as you stomp your way back to class, you are just daring him, in your thoughts, of course, to blink at you cockeyed.

Why are you now boiling? The sequence is very simple: You turned up the heat by adding your spoken words to your already seething thoughts, and now everyone had all better watch out because we know the progression that follows. Those out-of-control thoughts, compounded by out-of-control words, led to out-of-control feelings, which—watch out now—unless you are very careful, will lead to out-of-control behavior and then little Robert is not the only one who is going to be in trouble.

Our challenge... is to consciously learn to guard our thoughts about our students.

Our challenge then, should we determine to learn to care for all and not just some of our students, is to consciously learn to guard our thoughts about our students. Notice my use of the word learn. As we are learning our lessons, we must diligently practice them. We must zealously and consistently practice living them.

If we take weekly piano lessons and never practice during the week, never do the hard work it takes to become proficient, we will never learn to play soulful sonatas. But if we are passionately committed to our piano lessons, we will practice dutifully and ultimately compose music that resonates exquisitely with the souls of others.

But equally as important as guarding our thoughts, you will recall, is guarding our words. The more we verbalize something, the more we bind it to our thoughts, the more it "gets in us" so to speak. And then, often tragically, the more it can become our reality. The words give our thoughts more power.

If our thoughts about our students are positive and uplifting, and we combine them with positive and uplifting words, we are planting seeds of love in our own hearts, which enable us to love that unlovely child.

Every time we refuse to utter a harsh word, we are that much closer to victory over negative, destructive *thinking*. But be forewarned: Expect no victory over wrong thinking and wrong speaking if you vacillate. In time, by being consciously consistent with positive thought processing, you will no longer have to even think about your response, and you will not be able to even imagine going back to your former ways of careless thinking and speaking.

LOVE GIVES BLESSINGS

Mother Teresa once said, "We are not called to do great things, but to do small things with great love." I believe she meant that our love is most tenderly manifested by the small things we do for others. Mother Teresa, who went about doing good in the impoverished streets of Calcutta, blessed everyone in her path and in so doing became a blessing. She lived for no other purpose than to light up the darkness around her with unconditional love.

Why not you and me? Why not determine that we will go about doing good in our classrooms? Even more than just blessing others, why not become a blessing to our students? Why not wake up tomorrow and every day that follows with a personal pledge to be a blessing everywhere we go?

Once I chose to get serious about giving blessings rather than waiting to receive them, my life changed radically. The burden of my personal difficulties lifted, my life had greater purpose, my joy multiplied, I felt better physically and my heart began to overflow with love—not only for myself and others but for those who hurt or mistreated me. When our focus is on blessing others rather than on our own personal concerns and preoccupations, we forget ourselves. We go about doing good, and the world is a better place because we are in it.

LOVE HAS NO FAVORITES

St. Augustine said, "The value of a single child surpasses that of a galaxy of stars." I believe we can improve upon his maxim by adding the word *every*: "The value of *every* single child surpasses that of a galaxy of stars." Though most of us who teach would agree with Augustine in theory, I wonder how many of us can truly say that we value every one of our students to such a degree, for when we include the word *every*, we include the troublemakers, the clowns, the whiners, and the altogether obnoxious. We include those who cannot stop moving, and those who cannot grasp the concept even after we think we have exhausted our resources. We include those who sit in the back of the room and refuse to cooperate, and, we include the ones who intentionally defy every rule and question our authority— the ones who just seem to take pleasure in pushing our buttons.

We include the mean-spirited ones—those who pick on the class target and laugh when a classmate trips over a chair or gives the wrong answer. We include the difficult to love, and the ones we forget are the most trouble in our classroom because they are the most troubled.

And then there are what I call the "bright and beautiful." You know them. They are the smilers, the pleasers, the ones with the answers, the ones who respect the rules, the ones who never give us any problems. They are just so easy to love, and unless we are very, very careful, they are the ones who become our favorites.

Humbly, I admit my guilt: I have had favorites, many favorites. We never do this to intentionally hurt children, but how deeply we wound the unlovely when we regard their classmates above them! We may just as well tell them openly that we value them less than the others, yet they know it instinctively. We forget that children are so perceptive. They know so much—so much that they should never have to know.

NOT JUST A FIVE-MINUTE HURT!

When we base our treatment of children on their performance, we are giving them conditional love. We are saying, "I value you if you fit into my mold, if you meet my expectations, if you become who I think you should be." We do that to the precious children who fail to live up to our standards and expectations. Heaven help us to look at the truth and change our ways!

I once asked my students to share their feelings about teachers with favorites. Heather said,

> *"When my seventh grade teacher chose some students over others, I wanted to drop out of school so I didn't have to face her. I felt like I was completely invisible, like I didn't matter. My new teacher constantly shows that she has no favorites. Now I want to be in school. I don't want to miss a day. Now I feel important."*

Paul wrote,

> *"When teachers have pets, it makes me feel like I'm nothing or like I'm dumb. Teachers have no clue what it does to their students."*

THE PAINFUL TRUTH

I agree with Paul that I don't think teachers have any idea how much they damage children when they value some more than others. I can honestly admit that I had been teaching fifteen years before becoming acutely aware of the degree to which we injure young hearts with partiality.

I had claimed for so many years to love children. In truth, I did not love children—I was partial to some children. My "love" was selective, conditional, and performance-based. Today as I reflect back and consider my journey toward living the lessons of unconditional love in the classroom, I remember that the light turned on only dimly at first, revealing glimpses of the truth that I did, indeed, have favorites. From time to time, the subject would arise when a student accused me of favoritism. Though I vehemently denied the accusation and fiercely protected my innocence, I remember that little voice of conscience that impelled me to reconsider the truth. And as I grew more and more willing to listen, the light grew brighter and brighter until I clearly saw the painful truth: I had favorites!

Such moments of revelation hold the potential of changing the course of our path forever. We can embrace the truth about ourselves and, with tenacity and courage, choose to follow a new path, or we can do as so many do: ignore the truth, deny the truth, resist the truth, until finally… the light goes out. Millions of times men have faced their moment of truth and turned away, because looking at the truth hurts! I used to think that this pain had to do with ugliness of the truth, but now I think it has to do with our pride. We resist owning the truth because our pride refuses to accept that we are capable of committing something so atrocious as making a child feel invisible.

I KNOW WHO I REALLY AM

I remember the day I sat down with my students to humbly ask them if they thought I had favorites. After soberly announcing that I had a very important question to ask them, they gathered around me on the risers and in front of me on the rug. The moment of truth had arrived.

I knew what their answer would be even before I asked, but I was not prepared for the discussion that ensued. Never before had a teacher asked them such a question, particularly one about which they were so sensitive. It was a rare moment, and they were not about to let it pass.

One by one, they expressed their pain and anguish at having been dehumanized by teachers who valued them less highly than their peers. I listened intently, making sure that each was granted their moment to share. I looked into the eyes of each responder and thanked them for sharing. They knew I was valuing their feelings, and it was, in those revealing moments, the most important gift I could give them.

Then it was my turn. In a matter of thirty emotionally charged minutes, I made three decisions: First, without rebuttal, excuse, or denial of any kind, I decided to own and admit the truth to my students. Hearing an adult admit to being wrong has a way of softening a child's heart, which prepared them for my second decision: to ask for their forgiveness. Without hesitation, it was granted. By this time, the tears were flowing.

My third decision was not made lightly, but with conviction that I must diligently live this lesson, or I would lose my students' trust. Pledging to change my ways, I asked them to hold me accountable in the days to come. I explained that because I was unconscious of showing favoritism, it was their responsibility to bring it to my awareness the moment they perceived a breach of promise.

So began my commitment to valuing every one of my students equally. The journey to conscious loving is a process, not something to be gained in a year or even in many years. Indeed, we will still be learning it until that final bell.

Many times that year my students made good on their promise to hold me accountable; in fact, they relished every opportunity to pinpoint the smallest breach of agreement. As we all know, children have an extremely strong sense of and need for fair treatment.

WHEN WE "KNEW NOT WHAT WE DID"

I end this chapter with a heart-wrenching story that poignantly illustrates the deep scars that can result from our unconscious propensity to value some students above others.

Over the past several years, I have had the honor of sharing my "expertise" with many of the student teachers attending our local university. For the focus of one particular seminar I decided to talk about what I called my "pre and post Lovewalk years" in the classroom. Horizontally across the whiteboard I wrote the numbers one through thirty-one with a vertical line between fifteen and sixteen. As I explained it, the numbers one to thirty-one represented my years in the classroom, and the vertical line represented the division between my pre-Lovewalk and post-Lovewalk years. My objective for that seminar was to illustrate, drawing from my own real-life experiences, how to and how not to treat children in the classroom. The first fifteen years were the "how not to" years.

I began with my pre-Lovewalk days. Sparing no details, the student teachers learned the truth about my proud, unconscious, "all-about-me" days. Because I am widely known on the campus as a caring, compassionate teacher, they had difficulty comprehending the truth about whom I had been. I had to convince them with a story or two. As it turned out that day, the stories were about favorites. By the time I was finished, they were stunned believers.

At the conclusion of these seminars, the student teachers frequently approach to thank me and ask questions; that day was no different. But that day as I tried to converse with several simultaneously, I happened to look over their heads to see how many were waiting and was instantly drawn to a young woman whose sorrowful eyes pled for my immediate attention. She was obviously ready to burst into tears.

Politely pushing the others aside, I pulled her toward me, held her shoulders tightly, and turned us around so that our backs faced the crowd. After several moments of unsuccessful attempts to comfort her, she looked squarely into my eyes and asked if I remembered her. I hope you never have to face such a moment! God knows after several thousand students, we forget most of them, especially teachers like me, who have such a hard time with names!

And then she broke the silence with words I shall never forget: "I was one of those in your pre-Lovewalk years, one of those who was not one of your favorites." It got worse. "You did not even know my name. You wrote my name wrong in my yearbook."

As I recall now, she looked away as I held her close and implored her to forgive me. Over and over I pleaded for her forgiveness until finally she conceded with reluctance, "I forgive you only because you say you no longer have favorites." And then she pulled away and disappeared. I never saw her again.

These are the times when we must forgive ourselves, for "we knew not what we did."

I know Mrs. LaField loves me because...

when I would do Somthing bad miss lafield would Be mad but she would Still love me. David

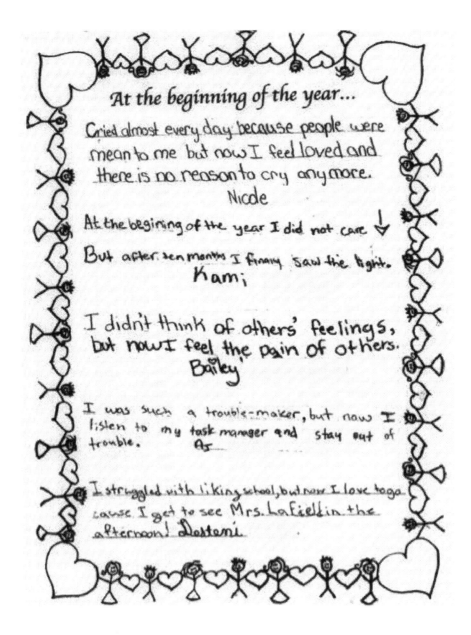

At the beginning of the year...

Cried almost every day because people were mean to me but now I feel loved and there is no reason to cry anymore.
Nicole

At the begining of the year I did not care ↓

But after ten months I finally saw the light.
Kami

I didn't think of others' feelings, but now I feel the pain of others.
Bailey

I was such a trouble-maker, but now I listen to my task manager and stay out of trouble.
AJ

I struggled with liking school, but now I love toga cause I get to see Mrs. Lafield in the afternoon! Destani

CHAPTER 26
Keeping Promises

*T*he story you are about to read is not one more victory among others. It was my Super Bowl, the big test. My test came in the form of a child in desperate need of assistance: a child named Peter.

In thirty-plus years in the classroom, I cannot think of a single student who tested my limits over a longer period of time than Peter. Our breakthrough did not come until two weeks before the end of the school year. It literally went on and on, and with the exception of a good day or two, *it never got better.*

What was it about Peter that tested not only my limits but those of the rest of the class? To begin with, he refused to assume responsibility for his actions, and his issues were "always someone else's fault." As you may have noticed, it is nearly impossible to assist someone who won't first assume responsibility for his or her actions. But Peter was simply "too wounded to be wrong."

Peter also had what we might call a persecution complex. In his mind, everyone hated him. His obnoxious behavior perpetuated his persecution complex because the longer he disrupted our classroom, the more the other students really did start to "hate" him. Peter was the victim of that vicious cycle that just keeps growing more vicious throughout someone's lifetime—unless it is broken.

Along with those two problems, Peter was the epitome of pessimism, a true-to-life prime example of all those "D" words that often plague that personality type: desperate, dejected, depressed, disturbed, distraught. Put them all together and you have a thoroughly defeated child... a Peter.

A contributing factor to Peter's sorrowful saga was the enabler in his life, his well-meaning stepfather. That's another story in itself. I'll skip a detailed explanation of the countless times I called him with the same issues. In fact, I called so many times that the checks by Peter's name finally exceeded the length of my call log. A first for me.

Despite the challenges, I remained positive, and if Peter actually had a good day, I would call his stepfather with a positive report. When spring came and there was still no improvement, I invited his stepfather to visit our classroom. I wanted him to see—not just hear about—our supportive environment so that he could not blame-shift Peter's problem onto our classroom. He was impressed; in fact, he was amazed. But did anything change? Unfortunately, no.

PETER—UNWANTED AND ALONE

By April, Peter had been asked to leave every group into which I tried to place him. You see, with Peter in the group, the group couldn't reach community, and everyone was committed to reaching community. So when Peter once again refused to listen to a patient, but exasperated Task Manager, that Task Manager would finally come to me with, "Ms. LaField, we don't want Peter in our group anymore." When one of my Task Managers reaches the point when the responsibility of being a Task Manager is no longer enjoyable, I know the situation has become dire.

So we were in the same situation again, Peter without a home, and me faced with, "What shall we do now, Peter?" I'd sit on the bottom step of the risers with Peter. It was a circular discussion that went around and around until we ran out of time to talk, and I'd send him off to that solitary desk in the front of the room that always awaited him.

That often-repeated promise to never abandon Peter was the key that unlocked the happy ending of his story.

But always, before I sent him off, I'd hug him and—without fail—promise to never abandon him. Then I'd say with sincere intensity, "Who loves you, Peter?" And he'd reply, "You do, Ms. LaField." When Peter walked away, he may have felt completely misunderstood and downcast, but he never felt rejected by me.

That often-repeated promise to never abandon Peter was the key that unlocked the happy ending of his story. It was certainly not something that I had promised others in the past. I may have said it once or twice to a couple of different students over the years, but with Peter I was impelled to say it every time we found ourselves back at square one. I just "knew" how important those words were to him.

I think I unconsciously knew, too, that if I didn't say the words aloud—that is, if I didn't make the promise in the first place—that maybe someday I just might reach my limit and do something I'd regret all my life. That promise held me accountable. I was teaching my students to be people of honor and integrity who kept their word, and I had better do the same. I had no idea that the day would come when that promise would be tested to the limit.

THE FINAL STRAW

Everything came to a head one day in mid May when I was in the room next door for a couple minutes and Peter had a problem with Richard, his Task Manager. Now Richard, along with his buddy Evan, had agreed in early May to allow Peter into their group on one condition: He would stay in their group on a five-minutes-at-a-time basis. In other words, if he refused to listen to the boys for more than five minutes, he was out of the group for the rest of the day. But the positive side of the plan was that he could join the group the next day with a fresh start. It was a brilliant, student-devised plan. In all my years of teaching kids how to work together cooperatively and reach community, I had never once thought of it.

On a day I was momentarily out of the room, Peter refused to listen to Richard's request for him to come back to their group and sit down, so Richard walked over to the other side of the room where Peter was "hanging out" and proceeded to bring him back—gently but forcefully.

Now the part of the story that will always perplex me is that Peter, the boy with the persecution complex, who whined pathetically if anyone so much as looked at him cross-eyed, never uttered a single syllable to me about the incident with Richard. As far as I knew from Richard's explanation, there had been a little problem with Peter, but it had been resolved. I never gave it a second thought—until the next morning, that is, when my vice-principal called my room before school to inform me that Peter's stepfather and mother were in the office claiming that Richard had grabbed Peter by the throat, thrown him against the wall with his legs dangling off the ground and threatened to hurt him.

That's what Peter told his stepfather after school without even so much as a syllable of complaint to me when I came back to the classroom following the "supposed" incident, and that's what Peter's step-father believed explicitly without even conferring with me.

Since it was my prep period and because I trusted that his stepfather and I had developed what I believed was a substantially stable, mutually cooperative relationship, I encouraged my vice-principal to send them up to my room. I was confident we could solve the problem without the help of the administration. I was wrong.

AN UNHAPPY MEETING

It was not a happy meeting. When a parent is not acting rationally, wisdom calls in the administration, and that is exactly what I calmly and respectfully informed Peter's parents that we needed to do. I stood up to indicate that the meeting was over, they followed suit, and Peter, who had been sitting there the whole time, looked at me as if to ask, "What am I supposed to do now, Ms. LaField?"

It seemed obvious to me that Peter should leave with his parents so he could return to the class he was missing. That was when I said the one thing that led us into the climax of the story: "I think Peter should go with you." That was when his mother said, "You want Peter in another class, don't you?" That was when I replied with the one thing I regret most out of the entire convoluted incident: "I think that would be a good idea." And I said it right in front of Peter—right in front of the little boy I had promised never to abandon. As they all walked away, his mother left me with, "You're not who I thought you were!"

What followed was as bad as it gets. The stepfather wrote a written letter of complaint to the principal and the superintendent, and Peter was removed from my class. It would have been all over at that point except for a promise.

EXCEPT FOR A PROMISE

I can only wonder at the number of times that promise reverberated in my mind that night. All I knew was that I had to get Peter back in our class, and that just doesn't happen—at least never before to my knowledge. Once a student is transferred, that's it. It's official.

The following morning, I went to my vice-principal in tears and begged her to help me get Peter back. Obviously, we both wanted only what was best for Peter, and his best was definitely not being transferred to another class for the last two weeks of school. She knew it and I knew it, but we had to somehow convince Peter's stepfather.

Feeling strongly that we could work out our problems and end Peter's school year on a positive note, we decided to request another meeting on his behalf. My immediate job was to make sure that Peter knew I wanted him back.

Knowing that his birthday was the following day and that none of his peers at school would care one way or another, I decided to bring a cake to school the next day. On his way to science that next morning, I motioned him over to my refrigerator and showed him the cake. Lovingly, I apologized for saying it was a good idea for him to transfer and humbly asked his forgiveness. Peter quickly recognized that I was keeping my promise. I told him of our plan to move him back into our class. Incredulous might be the best word to describe the look on his face.

Actually, shocked might be the stronger, even more appropriate word. Peter was shocked that I truly wanted him back, and that was when he finally believed that Ms. LaField really cared for him. I had to prove it to him before he would finally believe it.

Next, I had to prepare the class for Peter's possible return. What an opportunity it was, a truly teachable moment, to talk once again about the world's desperate need for unconditional commitment. One of the kids pointed to one of our favorite quotes on the wall: "People are not bad. They are wounded." Peter was not bad—though he had carried that label around for many years—he only needed his wounds healed. And then I wrote on the board "Love heals all wounds." Peter needs our love to heal his wounds, I told the kids. They were with me all the way.

I had convinced my vice-principal, Peter, and the kids. All that was left was to convince his stepfather, who later that day agreed to a meeting. As I knew she would, my vice-principal, a woman of honor and integrity, had kept her word.

WHAT WOULD YOU HAVE DONE NEXT?

Seriously consider the situation and try to decide how you would have handled this situation. Would you have responded in the same way? If so, how and why? Would you have stopped pursuing an unruly student after his stepfather had written a scathing complaint letter to your principal and superintendent (after you had tried to be patient for eight and a half months)?

Unconditional love—the real McCoy kind—doesn't even entertain going a certain distance, and then giving up. It doesn't love for eight and a half months and then decide to "throw in the towel." It patiently perseveres.

After I decided to honor my commitment to unconditional love, I still had to convince Peter's step-father to let him come back. I knew what I must do: I would humble myself.

It didn't matter that I had given Peter my all. It didn't matter that they couldn't see my efforts with Peter in the classroom. It didn't matter that I had spent so

Love obtained the victory that day and gave Peter back to me so that I could keep a promise.

many evenings on the phone. It didn't matter that they had filed a written complaint and sent it to my superiors. It didn't matter who was right or who was wrong. At that point, all that mattered was a promise. There in that conference room, hearts softened, tempers were diffused, minds changed, and wounds were healed.

However, the story gets even better. Peter's peers opened wide their arms and welcomed him back into the fold. I wish you could have been there. I wish the whole world could have been there.

Every time I turned around, Peter was by my side—close to cuddling, comfortable in his own skin, smiling radiantly up at me. No more pessimism, no more persecution complex, no more pointing the finger of blame, Peter was at peace with himself. For two whole weeks he was a happy boy who was finally a part of our family and knew it…and wonder of wonders, he actually completed a project!

I know Mrs. LaField loves me because...

...she always asks how my life is going, whether its about family, friends, sports, or girls.

Even when I was a brat Miss LaField Still smiled at me. Kami

She expresses her love even when I make a mistake, because she has unconditional love for me.
—Amanda

... She makes me feel wanted and she made me realize I'm special.
— Angela

even when I forget my reading logs she still loves me ~ashley

When I talk on Red Light she forgives me. Tiffany

CHAPTER 27

Authenticity

*H*er name was Amber. She came through my door that first day wearing a dark scowl that may as well have been a sign hanging around her neck announcing an angry warning to all: Don't tread on me! In just fourteen short years, Amber had learned to hate the world. She came equipped with a seemingly endless supply of hate, anger, distrust, and a dangerously explosive temper. Welcome to our quaint little happy family, Honey!

Only love can decimate the walls that children like Amber erect. They are pain-avoidance walls. They are walls that warn all trespassers to keep out. They are walls of self-imprisonment. I had a choice to make in those first critical moments. It was a conscious choice. I decided to love her.

A PLEA FOR PATIENCE

As with every new student, the Task Managers met that first day to decide who would take her into their group. After warning them that she would be a "challenge," dear Tracy happily agreed to welcome Amber into her group. It took all of about five minutes for the first problem to surface—Amber immediately and adamantly refused to listen to a single word that Tracy had to say. The battle had begun. What had once been a happy, peaceful caring community quickly dissolved into a veritable hornet's nest.

That first day I privately pleaded with each member of the group, challenging them to respond with patience to Amber's blatantly abominable behavior. Nick, in particular, was vehemently opposed to the whole idea. Brazenly, Amber had already ordered him to shut up, and Nick, one of the fiercest wrestlers in our school, was spitting nails as I worked to calm him down. As it turned out, after effusive persuasion, all reluctantly agreed to give her a chance.

PENETRATING WITH AUTHENTIC LOVE

My chance to privately connect with her came during lunch that day. Along with a "big picture" explanation of the dynamics of our classroom, I matter-of-factly, yet with great care, explained that her offensive attitude with others was the cause of much of her obvious unhappiness. She was, as I expressed in terms to which I knew she could relate, cutting her legs out from underneath herself. By the time lunch ended, Amber knew that I *felt* different. There, by my side on the beanbag, I hugged a child who was hungry for acceptance. If I recall correctly, she turned and smiled a bit as she left for her next class. I breathed a sigh of relief.

The first breakthrough came the very next day when once again Amber told Nick to shut up. I asked the whole group to join me on the rug where we peacefully resolved the conflict. After inviting each member to share his or her side of the story, it was obvious that Amber—no surprise to anyone—was the guilty party. Softly and without a hint of reprimand, I asked her if she had ever apologized to anyone in her life. "Only once," was her reply.

Can you see this in your mind? We were gathered closely together in a circle on the rug in front of the risers. It was perfectly quiet except for the muffled on-task conversation behind us. We were waiting. No one was moving. I was silently believing for a miracle. Amber was the focus of attention, and she knew it. And then she said them. The words that, for a child who has lived with undeserved pain, don't come easily—if ever. Three miracle words: "I'm sorry, Nick." And she really meant it. With a quick squeeze I thanked her, and the kids returned to their desks. For a few precious moments I sat alone, rejoicing at the remarkable event that had transpired.

FIGHTING FOR HER LIFE!

My next important move was to talk to the counselor. This child had a story, and I was anxious to hear it. Amber's mother, I learned, did not want her. Why would a mother not want her own child? In this case, it was a matter of choosing her boyfriend over her daughter. Her boyfriend, who had been sexually abusing Amber for over a year, was found out and instead of casting him out, her mother chose instead to cast out her own daughter.

The father, who lived several hundred miles away with his girlfriend, had also deserted her. At this time, we learned that Amber was temporarily living with an aunt who was rapidly reaching her limit. It all made perfect sense: Amber was fighting for her life. "Okay, Honey," I thought, "I'm in your corner now."

One of the first things we learn from the "Ambers" in our classroom is that we can expect them to be predictably unpredictable. From one day to the next, I could never be sure of Amber's state of mind. Some days she was perky, positive and all smiles; other days she was a rattler ready to strike. This encouraged me to expend more energy to be infinitely predictable, especially on her dark days.

It is highly doubtful that Amber had ever known unconditional love in her life. Up to that point, people had "loved" her—or not—depending on her behavior. That, of course, is the conditional, performance-based brand of love. She recognized it for what it was and utterly rejected it. Amber learned to trust me, and it was my privilege to care for her consistently despite her erratic behavior.

THE HARDEST PART

What was the hardest part of loving her? First, last, and everywhere in between, my level of patience was tested. Every day Amber took me a little deeper into living the lesson that children are infinitely valuable. As long as I remained patient, we were able to work through every problem. As long as I maintained my patience, I could avoid the next hardest part: not personalizing her attitude and behavior.

Sadly, one day Amber did not return to my classroom. She had left school unexpectedly, and I was not informed of where she would be moving. I thanked God I had loved her well, that I had risen to Augustine's high standard. No one knows how many "Ambers" we will have in our classrooms. We must prepare ourselves for their arrival so we are ready with a reservoir of commitment. Put simply, we must not misconstrue a student's problems with their person, we must not internalize their acting out as personally offensive, and we must be committed to the our difficult students despite their best efforts to reject such commitment.

CHAPTER 28
Never Failing

*I*magine a world where all children, in every classroom, are highly valued; a world where they are safe to be themselves, and not devalued because of obnoxious behaviors or emotional "baggage." Imagine if no one ever considered them a failure or a misfit. Imagine teachers who patiently help them to conquer their personal mountains.

I am reminded of Annie Sullivan's tenacious commitment to Helen Keller. A classic example of the teacher who refuses to admit defeat, Annie saw past Helen's aberrant behavior and recognized that deeply buried beneath that flailing, self-centered, spoiled little child lay the potential for greatness. Annie valued Helen enough to not forsake her, despite the fact that everyone, including her own family, had lost all hope of salvaging her. It took only one teacher who believed, who persevered, who stood resolute in the face of adversity. Annie believed in the power of one, as did Helen who later quoted Edward Everett Hale, "I am only one, but I am one. I cannot do everything, but what I can do and should do, by the grace of God, I will do!"

WILL WE BE DIFFERENT?

Students who exhibit antisocial behavior force us to stop and deal with them. They force us to grow. Some of them do it purposefully, usually for attention. They don't care if it's negative as long as it's attention of some kind. Others do not intend to unnerve us; they simply cannot control themselves.

We can usually identify these extreme cases by the end of the first day, and we can be sure they are anticipating the same teacher reaction they've received since their early days in kindergarten. The teacher gets angry; they are in trouble.

The teacher gets angrier; they are in more trouble. The teacher now is angry most of the time; they know deep inside that the teacher does not like them. The teacher—they are now convinced—wishes they would disappear.

They are enacting a self-fulfilling prophecy. The scenario has repeated itself for so many years that they now expect to be a problem. They are not happy children. What do they need from us? They need nothing more or less than our unconditional acceptance. If we have done our homework, that is, if we are committed to *living the lessons,* we will surprise them. At first, they will not trust our uncharacteristic response; in fact, I have learned the hard way that before we can ever hope to make any significant progress whatsoever, we simply have to earn their trust. That takes time, patience and all the love we can muster.

...before we can ever hope to make any significant progress whatsoever, we simply have to earn their trust.

If we ever hope to earn our students' trust, we must strive to lay aside our initial expectations and accept our students *where they are.* If we begin with unrealistic expectations at the outset, we are setting the stage for ultimate failure. We must acknowledge each student's level of academic acumen and maturity, and then set realistic goals for them. Next, we must determine their maximum potential and begin guiding them towards it with baby steps. I make sure each student knows I believe in them without reservation, and that it is all right to fall down often—as long as they get back up every time.

Once they trust us and believe that we will not abandon them, miracles appear.

CHAPTER 29

Letters from Students

$\mathcal{T}$he following letters exemplify the result of my dedication to meeting the needs of the children in my care. Upon reading them, note that Gretchen and Ethan eloquently expressed divergent needs.

Gretchen, on the one hand, was basically a *whole* child before we met. Her intellectual needs were stimulated on a higher level by my challenging lessons, and her emotional needs were further met by my example. Admired by all her peers for her kind deeds and joyful demeanor, Gretchen was socially adept in every way. Born into a stable, fully functional moral home, her parents had successfully met all of her developmental needs. With feet firmly planted on the right path and headed in the right direction, Gretchen was a veritable sponge, ready and eager to soak up more of everything I could give her. Please see following page for Gretchen's letter.

Dear Mrs. Lafield,

I just wanted to take the time and tell you that I look up to you as a fabulous role model, teacher, and friend. All through my life I have wanted to "be many different things: a vet, doctor, and a lawyer. In my spare time I wanted to write books and I still do to this very day. Now I want to be a teacher —English— just like you. Since the Right Heart Club, even since the day I walked into your room, I have been changing my life in many ways. I will come and see you every day, every lunch, even when I leave 8th grade. Even then I will come see you. All the colors and quotes on your walls make your room the best place to be when I'm down. Before I came to you, before I talked to you, I could not forgive anyone. Now I have forgiven people that I needed to forgive. I just want to sit and talk to you about nothing, just to be your friend. I want to write like you, teach like you, love like you, and be like you. If I ever become a teacher, I want my room to look just like yours, and feel as good as I do when I'm in your room. I love you Mrs. Lafield. I want to thank you for being ther for me, teaching me how to love, helping me forgive, and loving me. Love always,

Gretchen

Ethan, on the other hand, was operating on an empty tank from the moment he walked in my door. As a result of his unresolved, deep-seated emotional issues, he had effectively sabotaged any possibility of healthy social interaction with his peers. Predictably, behavior issues arose, and though not expelled for fighting in sixth grade, Ethan was a prime candidate for a grim future within the penal system. Fractured and defeated, despite his troubled past, Ethan clung to one hope: Everything could change. He believed his life could get better. He was looking for help, and I was ready with the life-line. As you will gather from his letter, I chose the "tough love" approach. I pushed hard and relentlessly expected his best. I never lowered the bar, and he soon began to rise to my expectations, to see himself in a whole new light. And that's when his life started getting better. Never forget: Love heals all wounds.

Dear Miss Lafield,

Last year was really bad at school. I was always mad about something. Nobody liked me and kids made fun of me so I only had one friend—Julian. So I was really mean—even to girls. I got in four fights but they never kicked me out for some reason.

I had really long hair and you couldn't see my eyes. The teachers got mad at me for that. They were always telling me Ethan cut your hair. I felt like I disappointed everyone mostly myself.

It was really hard to learn because I can't read and I couldn't pay attention in class. It made me feel really stupid and I had really bad grades. So the teachers gave up on me except for my math teacher. He made me come to study hall every day.

But this year is different. On the first day of school when I got in your class I thought she's going to help me. I was glad I cut my hair before school started. Even though you told me and Julian we were immature you told us you were going to help us stop acting stupid. You didn't say stupid but it was the same thing.

I decided to start trying hard. You kept yelling at me and saying Ethan where is your reading log? Then I started reading at night and my task manager helped me listen in class and you were always talking to me about that I had to care about my life. So guess what? It worked!

Now I'm confident and I definitely feel smarter. Julian is still my friend but now I have more friends. I only got in one fight so far this year but I told him I was sorry and now he's my friend. Nobody can believe I got the Skills of Independence. I was so excited I showed the counselor my badge and he was proud of me. And then I got the cake at our little red hen party. I feel like a new person.

So now I want to help people like you do. I want to be like that. I want to learn to inspire other kids like you inspired me to care about my life. You asked me to give teachers advice. It's that they should never give up on their students even if they give up on themselves. And you asked what is my favorite quote. It's if a man does his best what else is there? You always try your best Miss Lafield. You always love me.

Your student,
Ethan

THE BOTTOM LINE

Throughout the pages of *Living the Lessons,* I have elaborated on my unusual approach to meeting the needs of the Whole Child. I have endeavored to substantiate my premise that because I strive to meet the social, emotional, and moral needs of my students, their intellectual needs are met to substantially greater degrees, and, that as a result, my staunch commitment to the Whole Child philosophy has generated considerably higher test scores in my own classroom.

But *Living the Lessons* is not a "how to" for achieving high test scores! First and foremost, it is a book about the key to it all: strong personal relationships with our students. Meeting the needs of the children in our classroom is an impossibility unless they are convinced that we authentically care about their welfare. Personal relationships are the bottom line. When our students know we care, they are ready to listen and learn because they *want* to, not because they *have* to. Ultimately, *Living the Lessons* is the story of a teacher devoted to valuing her students beyond a galaxy of stars!

My Students Say, "Thank You!"

"Thank you for helping me through hard lessons this year and for teaching me how to deal with man's inhumanity to man."
★ Loren

"Thank you for showing me how to be a humble servant and for never giving up on me. You believed in me. You convinced me I could be a Valued Employee and I became one!"
★ Maile

"Thank you for getting me to a state of happiness and liking myself. You firmly pushed me to not be depressed, and that has changed my life so much that I wouldn't be the same person without you."
★ Zack

"Thank you for teaching me integrity by reading 'Horton Hatches the Egg.'"
★ Jordan

"Thank you for helping me get on the honor roll, be a Task Manager, and be a Valued Employee!!! You made me believe I could do it!"
★ Alexis

"Thank you for making our class fun. It made me want to come to school every day."
★ Victoria

"Thank you for teaching me the value of the truth."
★ Zartan

"Thank you for teaching me much more than English and history."
★ Shay

"Thank you for teaching me to forgive others."
★ Jordan

"Thank you for teaching us a lot of highly advanced material, such as sentence patterns."
★ Ben

"Thank you for spending back-breaking time teaching me how to correctly use colons!"
★ *Katrina*

"Thanks for opening the doorway that lead me to strive to do my best!!"
★ *Daniel*

"Thank you for teaching me to follow my dreams and for helping me through some of the hardest times of my life."
★ *Katherine*

"Thank you for showing me how to write magnificent essays!"
★ *Lane*

"Thank you for teaching me the real meaning of a true community."
★ *Billy*

"Thanks for teaching me to have an ecstatic right heart.
★ *Alisha*

"Thank you for changing my life by teaching me to love myself."
★ *Ashley*

"Thank you for teaching me how to do my ABSOLUTE best on everything I do."
★ *Katie*

"Thank you for teaching me to tell the truth."
★ *Colby*

"Thank you for making me strive for excellence in all subjects."
★ *Dylan*

"Thank you for being a wonderful history teacher who doesn't focus on the dates."
★ *Toria*

"Thank you for teaching me what I can do with my life with excellent writing skills."
★ *Amber*

Endnotes

Chapter 3

1. Goleman, Daniel. Emotional Intelligence. NY: Bantam, 2006, 81-2. Used with Permission.
2. Ibid.
3. 43.
4. 87.

Chapter 5

1. Goleman, Daniel. Emotional Intelligence. NY: Bantam, 2006, 272. Used with Permission.
2. Ibid, 285.

Chapter 6

1. Mizer, Jean. "Cipher in the Snow." NEA Journal, 50 (1964): 8-10.

Chapter 7

1. Williamson, Marianne. A Return to Love: Reflections on the Principles of "A Course in Miracles." NY: Harper Paper backs, 1996, 75.
2. Peck, M. Scott. The Different Drummer: Community Making and Peace. NY: Touchstone, 1998.
3. Peck. A Different Drum, 29.
4. Ibid, 47.

Chapter 8

1. Dr. Seuss. The Sneetches. NY: Random House, 1961.

Chapter 24

1. Eldredge, John. Journey of Desire: Searching for the Life we Always Dreamed of. Nashville: Thomas Nelson, 2000, 165.

Acknowledgements

…to my father and mother, whose support from "behind the curtain" was felt in my deepest parts. Though I could not audibly hear you, I know you were clapping loudest.

…to my dear friend and mentor, Dr. Thomas Forbes, who planted the idea for a book in my heart and nourished it graciously with infinite encouragement, support and technical wizardry. How deeply honored I am to be called your friend.

…to Rosanne Forbes, who time after time after time supported the cause with a sweet spirit and a right heart. Thank you, Rosie, for smiling all the way!

…to my one and only angel daughter, Layna Jayne, whose warrior spirit, indomitable courage, and selfless purity of heart impart light, love and healing to a troubled world.

…to my precious big sister and best friend on the planet, Valerie Jayne, who loves me unconditionally as no one else. Thank you for your editorial expertise. Only you know how much it means to me that you are proud of your little sister!

…to my faithful friend, Francie Parr, who walked closely beside me every step of the way on my journey to wholeness. How incredibly blessed I am to be a flower in your garden.

…to Dr. Al Rocca, whose steadfast support and enthusiastic encouragement over the years have embellished the journey with a thousand smiles. Al, you are a testimony to the power of one!

…and finally to M. Scott Peck. Thank you, my friend, for helping me learn to love the truth—at all cost! You have blessed my life beyond the telling.

P R O S P E R I T Y
—— W I T H ——
P U R P O S E

Recently I sat in a coaching meeting, and listened to an executive vice president state an all too familiar phrase.

"To be honest, Mike," he said, his impatience becoming evident, "all I want to know is how you became successful."

Despite his burgeoning career, a comfortable family life, and financial wealth, he was looking for a shortcut to what he referred to as "success." You might think, "What was he missing? His life sounds great!"

Some describe it as a gnawing, an empty feeling of the unknown that leaves you questioning, Is this all there is? After years of doing what he thought would bring him happiness, he had come to understand, "There's more." He just didn't know how to get there.

I understand his frustration well. I have lived a financially abundant life—yet for many years, I was drowning in superficiality. When unexpected tragedy occurred, I realized that what I was pursuing, and had sacrificed everything for, wouldn't bring me the fulfillment I desired.

What people often don't understand is that to live in prosperity, meaning to be fulfilled in every area of life, we must first go on a personal journey. And sometimes, we have to sacrifice the very thing we've strived to attain. I share my story, in a daringly vulnerable way, in hopes that my successes and mistakes will act as a guide to help you live a life of courage, and ultimately arrive at the place for which you dream.

Read more about Mike's journey to becoming one of the wealthiest and most prosperous men in America in his autobiography, Prosperity with Purpose, at redarrowmedia.com.

red arrow

Red Arrow Media is a company of media professionals with diverse, cosmopolitan backgrounds and a wealth of experience, all united by our desire to create, produce, and distribute excellent literary texts and other media worldwide. We offer a comprehensive menu of publishing services and specialize in helping both budding and seasoned authors find their literary voice, write and edit their texts, and create powerful and pleasing interior and exterior designs. We also connect our authors with a plethora of other media services, from printing and distribution to bookselling, website development, publicity campaigns, photography, and video production.

www.redarrowmedia.com

13134501R00150

Made in the USA
Charleston, SC
18 June 2012